Developmental Psychopathology and Its Treatment

Ellen D. Nannis, *Editor*
University of Maryland, Baltimore County

Philip A. Cowan, *Editor*
University of California, Berkeley

NEW DIRECTIONS FOR CHILD DEVELOPMENT

WILLIAM DAMON, *Editor-in-Chief*
Clark University

Number 39, Spring 1988

Paperback sourcebooks in
The Jossey-Bass Social and Behavioral Sciences Series

Jossey-Bass Inc., Publishers
San Francisco • London

Ellen D. Nannis, Philip A. Cowan (eds.).
Developmental Psychopathology and Its Treatment.
New Directions for Child Development, no. 39.
San Francisco: Jossey-Bass, 1988.

New Directions for Child Development
William Damon, *Editor-in-Chief*

New Directions for Child Development is published quarterly by
Jossey-Bass Inc., Publishers (publication number USPS 494-090).
Second-class postage paid at San Francisco, California, and at
additional mailing offices. POSTMASTER: Send address changes to
Jossey-Bass Inc., Publishers, 350 Sansome Street, San Francisco,
California 94104.

Editorial correspondence should be sent to the Editor-in-Chief,
William Damon, Department of Psychology, Clark University,
Worcester, Massachusetts 01610.

Library of Congress Catalog Card Number LC 85-644581

International Standard Serial Number ISSN 0195-2269

International Standard Book Number ISBN 1-55542-914-9

Cover art by WILLI BAUM

Manufactured in the United States of America

Ordering Information

The paperback sourcebooks listed below are published quarterly and can be ordered either by subscription or single copy.

Subscriptions cost $52.00 per year for institutions, agencies, and libraries. Individuals can subscribe at the special rate of $39.00 per year *if payment is by personal check*. (Note that the full rate of $52.00 applies if payment is by institutional check, even if the subscription is designated for an individual.) Standing orders are accepted.

Single copies are available at $12.95 when payment accompanies order. (California, New Jersey, New York, and Washington, D.C., residents please include appropriate sales tax.) For billed orders, cost per copy is $12.95 plus postage and handling.

Substantial discounts are offered to organizations and individuals wishing to purchase bulk quantities of Jossey-Bass sourcebooks. Please inquire.

Please note that these prices are for the academic year 1987–88 and are subject to change without notice. Also, some titles may be out of print and therefore not available for sale.

To ensure correct and prompt delivery, all orders must give either the *name of an individual* or an *official purchase order number*. Please submit your order as follows:

Subscriptions: specify series and year subscription is to begin.
Single Copies: specify sourcebook code (such as, CD1) and first two words of title.

Mail orders for United States and Possessions, Australia, New Zealand, Canada, Latin America, and Japan to:
Jossey-Bass Inc., Publishers
350 Sansome Street
San Francisco, California 94104

Mail orders for all other parts of the world to:
Jossey-Bass Limited
28 Banner Street
London EC1Y 8QE

New Directions for Child Development Series
William Damon, *Editor-in-Chief*

CD1 *Social Cognition,* William Damon
CD2 *Moral Development,* William Damon
CD3 *Early Symbolization,* Howard Gardner, Dennie Wolf

Contents

Editors' Notes

Developmental researchers are becoming increasingly involved in applications of their findings to children and families in psychological distress. Child clinicians are increasingly interested in how their assessment and treatment plans can be enriched by a consideration of theory, method, and findings from studies of normal development. A marriage of the two fields has recently occurred, and developmental psychopathology is its latest offspring.

Developmental psychopathology is not yet old enough to have a well-defined identity, but various portraits of this new field reveal distinct family resemblances. By virtue of their intellectual origins, developmental psychopathologists pay attention to phenomena often overlooked by investigators interested only in normal behavior. We are describing more than a new perspective on old issues. By considering and integrating questions, concepts, methods, and findings from different bodies of knowledge, developmental psychopathologists attempt to understand how pathological behavior emerges, and how it sometimes fails to emerge, even when expected.

We believe that the most promising theoretical advances in developmental psychopathology are coming from those who seek to combine Piagetian-informed and Werner-informed cognitive theories with psychoanalytic theories of socioemotional functioning. These theoretical approaches are based on the assumption that cognition and emotion are inextricably linked domains, though explanations of how advances or deficits in one domain carry over to the other differ from one theory of developmental psychopathology to another.

Some of the new approaches emerging from the combined cognitive-psychoanalytic perspectives tend to emphasize the role of cognition, whereas others focus on emotion and human relationships in their explanations of both normal and abnormal behavior. In this volume we bring together theorists who range from cognitively based to psychodynamically based and who cover a wide range of problems from reactive fears to autism. The message of this volume is that the study of developmental psychopathology opens exciting new windows on understanding and alleviating psychopathology.

In Chapter One, Cowan provides a schematic outline of current theories of normal and pathological development. He shows that every theory of normal development contains within it an explicit or implicit theory of psychopathology, and that every theory of psychopathology implies a specific set of intervention strategies. Second, he demonstrates that theories of development and psychopathology can be classified in a nine-cell matrix according to whether they focus on internal, external, or interactive forces producing developmental change and whether they focus on biological, individual psychological, or interpersonal levels of analysis. His conclusion is that no single current theory provides an adequate foundation for developmental psychopathology. Clinicians interested in this new approach must consider all nine cells whenever they attempt to diagnose or treat a child or family in distress.

Chapter Two by Nannis and Chapter Three by Gordon discuss individual differences in the structure and function of cognition and how these differences affect children's and adolescents' emotional experiences and interpersonal problem solving. Nannis maintains that cognitive structural development influences emotional understanding, which in turn influences how emotional experiences are internalized and conceptualized. She discusses the implications of her analysis for the assessment and treatment of children and adolescents referred for therapy.

Gordon outlines the dual role of structural and functional developmental concepts in assessing and treating peer and parent-child relationship difficulties. She suggests that limitations or immaturity of specific formal operational skills lead to dysfunctions in adolescents' social adaptation. When adolescents have difficulty generating and evaluating alternative hypotheses, solving problems, and understanding the world from another person's point of view, their interaction with peers, parents, and teachers become problematic. An imbalance in the use of assimilative and accommodative strategies also limits effective interpersonal problem-solving abilities. Gordon presents therapeutic intervention strategies for adolescents derived from her cognitive developmental model.

Slotnick's account in Chapter Four of her research with autistic children describes similarities and differences between the structure and function of their thought and behavior and that of a group of significantly younger normal children who were matched for developmental level on a classification task. Her chapter suggests that severe psychopathology is not adequately defined by a marked delay in development. Rather, over and above their slowness of developmental progress, autistic children interact with the physical and social world in a way that is qualitatively different from normal children of the same cognitive level. In addition, Slotnick demonstrates the interdependence of cognitive and social development in a severely disturbed sample; social dysfunctions may limit opportunities for cognitive development, and cognitive deficits may make social development more difficult.

Noam in Chapter Five discusses the usefulness of assessing cognitive-developmental levels of patients, but he departs from a Piagetian orientation to the assessment of psychopathology. He suggests that life events experienced by patients are to be understood in terms of the cognitive structures that they used to make sense of these events when they first occurred. Transformations of experiences reoccur throughout development. Memories of the events become encapsulated at early points of development (not unlike fixation points) and can become dysfunctional when transformed and incorporated into later personality structures. Expanding on theories of the development of the self, Noam goes on to present a theory of psychopathology based on the incorporation into the self of transformation or lack of transformation of events occurring in earlier years of development. He bridges more psychodynamic concepts by including the idea of "self-strength"—not unlike the notion of ego strength. Self-strength refers to the success with which earlier experiences have become integrated and synthesized as transformations occur.

Of the authors in the present volume, Cicchetti, Toth, Bush, and Gillespie describe in Chapter Six a theory of developmental psychopathology most heavily influenced by concepts derived from psychodynamic developmental theories. They emphasize socioemotional influences on both normal and pathological development. They describe stage-salient issues (such as the development of secure attachment), each having a specific effect at specific periods of development. Unlike Erik Erikson, they argue that individuals continue to deal with all of these issues throughout their lives. Also departing from psychoanalytic theory in their adoption of a transactional model, Cicchetti and his colleagues show how different combinations of biological and caretaking events have different influences on four illustrative diagnostic conditions: (1) Down syndrome, (2) nonorganic failure-to-thrive syndrome, (3) offspring of parents with a major depressive disorder, and (4) child maltreatment.

Finally, complementing Cowan's opening attempt to locate developmental psychopathology in the pantheon of theories of normal and dysfunctional development, Breslow in Chapter Seven discusses each author's attempt to apply cognitive-developmental and social-emotional-developmental theories to the understanding of the diagnosis and treatment of dysfunction. He suggests that the authors can be categorized into those who seek to build a bridge between cognitive-developmental and social-emotional theories and those who use cognitive developmental concepts to construct a new theoretical tower. Breslow articulates the advantages and the pitfalls associated with each approach and presents additional cautionary notes for those who seek to define and extend developmental psychopathology and its treatment.

Developmental psychopathology, the young offspring of clinical and developmental psychology, is now reaching adolescence. There is, as yet, no firm identity in the form of developmental psychopathology. What binds this volume together is the commitment of each author to understanding developmental psychopathology and psychological dys-

4

functions as phenomena that are always in the process of emergence and developmental transformation. There is a wealth of ideas from developmental psychopathology ready to be applied systematically in clinical interventions and tested systematically in empirical research. The new kid on the block is certainly coming of age.

Ellen D. Nannis
Philip A. Cowan
Editors

Ellen D. Nannis is assistant professor of psychology at the University of Maryland, Baltimore County. Her clinical interests include assessment and intervention with children, adolescents, and their families.

Philip A. Cowan is professor of psychology at the University of California, Berkeley. A former head of the clinical program there, he now codirects, with Carolyn Pape Cowan, a longitudinal research intervention study of marital quality, parenting styles, and child development.

*There are nine ways of explaining how development goes right
and how it goes wrong. Which one is correct? All of them.*

Developmental Psychopathology: A Nine-Cell Map of the Territory

Philip A. Cowan

As a clinical-developmental psychology student trained in the late 1950s
and early 1960s, I was puzzled about the lack of integration between
developmental and abnormal psychology. Although there were frequent
professions of faith that principles of normal development and psychopathology must be intimately interconnected (Erikson, 1950), there were
few detailed discussions, and even fewer empirical studies, examining the
links between ideas about how some children grow up to be well-func-
tioning adults, while others experience temporary or permanent setbacks
along the way.

Later, during my clinical training, it puzzled me that there were
few explicit references in the psychotherapy literature to concepts and
studies of normal development, and that in articles on developmental
theory and research I rarely found references to psychopathology and
treatment. This lack of integration continued until the recent spurt of

This chapter was written while I was receiving partial support from
NIMH grant MH–31109. I wish to thank Carolyn Pape Cowan for her helpful
comments on earlier drafts of this chapter.

E. D. Nannis, P. A. Cowan (eds.). *Developmental Psychopathology and Its Treatment.*
New Directions for Child Development, no. 39. San Francisco: Jossey-Bass, Spring 1988.

interest in developmental psychopathology (Achenbach, 1982; Cicchetti, 1984; Rutter and Garmezy, 1983; Santostefano, 1975; Sroufe and Rutter, 1984).

I am far from the first to note that there are close connections between theories of normal development, psychopathology, and intervention. My hope in this chapter is to show that these connections stem from the fact that developmentalists, diagnosticians, and therapists are all fundamentally concerned with the same question: How do we understand stability and change across situations and over time? Once we accept the centrality of this question, I believe it becomes clear that theories of adaptive and maladaptive development tend to converge on a common set of issues. As yet, these common issues give rise to no single theoretical solution. Instead, we are faced with an array of theories or schools, each claiming to follow the royal road to truth and to avoid the quagmires and bramble patches scattered along alternative pathways. My own work has explored the application of cognitive-developmental theory to psychopathology and intervention (Breslow and Cowan, 1984; Cowan, 1978), but my goal in this chapter is not to persuade the reader that this is the only reasonable point of view. I intend, rather, to provide an integrated, schematic map of the territory, describing cognitive-developmental theory as offering fresh ideas in a marketplace that includes nine major attempts to understand normal development and psychopathology.

The chapter begins with a brief outline of psychopathology from a developmental perspective. I believe that developmental psychopathology shifts our focus from the endless and perhaps fruitless debate about what psychopathology is, to how dysfunction emerges and is transformed over time. This question necessarily directs our attention to different and sometimes conflicting principles advanced in current theories of normal development, abnormal development, and intervention. Following the lead of developmental psychopathology, I argue that the best chance for integrating these theories lies in understanding how each has conceptualized the forces leading to individual stability and change.

As an organizing rubric for comparing and contrasting points of view, I propose that theories of normal development, psychopathology, and intervention come in "matched sets." Every theory of normal development contains within it an explicit or implicit theory of psychopathology. Conversely, every theory of psychopathology contains within it an explicit or implicit conception of normal development. Furthermore, every theory of psychopathology explicitly or implicitly dictates a course of action leading to prevention or treatment, though I will show at the end of the chapter that there is no necessary connection between theories of causation and the potential effectiveness of our choices concerning how, when, and where to intervene.

Developmental Psychopathology

The definitions of normality and psychopathology are open to widespread, sometimes vehement, dispute, particularly over the criteria that should be used to distinguish between normal and abnormal functioning. Traditional approaches look to statistical norms, social rules and values, or various conceptions of ideal psychological adaptation to define standards of normality. Marked deviations from these standards are labeled as pathological or dysfunctional. Diagnosis tends to be equated with the application of a categorical label summarizing a collection of symptoms indicating the presence of a specific form of mental illness (for example, schizophrenia, depression). The dominant diagnostic system now in current use in the United States, the newly revised *Diagnostic and Statistical Manual* of the American Psychiatric Association (DSM-IIIR), does not claim that every category of disorder represents a mental illness, but the classification system has its conceptual roots in the medical model of psychopathology, with its assumption that psychopathology is a disease located somewhere in the patient.

In the past decade, the newly emerging field of developmental psychopathology has begun to challenge the current static focus on classification of psychopathology at a single point in time (Cicchetti in Chapter Six; Sroufe and Rutter, 1984; Rutter and Garmezy, 1983). Investigators within this tradition concluded, in effect, that it is not possible to answer the question of what constitutes the essence of normality and abnormality, so they accepted commonly used assumptions, procedures, and diagnostic categories. Their view is that important questions, centrally relevant to psychopathology, can be answered if we focus on the understanding of stability and change over the course of development. Adopting a longitudinal perspective and following individuals over time, they argue that we should pay attention to four developmental patterns, each one requiring an explanation of how it is that individuals come to follow that pathway:

a. Some individuals are symptom-free at Time 1 and remain so at Time 2.

b. Some individuals are symptom-free at Time 1 but develop symptoms or syndromes at Time 2.

c. Some individuals have clinically diagnosed symptoms or syndromes at Time 1 and continue to have them at Time 2.

d. Some individuals have clinically diagnosed symptoms or syndromes at Time 1 but have recovered by Time 2.

Developmental psychopathologists are concerned with understanding both group trends and individual variations as people change over time, with a special interest in factors that place some children at risk for dysfunction or that protect and buffer them from life's slings and arrows

(Garmezy, 1981). Developmental psychopathology begins with an interest in normal development and descriptions of the normative life course, and it attempts to explain how some individuals seem to be less vulnerable than others to developing clinically diagnosable symptoms or disorders (Pattern *a*). Developmental psychopathologists then seek to understand the emergence of psychological disorders (Pattern *b*). They do so by attempting to learn why some symptoms or syndromes tend to show relatively high incidence at specific developmental points in a population (for example, autism in early childhood, schizophrenia in adolescence), and why a particular disorder emerges at a given time in a single individual.

These theorists do not stop with the initial diagnosis. They assume that even though individuals may exhibit psychological disorders continuously over time, their symptoms and syndromes may show systematic transformations (Pattern *c*). There may be continuity in the fact that early problems predict later ones, but the form or category of the problem may change markedly over time. We know that some symptoms identified early in development (for example, trouble with peer relationships in the early years of elementary school) predict a variety of negative outcomes of adolescent development (learning problems, aggression, delinquency). However, there is no one-to-one correspondence between early and later symptoms (Kellam, Brown, Rubin, and Ensminger, 1983). Somehow we must begin to trace the developmental pathways from one form of psychopathology to another. We also must discover principles of continuity and transformation in the fact that a schizophrenic child may grow into a schizophrenic adult, maintaining the same label but changing most of his or her behavior.

Finally, developmental psychopathologists are interested in the fact that many individuals are at risk for psychopathology, or have actually been diagnosed, but the symptoms disappear after therapy, or even without treatment (Pattern *d*). In summary, contrasting individuals in Pattern *a*, who remain symptom-free, and Pattern *b*, who become dysfunctional, will tell us a great deal about the emergence of psychopathology. Studying individuals in Pattern *c*, who remain dysfunctional but may change their diagnostic category, and those in Pattern *d*, who manage to give up their symptoms, will reveal a great deal about the curative factors that can be harnessed for deliberate intervention. The central message of developmental psychopathology is that researchers should be less concerned than they currently are in distinguishing between normality and abnormality, and more concerned with understanding the conditions regulating stability and change in development.

The Unifying Question: How Do We Explain Stability and Change?

Understanding change is a central task of the developmentalist, the clinical diagnostician, and the therapist. No matter how the concept of development is defined, it always involves some degree of modification between successive measurement periods and responsiveness to alterations in situation or context. Too much change, however, is usually taken as a sign that something is wrong: sudden shifts in behavior over short periods of time, or hyperresponsivity to the slightest alteration in external or internal stimulation, are often interpreted as symptoms of psychological distress or dysfunction.

Stability is also a central defining attribute of both normal and pathological development. Normally, individuals of all ages display a great deal of predictability over time and consistency across situations. However, individuals of families who come to therapists often show excessive stability in that they fail to move past a given developmental milestone at the usual rate, or they cannot shift their behavior in response to changing environmental demands.

Let me introduce Robert, a ten-year-old boy, brought by his parents to a clinical psychologist:

> A creative, charming child, Robert has nevertheless been a source of great distress to his fourth-grade teacher. He talks out in class. He appears unable to sit still. Though he has generally excellent IQ test scores (on individually administered tests), he make obvious mistakes in reading and fails to complete assignments. Robert's papers can often be seen, crumpled and messy, stuffed into his backpack, his pockets, or the wastebasket. At home his behavior is similar but even less controlled. Robert does not follow his parents' instructions, frequently flares into tantrums, and hits his younger brother and other children in the neighborhood.

There is no doubt that Robert's behavior presents a problem both in the family and in the school. Whether it can be considered as abnormal, symptomatic of some underlying psychopathology, is, as we have seen, open to debate. But each question about the nature of Robert's psychopathology can be transformed into further questions about how Robert came to display this collection of behaviors, what conditions are maintaining them, and how a change in the direction of more acceptable behavior might be facilitated. At present Robert's behavior may be too stable in some respects (he does not adapt well to changing situations and demands) and too changeable in others (he responds to distractions that other children are able to ignore). Systematic information about what maintains stable behavior in this child and what induces change will be essential to understanding the meaning of his present symptoms and to forming a plan for treatment.

Nine-Cell Matrix

Following Piaget's epistemological analysis (Piaget, 1971), I suggested previously that theorists tend to hold one of three basic assumptions about the origins of both stability and change (Cowan, 1978). Some look to internal forces (biochemical mechanisms, id forces, moral values) that encourage stability or stimulate change from within the person. Others explain stability and change primarily in terms of external forces that impinge on individuals and influence them to maintain their behavior or to alter it (stimulus organization, parental discipline, societal values). Still others adopt interactive theories in which change or stability is a joint product of specific internal events in specific environmental contexts.

Within internal, external, and interactive alternatives are theories that focus on different levels of analysis. Some are primarily concerned with the biological substrates of behavior (genetic, physiological, neurochemical). Others attempt to understand normality and pathology in terms of the impact of external events on individual psychology and behavior. Finally, some theories focus on the ways in which the quality and structure of interpersonal relationships are implicated in the maintenance of an individual's stability and in the stimulation of change. Thus, we can construct a 3 × 3 matrix of "cells" (see Figure 1), each containing a set of theories that explain normal development, psychopathology, and approaches to preventive or therapeutic intervention. Each cell will be described as if it represented a sufficient explanation of individual stability and change. As I will argue below, all of the alternatives may be relevant to the explanation of growth or dysfunction in a single child or family.

Physical/Biological Level of Analysis. In the top row of Figure 1

Figure 1. Nine Explanations of Stability and Change

	Internal	External	Interactive
Physical/Biological	Cell 1	Cell 2	Cell 3
Individual/Psychological	Cell 4	Cell 5	Cell 6
Relationship	Cell 7	Cell 8	Cell 9

Note: This nine-cell matrix focuses only on explaining stability and change in individual psychological functioning. A more complicated version could be constructed to examine the impact of biological, individual psychological, and relationship variables on biological, psychological, and relationship adaptation; I will comment on this possibility toward the end of this chapter.

are located explanations of stability and change that rely on biological characteristics of the organism and physical characteristics of the environment that affect biological functioning.

Internal Views: Cell 1. Included in the top left cell of Figure 1 are what I would call the unidirectional, traditional organic/biological explanations of how individuals normally function. Genetic, biochemical, and neurological factors operating inside the person are said to shape the course of development. Genetic factors transmit developmental messages, biochemical factors influence mood, and neurological factors affect information-processing accuracy.

Psychopathology, in this view, results directly from genetic inheritance (for example, phenlyketonuria, a specific form of mental retardation), or from biochemical or neurological dysfunction. Robert, the hyperactive child I described in the brief vignette, may be suffering from some form of physiological impairment that affects his focus of attention and his ability to process information. Despite my characterization of the biological internal formulation as traditional, it currently enjoys renewed popularity, especially in psychiatric explanations of serious disturbances such as schizophrenia (Gottesman and Shields, 1972) and depression (Asberg and others, 1976). The assumption is that the distortion of mood and perception in these conditions is directly attributable to underlying biological events.

There are two types of intervention stemming from the biological internal view of stability and change. First, there is the preventive thrust of genetic counseling, which attempts to give parents information to make informed decisions about starting a family or about continuing with a pregnancy, based on genetic, family history, and medical information. Second, of course, is the psychopharmacologic approach, which attempts to influence physiological and biochemical imbalances with various forms of drug treatment (for example, Campbell and Small, 1978).

External Views: Cell 2. It would be absurd to suppose that internal biological events could take place in the absence of an external environment. The weak form of the external view is simply that a good enough environment is necessary as a supportive context in which biological processes unfold. The stronger form of the environmental view traces specific variations in biological processes to specific variations in the external environment. Researchers adopting the biological external view may examine the adequacy of available nutrition or the organization and quality of stimulation in the home in their attempts to account for the child's cognitive developmental progress.

When they attempt to account for psychopathology, these theorists also turn to external factors. Toxic waste or substances in the home can produce symptoms of psychological disturbance. Birth injuries or physical traumas later on can impair the child's neurological functioning.

Ten-year-old Robert, in our example, may be suffering from some neurological damage incurred during the birth process and from severe stimulus disorganization in the home or the classroom.

Theorists who adopt an external view of change and stability and focus on the physical or biological level of analysis tend to maintain this perspective when they consider ways of affecting human distress. Public health researchers emphasizing prevention point out that it is possible to decrease risk or promote health by altering the child's physical environment (including the prenatal state of the mother). Once the toxic effect has occurred, mental health workers, teachers, and parents know that it is often possible to treat the child by altering his or her physical environment to alleviate psychological distress.

Interactive Views: Cell 3. In Cell 3 are what I would describe as new organic and biological theories. Certainly there are important neurological and biochemical effects on emotion and cognition, but emotion and cognition also affect biological states. In normal development, the genetic and biological substrates of behavior push the individual toward certain levels of adaptation, but activity and incoming information also influence the development of neurological pathways and endocrine functioning and shape the unfolding of genetic potential (Plomin, 1987).

While we all give lip service to the importance of an interaction between external or internal forces in accounting for behavior, some theorists adopt a very precise definition of the term: it is impossible to understand any behavior unless we specify properties of both the person and the stimulus. It is impossible to determine the effect of the stimulus without knowing about the properties of the person, and it is impossible to understand the functioning of the person without knowing about the properties of his or her situation. It is this precise view of interaction with which I am concerned in presenting the nine-cell matrix describing the origins of stability and change in individual adaptation.

The interactive view of psychopathology at the biological level of analysis has been called the diathesis-stress model (Rosenthal, 1970). Biological factors, especially genetic inheritance, may create a predisposition (diathesis) for the development of a particular form of dysfunction, such as schizophrenia or depression, but whether the end result is pathological depends a great deal on whether external circumstances in the child's life augment or buffer the child's experience of stress. It may be that schizophrenic symptoms are amplified by a dopamine imbalance present from birth (Wyatt and others, 1978), but it is also the case that prolonged psychological distress can alter the levels of dopamine in the system (Buchsbaum, Coursey, and Murphy, 1976). Ten-year-old Robert may have been born with a mildly dysfunctional central nervous system, but his disability may be noticeable only when the physical conditions of his environment are in relative disarray.

Recent research within the diathesis-stress model has focused on the potential for identifying children or adolescents at risk for dysfunction (for example, Baldwin, Cole, and Baldwin, 1982; Goldstein, 1981; Sameroff, Seifer, and Zax, 1982), in the hope of developing programs emphasizing prevention or early intervention. Also consistent with the diathesis-stress model are therapies that combine drug and psychological treatments in an attempt to reduce stress and to interrupt the internal patterns that shape the disordered behavior (Weissman, 1978).

Individual Psychological Level of Analysis. Now we turn to explanations of stability and change that focus on the psychological functioning of the individual.

Internal Views: Cell 4. Theorists who adopt an internal psychological view of individual change and stability tend to use the metaphor of the flowering seed. Of course, there must be favorable external conditions of soil, water, and sun, but just as the seed eventually becomes a flower, the child will continue to grow as long as adequate environmental conditions persist. External events sometimes affect the rate at which the child develops, but by and large, change and stability tend to be regulated internally.

In this cell we have two very different types of theories—humanistic (Maslow, 1962; Rogers, 1966), and psychoanalytic (Freud, 1933; Jung, 1917). The humanists optimistically assume that there are innate inner forces pushing individuals toward self-actualization. Freud's equilibrium, tension-reduction model proposes that stage changes in the locus of pleasure (oral, anal, and so on) occur in a process of psychological unfolding driven by underlying biological transformations. Although parents' behavior may affect the rate of development, the shift from one stage to another is internally regulated. Given a good parent (Bettelheim, 1987; Winnicott, 1953), development toward increased levels of adaptation will inevitably occur.

The problem, of course, is that external forces do interfere with the child's development. In both humanistic and psychoanalytic theories, mothers are often criticized when children fail to progress toward adulthood, and fathers and societal institutions are awarded at least a partial share of the blame. As I interpret these theories, external events are given the status of distal causes of psychopathology, setting in motion a chain of events resulting in an internal proximal cause of stability and change. For example, external disruptions create internal anxieties, mobilize defenses, and unbalance the relative influences of id, ego, and superego on behavior. In humanistic theories, these events are described as creating barriers to the natural growth process. Even when the child is reacting to extremely noxious family circumstances (distal), psychopathology is a product of internal psychological imbalances and barriers (proximal). Not only the proximal cause, but the locus of psychopathology rests inside the person. According to the psychological internal view, Robert's difficulty in the classroom and at home may be a consequence of his anxiety. His defense mechanisms are not helping him to master or repress his tension, with the result that his anxiety interferes with his current level of functioning.

Preventive interventions planned by clinicians holding a psychological internal view of stability and change tend to focus on parent and teacher education designed to encourage a benign environment for children's growth. The primary emphasis in the psychoanalytic literature, however, is not on prevention but rather on individual treatment of the child. Parents are seen less frequently and appear to play an ancillary role. The distinction between distal and proximal causation may help to explain why psychoanalysts direct a great deal of their attention to parental inadequacies but focus their treatment on the child in the playroom (Haworth, 1965), with the goal of creating a psychologically safe place in which the child can experience and express previously repressed thoughts and feelings. Once the barriers to growth are removed, it is assumed, the child's natural disposition toward active mastery will result in developmental progress.

External Views: Cell 5. The metaphors best capturing the approaches in Cell 5 consider the child to be a clean slate to be written upon or an empty vessel waiting to be filled. Stability, consistency, and change are regulated by shifts in the external environment. Theories of classical and operant conditioning and social learning belong in this cell (Pavlov, 1927; Skinner, 1953; Bandura and Walters, 1963). So do traditional views of socialization that focus on the behavior of mothers or fathers as it affects the development of their children. In this case, parent behavior is considered a proximal force, rather than a distal link in the chain as it is in psychoanalytic or humanistic theories. Conditioned emotions, rewards for conformity, and adult or peer models all contribute to the child's propensity to behave in a normal, socially desirable fashion. What changes or remains stable in the child's behavior depends on what happens in his or her environment.

Learning and socialization theories need no new principles to explain psychopathology. Everything is learned. Fears are conditioned responses. Aggression grows more frequent when it is reinforced or modeled by adults or peers in the child's environment. Specific parenting behaviors result in specific child outcomes. Robert, in our example, may have been ignored when he was working quietly and rewarded with attention when he began to move around the room. This reinforcement pattern might have increased his off-task behavior and decreased his tendency to focus on his assignments.

Behavior modification and parent training are the treatments of choice by those who adopt an external psychological view of stability and change (for example, Blechman, 1985; Patterson, 1976). Classes or therapy sessions guided by this model focus on teaching specific skills to help parents gain more appropriate control of their children's behavior.

In giving examples of internal and external psychological events that affect individual adaptation, I have shown how parents and others help to maintain stability or facilitate change. In my view, the simple presence of other people, or an account of their specific behaviors toward the child, do not signify that we are using the relationship level of analysis. It is not too far fetched to imagine that at least some of the parent or teacher reinforcement effects could be administered effectively by machine. When we discuss the bottom three cells of Figure 1, I will show how factors internal and external to the quality of relationships between people can affect children's development. Here, the focus remains on individual psychological factors affecting stability and change.

Interactive Views: Cell 6. Piagetian and other cognitive developmental theories are located in the right column of the middle row in Figure 1. I have used the metaphor of a generator-transformer to characterize their view of the child (Cowan, 1978). This admittedly inelegant phrase attempts to summarize the assumption that the child's "output" is shaped by incoming stimulation, but that the child transforms the meaning of the stimulus to fit his or her current level of cognitive structure. For example, in a study of children's understanding of where babies come from, Anne Bernstein and I (Bernstein and Cowan, 1975; 1981) found that children transform what parents tell them into concepts consistent with their cognitive developmental level. One five-year-old girl, performing at Piaget's intuitive stage in other cognitive tasks concerned with identity and causality concepts, believed that "if you want to get a baby, buy a duck." It turned out that this innovative solution came from hearing her parents read a book about babies that began with a discussion of ducks and ended with an account of human conception. She assumed that the sequence of topics in the book had causal implications, probably because sequence is the major cue to causality in children at the intuitive stage.

In a similar vein, Nannis in Chapter Two shows how children's understanding of emotions in the self and others follows the same structural patterns as their understanding of other cognitive and social concepts. Cognitive developmentalists assume that meaning in each specific content area is shaped by the individual's underlying cognitive stage (transformational system). Examples of how cognitive schemes guide adult understanding and behavior can be seen in studies of parenting beliefs by Sigel and his colleagues (McGillicuddy-DeLisi, 1982; Laosa and Sigel, 1982).

The concept of cognitive stage, by focusing on the common structure underlying different concepts and behavior, helps to explain why children's responses are relatively stable over time and consistent across situations. How, then, does change occur? Interactions with the environment produce unexpected and disequilibrating information. Children can either assimilate this new information, transforming it to their existing way of thinking, and thus remain the same as before, or accommodate to changes in stimulation by altering their ideas and behavior. The outcome is a joint product of the nature of the stimulus challenge and the nature of the child's cognitive organization. When the structure of the stimulus is above but close to the cognitive stage of the child, developmental progress is facilitated (Turiel, 1966). If the challenge is too little or too great, change is not likely to occur. Without an explicit stage theory, Vygotsky (1978) also portrays the child's development as proceeding best when parents provide a sensitive scaffolding—reducing the complexity of tasks and matching their intervention to the level where the child can use help but not being so intrusive and helpful that the child is stifled or bored.

Cognitive developmentalists tend to define normal development in terms of both structure and process: From the structural point of view, children are developing normally when their stage level roughly approximates that of their peers and when there is relative synchrony in their levels of performance across different tasks or domains. From the functional point of view, normality is defined by the degree of balance and coordination between the processes of assimilation and accommodation (Block, 1982; Breslow and Cowan, 1984; Cowan, 1978). When assimilation predominates, the child may be more engaged in symbolic play, transforming real objects into fantasies. When accommodation predominates, the child may be engaged in imitation or other forms of self-change in response to environmental demands. Piaget assumes that in the normal course of events there is a self-regulating equilibration process that brings these two processes into adaptive balance. Individuals can transform new events on the basis of already established schemes to fit them into existing categories and belief systems, and modify schemes to solve new problems and meet new challenges. In this process there is a flexible balance established between stability and change.

Structural and functional perspectives are also central to the description of psychopathology. From a structural point of view, individuals diagnosed as severely disturbed are far behind their age-mates in Piagetian developmental stage or show marked discrepancies between their levels of performance in different domains (Cicchetti, Toth, Bush, and Gillespie in Chapter Six; Cowan, 1978; Gordon in Chapter Three; Noam in Chapter Five; Slotnick in Chapter Four). There are very few empirical studies focusing on functional imbalances in psychopathology. It is possible that disturbed children show a chronic overemphasis on accommodation or assimilation (Block, 1982; Gordon in Chapter Three;

Slotnick in Chapter Four) or that they flip-flop rapidly from one mode to the other (Schmid-Kitsikis, 1976). Breslow and Cowan (1984) showed that above and beyond the fact that psychotic children are delayed in their progress through the developmental stages, they seem to demonstrate a tendency to focus on concrete details of their immediate environment (they overemphasize accommodation) and to have difficulty using their normal assimilative mechanisms to regulate the degree of flexibility and stability in their environment.

The psychological interactive perspective on stability and change has one important implication for the definition of psychopathology. In the internal view, psychopathology is located in the child. In the interactional view, psychopathology is located in a nonoptimal mismatch between environmental demands and child characteristics. In the brief vignette about Robert, cognitive developmentalists would focus on the mismatch between the level of reasoning he is able to use and the level required to solve a problem or to meet the demands of his teacher or parents. It may be that while he is able to be socially charming, Robert has not yet developed a cognitive level appropriate to the demands of a fourth-grade curriculum. Similarly, Robert's problem would not be defined by his tendency to overaccommodate, responding to every change in stimulation, but by the mismatch between his cognitive style and the demands for impulse control in the family or classroom. In this view intervention is not directed primarily to changing the child but rather to changing the relationship between the child and his major environments.

Clinicians are beginning to use cognitive-developmental principles to assess children or adults and to plan a course of treatment (Noam, 1987; Santostefano, 1975). For example, in addition to knowing that an individual has a diagnosis of schizophrenia, it is possible to determine his or her predominant structural level of understanding (Cowan, 1978). Some schizophrenic children and adults appear to be using sensorimotor reasoning without having achieved object permanence. Some have achieved object permanence and the formation of a representative symbol system but do not conserve quantities or use two-dimensional classification systems. Still others at the older age ranges may have mastered concrete operations but are unable to use formal abstract reasoning. This information can be used as a guideline for clinicians to provide appropriate scaffolding—to match the level of their demands more closely to the level of the patient's system of meanings. For example, peekaboo or hiding object games might be more appropriate for a psychotic child who does not appear to have object permanence than would word games or verbal instructions, even if the child seemed to have the use of language.

Similarly, and this is even more speculative, it may be possible to match interventions more appropriately to the individual's tendency to overassimilate or overaccommodate. Children who are withdrawn into a fantasy world may benefit from some of the externally based attempts to bring their behavior under the control of events and people. Gradual applications of behavioral reinforcement techniques may help the child to pay more attention to the outside world than to his or her own inner distress. Children who are overreactive and impulsive may benefit from a play therapy approach that ultimately encourages assimilation by helping the child to impose structure and stability on an ever-changing world. These suggestions may seem paradoxical. At present, behavioral therapies tend to be used with children and adults who are aggressive, impulsive, and overreactive to incoming stimulation. Play therapies tend to be used with internalizing children who withdraw from social situations and become preoccupied with inner conflicts. I am suggesting that although these approaches may match the child's initial tendencies, it might be important to shift gradually to the opposite functional mode in order to facilitate equilibration and adaptation. Note that the spirit of the interaction perspective does not require us to abandon interventions conceptualized from internal and external points of view. Rather, it forces us to consider the match between the nature of the intervention and the nature of the specific child.

Relationship Level of Analysis. The bottom three cells of Figure 1 focus on the child's relationship life. I will be looking at how relationships symbolically represented by the child (internal) and relationships occurring in transactions between people (external, interactive) affect developmental stability and change.

Internal Views: Cell 7. We usually think of relationships in the context of interactions between people, but from some time during the first year of life, symbolic representations of these relationships are located inside the child. These symbolic representations have variously been called object relations (Buckley, 1986), working models (Bowlby, 1980), and relationship schemes (Raush, Barry, Hertel, and Swain, 1974). In his theory of the Oedipus complex, Freud (1933) discussed the impact of fathers and mothers on superego development in the child. In fact, Freud's emphasis was on the child's internalization of idealized parent characteristics. What is internalized is not an accurate "photograph" of the parent-child relationship but rather a "scheme" representing the parents' rules about which aspects of the pleasure principle the child should and should not attempt to satisfy. The importance of the real relationship is downgraded and the operation of the child's "screened memories" and fantasies is emphasized.

British object relations theorists Klein, Fairbairn, Guntrip, and Winnicott (Buckley, 1986) and Bowlby's (1980) theory of attachment and loss tend to take actual parent-child relationships more seriously. Still focusing on the child's internal representations, these theorists point to the quality of the earliest bond or attachment between caretaker and child as laying the essential foundation for later child development and adaptation. That is, it contributes both to stability across time and situations, and to the child's willingness to try something new when old strategies no longer work.

Drawing on Bowlby's writings, American attachment theorists have begun to examine how working models of early parent-child attachment may be implicated in consistency of adaptation across three generations. Main, Kaplan, and Cassidy (1985) and Ricks (1986) showed that adults' memories of early security in the parent-grandparent relationship (assessed in interviews) predict security in the parent-child relationship (assessed in laboratory observations when the child is six). Furthermore, infants judged to show secure early attachments tend to show higher levels of cognitive and social competence at two years, three and one-half, and five years of age (Arend, Gove, and Sroufe, 1979). Though these data do not prove that early attachment in the parent, or early attachment in the child, causes later adaptation, they certainly support the hypothesis that the quality of early and continuing parent-child relationships may be important in the child's later progress through normal developmental stages or tasks.

Conversely, attachment theorists believe that early disruption in the parent-child bond leads to both internalizing disorders (anxiety and depression) and externalizing disorders (aggression) in later years. Empirical tests of this hypothesis have not yet led to clear-cut results (Bates, Maslin, and Frankel, 1986; Erickson, Sroufe, and Egeland, 1986). Applications of a Cell 7 approach to understanding Robert's troublesome behavior would focus on his construction of his early relationships with his parents and on how anxiety and distrust formed in the family crucible may have generalized to Robert's relationships with both adults and peers at school.

Is it possible to affect the quality of object relationships through psychological intervention? Preventive programs derived in part from object relations theory focus on strengthening the mother-child bond in children at risk for later distress (Fraiberg, Adelson, and Shapiro, 1975). Fathers, so far, have been ignored though Parke and his colleagues (Parke, Hymel, Power, and Tinsley, 1980) showed that a very simple early intervention can have a marked effect on father involvement and the quality of father-newborn interaction. Treatment approaches adopting the internal relationship perspective seem to maintain the general format of individual psychoanalytic or psychodynamic therapy, focusing even more strongly on material derived from memories of early parent-child relationships. There is some attempt to work with the child's actual parent (usually the mother), but she is seen separately from the child, often with the focus on her own dynamics rather than on a direct examination of the transactions in the parent-child relationship.

External View: Cell 8. In the psychological external Cell 5 above, I described traditional socialization theories that center on parents' behavior toward their children. Cell 8 is the home of traditional theories that focus on family relationships and the effects of other social institutions on child development. There has been a long sociological tradition investigating the impact of family structures on child development (Skolnick, 1973) and a newer set of psychological studies of the impact of changing family structures (for example, divorce) on the child's adaptation (Hetherington and Camara, 1984; Wallerstein and Kelly, 1980). In psychology and psychiatry, a number of family theorists focus on communication patterns between parents, and between parents and children, all of which may affect normal adaptation (for example, Schultz, 1984). Community psychologists (Sarason and others, 1966) and other ecological theorists (Bronfenbrenner, 1979) look at school systems and the structure of the relationships within them in order to explain individual differences in student competence. The approach in this cell is always from adult to child, examining how social relationships preserve stability and consistency of behavior while at the same time directing the child along certain developmental pathways.

Relationship theorists who emphasize the external view imply that pathology and the blame for psychological distress in the child is located either in dysfunctional relationships between the child and others or in dysfunctional relationship systems in which the child is embedded (for example, cultures, families, schools). Not surprisingly, intervention as conceptualized within this cell tends to have a political cast. In order to provide more optimal environments for children, many claim we must change national policies in support of the family, revise the welfare system, alter parental leave policies at work, and reorganize and revitalize the schools. On a more microscopic level of distress, it would be necessary to change the relationship between Robert and his teacher or the other students, and possibly to modify the structure of his classroom.

Interactive Views: Cell 9. The prototypic interactive view of relationship factors in adaptation can be seen in family system theories. At first these theories focused on families in treatment (Bateson, Jackson, Haley, and Weakland, 1956; Minuchin and Fishman, 1981; Satir, 1964; Wynne and Singer, 1963), but they are now beginning to be applied to the systematic study of normal families (for example, Reiss, 1981; Walsh, 1982). Their basic assumption is that each individual affects and is affected by all the individuals and all the relationships (dyadic, triadic, and so on) in the family system. Many, but not all, family theorists also assume that internal symbolic representations of relationships affect the quality of interpersonal exchanges, at the same time that interpersonal exchanges shape the quality of each individual's working models (for example, Ackerman, 1968; Bowen, 1978; Framo, 1981). Some community psychologists also have adopted an interactional perspective by showing, for example, that the impact of a given classroom structure depends on specific characteristics of individual students, including their perceptions of classroom events (Weinstein, Marshall, Sharpe, and Botkin, 1987).

Like the psychological interactive perspective, the relationship interactive cell requires a reconceptualization of psychopathology. The locus of dysfunction is no longer in individuals or in dyadic relationships but in the structure and function of all relationships in the system. From this perspective, Robert and his hyperactivity are not the central problem. Rather, Robert's personality characteristics and style may be getting him into trouble because he is unfortunately involved in a mismatch with the way things are done in both family and school.

Since they see psychological problems of individuals as located in social systems, most relationship interactive theorists propose some form of conjoint group intervention to prevent or alleviate both individual and system distress. For example, Carolyn Pape Cowan and I have been testing the hypothesis that in the early years of family formation, the arrival of a child has a marked impact on the couple relationship, and the couple relationship in turn affects the quality of parent-child relationships and the course of the child's development (Cowan and Cowan, 1987). Based on that premise, we created and assessed the effect of a couples group that met weekly for three months before and after the birth of a first child (Cowan and others, 1985; Cowan and Cowan, 1987). Trained leaders helped couples focus on marital and parenting issues to strengthen both marital and parent-child relationships during the transition to parenthood and the early period of family formation. The eighteen-month postpartum follow-up revealed that when couples in the intervention sample were compared with a control sample, their marital satisfaction declined less and they had all remained in intact relationships; by contrast, 12.5 percent of the control couples had separated or divorced. Two years later, we found intervention effects on parents' relationships with their three-and-one-half-year-olds and on their children's level of ego-resiliency (Block and Block, 1980). Intervention focused on the couple as the central dyadic relationship, then, may affect all the individuals and relationships in the family.

Multiple Cell Perspective

In each of the nine cells I described complementary conceptions of stability and change within theories of normal development, psychopathology, and intervention. I presented each cell as if it alone can serve as an explanation of an individual's current behavior or as a blueprint for planning intervention. This format has been dictated largely by the fact that each developmental and clinical theory is usually presented as if it describes the whole truth about stability and change. But it should be obvious by now that the nine alternatives I put forth are not mutually exclusive. However, in my experience, it is an extremely rare exception for a researcher or clinician to adopt a multicell perspective in attempting to understand normal development or to affect the course of psychopathology.

Let us take a final look at ten-year-old Robert. From a physical/biological perspective, it is possible that his behavior is indeed affected by neurological malfunctions (Cell 1), but that both his home and school environments are so full of sights and sounds (Cell 2) that he has great difficulty finding a central focus of attention (Cell 3). From an individual psychological perspective, it is also possible that he is anxious (Cell 4), that his parents covertly reinforce him for disobedience (Cell 5), and that there is a mismatch between his developmental stage and cognitive style and what the school and family demand (Cell 6). A relationship perspective is not easy to reconstruct from the details in the vignette, but it may be that Robert's working models of relationships stem from his early difficulties in establishing relationships with his mother and father (Cell 7), that his anxiety is exacerbated at home by his parents' frequent fights and at school by the level of disorganization in the classroom (Cell 8). It may also be that the characteristics and histories of Robert's parents and teachers make it difficult for them to deal sympathetically with Robert's combination of charming and annoying behavior (Cell 9).

I draw four conclusions from these speculations:

1. *It is necessary to consider all nine cells in understanding the normality and pathology of an individual child.* The issue is not a simple matter of eclecticism in which all ideas have equal value regardless of merit. Rather, each type of theorist has set out to solve a particular set of problems in understanding stability and change. In my view, different theories and approaches must be considered before making a final diagnosis and treatment plan. Why not simply pay attention to the three interactive cells in Figure 1 since they include both external and internal explanations of change? Until all the evidence is in, I prefer to suppose that there are both main effects and interactions. Sometimes it may be useful to focus primarily on external events because they actually create a large part of the problem. Sometimes it may be useful to focus on internal events, because there are severe difficulties located within the child. However, we should always keep in mind the possibility that external and internal variables act in combination to maintain stability and to produce disequilibration and change.

2. *It is possible that developmental outcomes are a product of interactions, not only among external and internal forces but also among biological, psychological, and relationship domains.* I am arguing here that levels of analysis and explanations of stability and change do not operate

independently. Biological internal events may amplify or reduce the impact of psychological and social stressors or buffer the individual from their harmful effects (for example, Gottman and Levenson, in press). Internal defense mechanisms or the qualities of intimate relationships may exacerbate or buffer the effects of genetic, hormonal, or physiological patterns.

3. *The influence or weighting of the importance of each cell may vary considerably from individual to individual.* For some children, internal biological events may have the most influence on level of adaptation. For other children, external psychological or interactional family system factors may be most relevant to the understanding and treatment of a specific problem. At this point in our knowledge, there is no way of determining the exact weights to be allocated in understanding a specific individual or family. In the analysis of a single case we will always need to rely on careful clinical assessment and a consideration of all the alternatives. As research in developmental psychopathology proceeds, we may be able to refine our ideas about the relative contribution of each cell to the emergence and course of developmental disorder.

4. *Stability and change may have their etiology in one cell but may be maintained by events more characteristic of another.* Hyperactive behavior may be triggered initially by neurological damage, but it may be maintained by how the child is treated at home and in school. Depression may have a strong biologically determined onset in a child, but the course of the difficulty may be affected by family dysfunction. Thus, principles governing the antecedents or causes of a given behavior in the past may be quite different from principles maintaining current stability and change.

Connection Between Etiology and Treatment

The fact that behavior can be caused by events located in one cell and maintained by events in another calls into question the assumption that the theory of etiology should determine our approach to treatment. For example, if we adopt a psychological internal theory of how problems come into being, we should not necessarily be committed to a psychodynamic or humanistic approach to therapy. A few examples are sufficient to demonstrate that the connection between cause and cure is not as inevitable as it seems:

• We are not limited to biological and physical treatments for children with neurological difficulties. These children also respond to more structured parenting and teaching strategies. Conversely, the impact of environmental traumas can be alleviated with drug therapies, especially in combination with psychological therapies.

• Children with internally caused anxieties may benefit from play therapy, but they also may be successfully treated with (external) behavior modification. On the other hand, the distress resulting from external stressors may be relieved with psychodynamic therapy.

• Family system problems can be affected through individual therapy, just as individual problems may be alleviated in conjoint family treatment.

I am not arguing here that we should disregard etiology when planning interventions. Understanding the factors leading to the emergence of dysfunction is still an important concern of developmental psychopathology researchers. Understanding the source of pathology may be important to clinicians and their clients. It may help therapists and patients to identify potentially successful and unsuccesful interventions. But the level at which clinicians intervene or their choice of focusing on internal or external factors may be quite different than that suggested by the cell in which the problems began. I should note that questions of etiology are essential to answer when we think about preventive intervention. Here it is necessary to identify the antecedents, if not the causes, of dysfunctions and disorders, before we can intelligently plan interventions to reduce the incidence or severity of individual distress.

What I am suggesting in the planning of an intervention for an individual child or family already in difficulty is that we must go beyond the limited question of how the distress occurred. We must turn our attention to more general issues of understanding how to maintain stability in some aspects of life and to facilitate change in others. The individual child does not live in a single cell of the nine-cell matrix. Rather, he or she is a biological, psychological, and social system, in which internal and external forces operate independently and in interaction. Regardless of where the proximal cause of the problem may lie, it is possible that an intervention directed toward internal or external change at any level of the system may have a desirable effect. This is not simply a rose-colored view that any intervention will be successful with disorders of any origin. Instead, I am attempting to question the automatic assumption that an environmentally caused condition will only respond to environmental manipulation, a biologically caused condition will only respond to physical or chemical treatment, an internal locus of distress must be addressed with internally focused therapy, and externally conditioned symptoms must be treated with behavior modification techniques.

If all forms of intervention are possible in a given case, how do we choose which ones to try? The nine-cell matrix I presented reminds us of all the alternatives. However, it would be overwhelming to both patient and therapist to institute them all at one time. There is as yet very little systematic evidence in the case of most disorders that suggests which cell or cells might provide the most effective guidelines for change. In part, the decision may be a practical one. Even if the major dysfunction is located in the family system, if some or all of the family refuses to become involved in treatment, it is still necessary to provide some support for the child in distress. A school psychologist who receives an inordinate number of referrals from one classroom might begin to wonder whether his or her energy may be more effectively spent consulting with the teacher and focusing on classroom interactions. A therapist with a severely depressed adolescent considering suicide may want to consider drugs as an adjunct to psychological treatment, just as a biologically oriented psychiatrist may want to consider family sessions to help parents deal with the painful daily interactions with a severely disturbed child.

By focusing on nine different approaches to understanding what leads to consistency across time and situations, and what leads to adaptive change, I have shown, I hope, that a comprehensive theory of normality, psychopathology, and intervention cannot be located conveniently in any single cell of the nine-cell matrix in Figure 1. Once we take the challenge offered by developmental psychopathology to examine stability and change in both normal and abnormal behavior across the life span, it becomes clear that no single-cell theory of psychopathology and intervention will suffice. We need a more unified and integrated theory of developmental psychopathology, even though it introduces additional alternatives into an already difficult research and clinical task. All of the individuals that we study, diagnose, and treat are biological beings, with individual minds, engaged in challenging and demanding relationships. They transform their worlds and, in turn, are transformed by them. As theorists and clinicians, we must do justice to the puzzling and challenging complexity of their unfolding lives.

References

Achenbach, T. M. *Developmental Psychopathology.* (2nd ed.) New York: Wiley, 1982.

Ackerman, N. W. "The Role of the Family in the Emergence of Child Disorders." In E. Miller (ed.), *Foundations of Child Psychiatry.* Oxford, England: Pergamon Press, 1968.

American Psychiatric Association Committee on Nomenclature. *Diagnostic and Statistical Manual of Mental Disorders.* Vol. 3. (rev. ed.) Washington, D.C.: American Psychiatric Association, 1987.

Arend, R., Gove, F., and Sroufe, L. A. "Continuity of Individual Adaptation from Infancy to Kindergarten: A Predictive Study of Ego-Resilience and Curiosity in Preschoolers." *Child Development,* 1979, *50*, 950–959.

Asberg, M., Thoren, P., Traskman, L., Bertilsson, L., and Ringberger, V. "Serotonin Depression—A Biochemical Subgroup Within the Affective Disorders?" *Science,* 1976, *191*, 478–480.

Baldwin, A. L., Cole, R. E., and Baldwin, C. P. (eds.). *Parental Pathology, Family Interaction, and the Competence of the Child in School.* Monographs of the Society for Research in Child Development, no. 197. Chicago: University of Chicago Press, 1982.

Bandura, A., and Walters, R. *Social Learning and Personality Development.* New York: Holt, Rinehart & Winston, 1963.

Bates, J. E., Maslin, C. A., and Frankel, K. A. "Attachment Security, Mother-Child Interaction, and Temperament as Predictors of Behavior-Problem Ratings at Age Three Years." In I. Bretherton and E. Waters (eds.), *Growing Points of Attachment Theory and Research.* Monographs of the Society for Research in Child Development, no. 209. Chicago: University of Chicago Press, 1986.

Bateson, G., Jackson, D. D., Haley, J., and Weakland, J. H. "Toward a Theory of Schizophrenia." *Behavioral Science,* 1956, *1,* 251-264.

Bernstein, A. C., and Cowan, P. A. "Children's Concepts of How People Get Babies." *Child Development,* 1975, *46,* 77-91.

Bernstein, A. C., and Cowan, P. A. "Children's Conceptions of Birth and Sexuality." In R. Bibace and M. E. Walsh (eds.), *Children's Conceptions of Health, Illness, and Bodily Functions.* New Directions for Child Development, no. 14. San Francisco: Jossey-Bass, 1981.

Bettelheim, B. *The Goodenough Parent.* New York: Random House, 1987.

Blechman, E. R. *Solving Child Behavior Problems—at Home and at School.* Champaign, Ill.: Research Press, 1985.

Block, J. "Assimilation, Accommodation, and the Dynamics of Personality Development." *Child Development,* 1982, *53* (2), 281-295.

Block, J. H., and Block, J. "The Role of Ego-Control and Ego-Resiliency in the Organization of Behavior." In W. A. Collins (ed.), *Minnesota Symposia on Child Psychology.* Vol. 13. Hillsdale, N.J.: Erlbaum, 1980.

Bowen, M. *Family Therapy in Clinical Practice.* New York: Aronson, 1978.

Bowlby, J. *Attachment and Loss.* Vol. 3: *Loss, Sadness, and Depression.* New York: Basic Books, 1980.

Breslow, L., and Cowan, P. A. "Structural and Functional Perspectives on Classification and Seriation in Psychotic and Normal Children." *Child Development,* 1984, *55,* 226-235.

Bronfenbrenner, U. *The Ecology of Human Development.* Cambridge, Mass.: Harvard University Press, 1979.

Buchsbaum, M. S., Coursey, R. S., and Murphy, D. L. "The Biochemical High-Risk Paradigm: Behavioral and Familial Correlates of Low Platelet Monoamine Oxidase Activity." *Science,* 1976, *194,* 339-341.

Buckley, P. (ed.). *Essential Papers on Object Relations.* New York: New York University Press, 1986.

Campbell, M., and Small, A. M. "Chemotherapy." In A. O. Ross and J. Egan (eds.), *Handbook of Treatment of Mental Disorders in Childhood and Adolescence.* Englewood Cliffs, N.J.: Prentice-Hall, 1978.

Cicchetti, D. "The Emergence of Developmental Psychopathology." *Child Development,* 1984, *55,* 1-7.

Cowan, C. P., and Cowan, P. A. "A Preventive Intervention for Couples Becoming Parents." In C.F.Z. Boukydis (ed.), *Research on Support for Parents and Infants in the Postnatal Period.* Norwood, N.J.: Ablex, 1987.

Cowan, C. P., Cowan, P. A., Heming, G., Garrett, E. T., Coysh, W. S., Curtis-Boles, H., and Boles, A. J. "Transitions to Parenthood: His, Hers, and Theirs." *Journal of Family Issues,* 1985, *6,* 451-481.

Cowan, P. A. *Piaget with Feeling: Cognitive, Social, and Emotional Dimensions.* New York: Holt, Rinehart & Winston, 1978.

Cowan, P. A., and Cowan, C. P. "Couple Relationships, Parenting Styles, and the Child's Development at Three." Presented at a Society for Research in Child Development Symposium on Transition to Parenthood, Baltimore, Md., Apr. 1987.

Erickson, M. F., Sroufe, L. A., and Egeland, B. "The Relationship Between Quality of Attachment and Behavior Problems in Preschool in a High-Risk Sample." In I. Bretherton and E. Waters (eds.), *Growing Points of Attachment Theory and Research.* Monographs of the Society for Research in Child Development, no. 209. Chicago: University of Chicago Press, 1986.

Erikson, E. H. *Childhood and Society.* New York: Norton, 1950.

Fraiberg, S., Adelson, E., and Shapiro, V. "Ghosts in the Nursery: A Psychoanalytic Approach to the Problems of Impaired Mother-Infant Relationships." *Journal of the American Academy of Child Psychiatry,* 1975, *14,* 387–421.

Framo, J. L. "The Integration of Marital Therapy with Sessions with Family of Origin." In A. S. Gurman and D. P. Kniskern, *Handbook of Family Therapy.* New York: Brunner/Mazel, 1981.

Freud, S. *New Introductory Lectures on Psychoanalysis.* New York: Norton, 1933.

Garmezy, N. "Children Under Stress: Perspectives on Antecedents and Correlates of Vulnerability and Resistance to Psychopathology." In I. A. Rabin, J. Aronoff, A. M. Barclay, and R. A. Zucker (eds.), *Further Explorations in Personality.* New York: Wiley, 1981.

Goldstein, M. J. (ed.). *New Developments in Interventions with Families of Schizophrenics.* New Directions for Mental Health Services, no. 12. San Francisco: Jossey-Bass, 1981.

Gottesman, I. I., and Shields, J. *Schizophrenia and Genetics: A Twin Study Vantage Point.* New York: Academic Press, 1972.

Gottman, J. M., and Levenson, R. W. "The Social Psychophysiology of Marriage." In P. Noller and M. A. Fitzpatrick (eds.), *Perspectives on Marital Interaction.* San Diego, Calif.: College Hill Press, in press.

Haworth, M. *Play Therapy.* (2nd ed.) Orlando, Fla.: Grune & Stratton, 1965.

Hetherington, E. M., and Camara, K. A. "Families in Transition: The Processes of Dissolution and Reconstitution." In R. D. Parke (ed.), *Review of Child Development Research.* Vol. 7: *The Family.* Chicago: University of Chicago Press, 1984.

Jung, C. G. *Collected Papers on Analytical Psychology.* New York: Moffat Yard, 1917.

Kegan, R. S. *The Evolving Self: Problem and Process in Human Development.* Cambridge, Mass.: Harvard University Press, 1982.

Kellam, S. G., Brown, C. H., Rubin, B. R., and Ensminger, M. E. "Paths Leading to Teenage Psychiatric Symptoms and Substance Abuse: Developmental Epidemiological Studies in Woodlawn." In S. B. Guze, F. J. Earls, and J. E. Barrett (eds.), *Child Psychopathology and Development.* New York: Raven, 1983.

Laosa, L. M., and Sigel, I. E. (eds.). *Families as Learning Environment for Children.* New York: Plenum Press, 1982.

Lazarus, R. S. "On the Primacy of Cognition." *American Psychologist,* 1984, *39,* 124–129.

McGillicuddy-DeLisi, A. V. "The Relationship Between Parents' Beliefs About Development and Family Constellation, Socioeconomic Status, and Parents' Teaching Strategies." In L. M. Laosa and I. E. Sigel (eds.), *Families as Learning Environment for Children.* New York: Plenum, 1982.

Main, M., Kaplan, N., and Cassidy, J. "Security in Infancy, Childhood, and Adulthood: A Move to the Level of Representation." In I. Bretherton and E. Waters (eds.), *Growing Points of Attachment Theory and Research.* Monographs of the Society for Research in Child Development, no. 209. Chicago: University of Chicago Press, 1985.

Maslow, A. H. *Toward a Psychology of Being.* Princeton, N.J.: Van Nostrand, 1962.

Minuchin, S., and Fishman, H. C. *Family Therapy Techniques*. Cambridge, Mass.: Harvard University Press, 1981.

Noam, G. "Marking Time in the Hardest Movement: Borderline Psychopathology in Lifespan Perspective." In K. Field, G. Wool, and B. Cohler (eds.), *Psychoanalytic Perspectives on Learning and Education*. New York: International Universities Press, 1987.

Parke, R. D., Hymel, S., Power, T. G., and Tinsley, B. R. "Fathers and Risk: A Hospital-Based Model of Intervention." In D. B. Sawin, R. C. Hawkins, L. O. Walker, and J. H. Penticuff (eds.), *Psychosocial Risks in Infant-Environment Transactions*. New York: Brunner/Mazel, 1980.

Patterson, G. R. *Living with Children: New Methods for Parents and Teachers*. (rev. ed.) Champaign, Ill.: Research Press, 1976.

Pavlov, I. P. (G. V. Anrep, trans.) *Conditioned Reflexes*. London: Oxford University Press, 1927.

Piaget, J. *Genetic Epistemology*. New York: Norton, 1971.

Plomin, R. *Genetics, Development, and Psychology*. Hillsdale, N.J.: Erlbaum, 1987.

Raush, H. L., Barry, W. A., Hertel, R. K., and Swain, M. A. *Communication, Conflict, and Marriage*. San Francisco: Jossey-Bass, 1974.

Reiss, D. *The Family's Construction of Reality*. Cambridge, Mass.: Harvard University Press, 1981.

Ricks, M. "The Social Transmission of Parental Behavior: Attachment Across Generations." In I. Bretherton and E. Waters (eds.), *Growing Points of Attachment Theory and Research*. Monographs of the Society for Research in Child Development, no. 209. Chicago: University of Chicago Press, 1986.

Rogers, C. R. "Client-Centered Therapy." In S. Arieti (ed.), *American Handbook of Psychiatry*. Vol. 3. New York: Basic Books, 1966.

Rosenthal, D. *Genetic Theory and Abnormal Behavior*. New York: McGraw-Hill, 1970.

Rutter, M., and Garmezy, N. "Developmental Psychopathology." In P. Mussen (ed.), *Handbook of Child Psychology*, Vol. 4: *Socialization*. New York: Wiley, 1983.

Sameroff, A. J., Seifer, R., and Zax, M. *Early Development of Children at Risk for Emotional Disorder*. Vol. 47. Monographs of the Society for Research in Child Development, no. 199. Chicago: University of Chicago Press, 1982.

Santostefano, S. *A Biodevelopmental Approach to Clinical Child Psychology*. New York: Wiley, 1975.

Sarason, S. B., Levine, M., Goldenberg, I. I., Cherlin, D. L., and Bennett, E. M. *Psychology in Community Settings: Clinical, Educational, Vocational, and Social Aspects*. New York: Wiley, 1966.

Satir, V. *Conjoint Family Therapy*. Palo Alto, Calif.: Science and Behavior Books, 1964.

Schmid-Kitsikis, E. "The Cognitive Mechanisms Underlying Problem-Solving in Psychotic and Mentally Retarded Children." In B. Inhelder and H. H. Chapman (eds.), *Piaget and His School: A Reader in Developmental Psychology*. New York: Springer-Verlag, 1976.

Schultz, S. J. *Family Systems Therapy: An Integration*. New York: Jason Aronson, 1984.

Selman, R. *The Growth of Interpersonal Understanding: Developmental and Clinical Analyses*. San Diego, Calif.: Academic Press, 1980.

Skinner, B. F. *Science and Human Behavior*. New York: Macmillan, 1953.

Skolnick, A. *The Intimate Environment: Exploring Marriage and the Family*. Boston: Little, Brown, 1973.

Sroufe, L. A., and Rutter, M. "The Domain of Developmental Psychopathology." *Child Development,* 1984, *55,* 17–29.

Turiel, E. "An Experimental Test of the Sequentiality of Developmental Stages in the Child's Moral Judgment." *Journal of Personality and Social Psychology,* 1966, *3,* 611–618.

Vygotsky, L. S. *Mind in Society: The Development of the Higher Psychological Processes.* Cambridge, Mass.: Harvard University Press, 1978.

Wallerstein, J. S., and Kelly, J. B. *Surviving the Breakup: How Children and Parents Cope with Divorce.* New York: Basic Books, 1980.

Walsh, F. *Normal Family Processes.* New York: Guilford Press, 1982.

Weinstein, R., Marshall, H. H., Sharpe, L., and Botkin, M. "Pygmalion and the Student: Age and Classroom Differences in Children's Awareness of Teachers' Expectations." *Child Development,* 1987, *58,* 1079–1093.

Weissman, M. M. "Psychotherapy and Its Relevance to the Pharmacotherapy of Affective Disorders: From Ideology to Evidence." In M. A. Lipton, A. DiMascio, and K. F. Killam (eds.), *Psychopharmacology: A Generation of Progress.* New York: Raven, 1978.

Winnicott, D. W. "Transitional Objects and Transitional Phenomena." *International Journal of Psycho-Analysis,* 1953, *34,* 89–97.

Wyatt, R. J., Potkin, S. G., Walls, P. D., Nichols, A., Carpenter, W., and Murphy, D. "Clinical Correlates of Low Platelet Monoamin Oxidase in Schizophrenic Patients." In H. S. Akiskal and W. L. Webb (eds.), *Psychiatric Diagnosis: Explorations of Biological Predictors.* New York: Spectrum, 1978.

Wynne, L. C., and Singer, M. T. "Thought Disorder and Family Relations of Schizophrenics: A Classification of Forms of Thinking." *Archives of General Psychiatry,* 1963, *9,* 199–206.

Philip A. Cowan is professor of psychology at the University of California, Berkeley. A former head of the clinical program there, he now codirects, with Carolyn Pape Cowan, a longitudinal research intervention study of marital quality, parenting styles, and child development.

As children's cognitive abilities develop and change over time,
so must the way in which they understand their emotional
worlds.

Cognitive-Developmental Differences in Emotional Understanding

Ellen D. Nannis

Mark, age three, was being scolded by his father. "You're mad at me," Mark declared. "Yes," his father replied. "Do you still love me?" Mark inquired almost cautiously. His father, somewhat taken aback explained, "I'm angry at you because of what you did, but yes, of course, I still love you. Do you understand that?" "I understand," responded Mark, "but it doesn't make sense."

Clinicians, teachers, parents, and all who work with children are aware of the dilemma facing Mark's father—that is, how do you talk about feelings in a way that children understand and that makes sense to them? With this question in mind, a burgeoning area of research examines children's knowledge about feelings, the bases of attributions of feelings, ideas about causality of feelings, control of emotional expres-

I would like to thank Philip Cowan for his assistance on the research that is the basis of this chapter, Peter Lifton for his editorial comments, and Terri Harold for her assistance in preparing the manuscript.

E. D. Nannis, P. A. Cowan (eds.). *Developmental Psychopathology and Its Treatment.*
New Directions for Child Development, no. 39. San Francisco: Jossey-Bass, Spring 1988.

sion, and how one understands the experience of feeling multiple feelings simultaneously. Many who study emotional understanding in children present results descriptively and within a developmental framework. Few of the reseachers, however, present their findings within the context of a general perspective of cognitive development. For example, it would be useful to focus on how age and stage changes related to cognitive development are connected with changes in emotional understanding.

In this chapter, I will focus on the development of children's understanding of feelings. Based on current research, I will present a coding system describing four levels of emotional understanding, with the different levels linked to developmental differences in nonsocial, cognitive abilities. I will use clinical vignettes to illustrate the utility of this cognitive-developmental perspective in clinical interventions.

An important distinction needs to be made at the outset. The area of emotional understanding is not synonymous with emotional development. Rather, it overlaps with the field of emotional development, focusing on how changes in cognitive development influence changes in emotional experience and the emotional repertoire. I will not address the question of whether there is a system of emotion that undergoes change and development. Rather, I will focus on how the child organizes his or her emotional system to act and react to the world. My basic assumption is that cognitive development serves as one organizer of emotion. This is not a unique perspective but rather builds on cognitive-developmental theory proffered by Piaget (1981), Cicchetti and Pogge-Hesse (1981), Sroufe (1979), Cowan (1978, 1982), and others. As children's cognitive abilities develop and change over time, so must the ways in which they understand their emotional worlds. This perspective suggests that structural differences in cognitive development influence how children and adolescents interpret and eventually internalize emotional experiences.

Children and adolescents have many emotional experiences for which they have neither labels nor adequate understanding. One source of emotional difficulties may be the mismatch between that which is experienced (the feeling) and the cognitive structure available to process the information. For example, a four-year-old may not be able to make sense of the fact that he is happy and angry at the same time despite a confusing surge of emotional experience. The inability to construct a way to understand the conflicting feelings may lead to a sense of lack of control over one's self and result in some dysfunctional behavior as a way to gain control.

Further along the age spectrum, an adolescent experimenting with hypothesis generating in formal operations may be able to take multiple perspectives and generate many possible explanations for why she feels sad. However, in considering the multiple possibilities, she may be unable to focus on what she herself feels. In the instance of the four-year-old, his cognitive structures are insufficient to deal adequately with his emotional experiences. In the case of the adolescent, the development of more complex thought leads to greater difficulty in limiting options and focusing more narrowly on her own emotional experience.

This chapter discusses different ways in which children and adolescents understand their feelings. Because of space limitations, I will not review the literature in the area of emotional understanding. I refer the reader to another paper by Nannis (forthcoming) for a more extensive discussion of previous studies.

Research concerning emotional understanding can be classified in four categories. Most common is research concerning children's knowledge of feelings (Carroll and Steward, 1984; Gnepp and Gould, 1985; Harris, 1983, 1985; Harris, Olthof, and Terwogt, 1981; Nannis and Cowan, 1987; Taylor and Harris, 1983; Tharinger, 1981; Thompson, 1985). This area is concerned with the basis of children's inferences about their own and others' feelings and some general ideas about how feelings work (for example, that feelings may wane in intensity after the precipitating event).

A second area of research involves children's ideas about control over emotional expressions. This includes children's understanding of social conventions about displaying feelings (Saarni, 1979, 1985) and the actual strategies used by children to manipulate their expressions, such as how children hide feelings (Nannis and Cowan, 1987; Tharinger, 1981).

The third focus of research concerns children's understanding about the ability to experience multiple feelings. This research was pioneered by Harter and her colleagues (Harter, 1977, 1980, 1983a, 1983b; Harter and Buddin, 1987). Those who study children's ideas about experiencing multiple feelings generally link this skill with the ability to experience ambivalence (Donaldson and Westerman, 1986).

The final area of research includes children's notions about the causality of feelings (Donaldson and Westerman, 1986; Gnepp and Gould, 1985; Harris, Olthof, and Terwogt, 1981; Nannis and Cowan, 1987). Studies addressing issues of causality include children's abilities to discern precipitants of feelings in themselves and others and children's ideas about how feelings develop (for example, where feelings come from and how they go away).

Regardless of the specific area of research about emotional understanding, studies conclude that there are age-related differences in children's emotional understanding. Three levels of understanding are usually elaborated. Younger children (approximately three to five years old) understand feelings as an external phenomena, precipitated by a single event, such as getting a present. Latency-aged children (approximately six to ten years old) view feelings as internal processes communicated by external signs, such as facial expression. By adolescence, more internal and mentalistic explanations are used. Adolescents acknowledge the importance of situations in precipitating or maintaining an affective state, though they recognize that there is an internal process under a person's control that will help them to evaluate situations and direct affective expressions.

Most studies explore children's ideas about one or two aspects of feelings. On the basis of age or grade children participating in these studies generally are presumed to be in the preoperational and concrete operational levels of thought. With relatively few exceptions, emotional understanding in adolescents is unexplored. Even fewer studies attempt to link emotional understanding to structural measures of cognitive stage (Carroll and Steward, 1984; Cowan, 1978, 1982; Harter, 1983a; Nannis, 1985, forthcoming; Selman, 1980; Tharinger, 1981). In an effort to articulate a cognitive-developmental framework for emotional understanding, I will discuss how four levels of emotional understanding are related to stages of cognitive development as described by Piaget.

Four Levels of Emotional Understanding

Emotional understanding at four age levels is summarized in Figure 1 and elaborated in this section. Each level is illustrated with interview data that I have gathered. In a series of studies, seventy children in four different grades (kindergarten, third, sixth, and ninth) and thirty-four college freshmen were interviewed about their knowledge of feelings, understanding of control over emotional expression, ideas about experiencing multiple feelings, and understanding about the causality of feelings. In addition, the children's and adolescents' cognitive levels were assessed by several nonsocial, cognitive tasks. The performances on the cognitive tasks were related to children's emotional understanding. The illustrations reflect optimal levels of responses. That is, older children do talk about feelings using explanations similar to their younger peers. However, unlike their younger peers, they are able to reason about feelings using more complex notions.

Level 1 (Three to Five Years Old). Level 1 responses are used primarily by the youngest children. Feelings are described as external, concrete phenomena—frequently, the facial expression that represents them. Feelings can change by changing the facial expression or the concrete object that causes them. Because feelings are the concrete external object, they cannot be feigned nor hidden—if the smile is not present, then one is not happy. One cannot pretend to be sad by frowning, since a frown always means one is sad. Children at this age believe one can have multiple, simultaneous feelings only if the two activities or facial expressions can occur simultaneously (for example, crying and smiling). That is, if

Figure 1. Levels of Explanations about Knowledge of Feelings, Control of Feelings, Multiple Feelings, and Causality of Feelings

	Knowledge	*Control of Expression*	*Multiple Feelings*	*Causality*
Level 1	Feelings are external, concrete phenomena.	Impossible since presence or absence of the external phenomenon or event is the feeling.	Possible if two different facial expressions can coexist.	Precipitated by presence or absence of event, object, or facial expression.
Level 2	Feelings are internal, concrete phenomena.	Possible since feelings are internal.	Possible if two different organs house the two feelings, or feelings are of similar valence, or explanations based on sequential experience of emotion.	Precipitated by internal organ. Changes occur by feelings going from one body organ to another.
Level 3	Feelings are an internal, diffuse process.	Possible. One can willfully misrepresent feelings.	Possible by attributing different feelings to different aspects of same feeling.	Precipitated by an external event; no explanation of how the external event leads to an internal phenomenon.
Level 4	Feelings are part of a larger scientific system (for example, physiological and psychological).	Control of feelings explained by using levels of consciousness and introspection.	Possible as part of normal emotional experience. May talk about it as a combined feeling.	Precipitated by physiological/biological/scientific process; child attempts to explain how external events precipitate internal processes.

one cannot make a happy and angry face at the same time, one cannot be angry and happy at the same time.

Children tend to understand the feelings of others in one of two ways. When asked how they know what others are feeling, they will say "I don't know," or they will give answers invoking concrete, external criteria, usually involving a facial expression. In the former case, it is uncertain whether the "I don't know" reflects an inability to understand the question or lack of knowledge about the answer. However, the lack of knowledge or understanding is more likely when children talk about causality, control, or multiple feelings. When asked about how they know a parent is happy, children at this age generally respond using the same level as when they talk about their own feelings. The content of the response often differs, though the level of explanation does not.

> *I:* How do you know you are happy?
> *S:* I'm smiling.
> *I:* Can you be sad and smile?
> *S:* No way. I'd have a frown on . . .
> *I:* How do you get to feel happy?
> *S:* I smile.
> *I:* Are there other ways?
> *S:* Eating candy.
> *I:* How does eating candy make you happy?
> *S:* I smile when I eat candy.
> *I:* Can you stop feeling happy?
> *S:* When the candy is gone . . . If there's no more candy, I'm not happy anymore.
> *I:* Can you be happy and angry at the same time?
> *S: (laughs and has contorted face)*
> *I:* It looks like you're smiling and trying to have a mad face.
> *S: (laughing)* Yeah . . .
> *I:* How do you know your mom and dad are happy?
> *S:* They laugh.
> *I:* Could they be happy and you wouldn't know?
> *S:* If I was in another room.
> *I:* How come that would matter?
> *S:* I couldn't see them.

As in other areas of preoperational thought, these children's thoughts are dominated by what they see. It is difficult to conceive of feelings being present without a direct referent. Causality of the feeling is the preceding event (eating candy). However, there is no appreciation of candy precipitating the feeling; rather, mere presence or absence of the candy is considered to trigger the presence or absence of the feeling.

Level 2 (Six to Nine Years Old). In my study, children in all age groups responded using Level 2 criteria, although children between seven and eight used this level of response more frequently than children at other ages, particularly in relation to their own feelings. Feelings are considered to be internal phenomena tied to such concrete objects as hearts, brains, and stomachs. Because feelings reside inside the body, they can be hidden, although the children do not think that one can willfully hide feelings. Children are beginning to make a distinction between having feelings—an internal process—and showing feelings—an external event. Children using this level of explanation are more likely to agree that one can pretend feelings than they are to admit that feelings can be hidden. This finding is not fully understood. It may reflect the fact that pretending to have a feeling requires more fantasy and thus is assimilative, whereas hiding a feeling requires altering the expression to meet external social demands and is therefore accommodative. Because assimilation may be an easier process (Block, 1982), using already existing structure, pretense may be accepted more readily.) Despite this distinction, there is no difference in the level of explanations concerning pretending and hiding feelings.

Multiple feelings, such as feeling both happy and sad, are easily explained by having one feeling in one organ and a second feeling housed in a different organ. Some children explain multiple feelings as two feelings about two different events, or two feelings that are actually sequential, not simultaneous. A child's belief that one cannot hold multiple feelings is explained in terms of a person being all one thing or another; the body cannot hold the two feelings because the two feelings cannot mix.

Because they believe that feelings are internal, it follows that children operating at Level 2 will state that they never know what others are feeling unless others tell them. The few exceptions to this rule are fanciful responses stating that mind reading, magic, and X-rays can help them to know what someone else feels. In discussing any of the four aspects of feelings, children at this age tend to use a similar level of reasoning whether they are talking about their own or another's feelings.

I: How do you know you are happy?

S: My brain tells me.

I: How does your brain know that those are happy feelings?

S: I don't know; it just does.

I: Is there any other way to figure out you're happy?

S: You mean if my brain didn't tell me? *(nods yes)* Well, maybe my stomach would tell me . . .

I: Can you hide your happy feelings?

S: Yeah, they're inside you.

I: Well, is there any way I'd be able to tell what you're feeling?

S: No. *(pause)* Well, maybe if you took an X-ray.

I: Any other way?

S: If you could read my mind . . .

I: How do you know your mom and dad are happy?

S: They'd tell me.

I: What if they didn't tell you?

S: I don't know, I'd have to ask them . . .

Children's responses to feelings at this level reflect the beginning and middle stages of concrete operational thought. Children are able to break the dominance of their perceptions, thereby allowing feelings to be an internal event. However, the break from the immediately perceptible is not a break from the concrete and tangible. Hence, although internal, feelings are linked to concrete objects, such as hearts or brains.

Children at this age are able to classify using simple matrices—that is, an object can fall into two classes. Classification skills underlie Level 2 responses, particularly in response to questions about multiple feelings. Children understand that one person may be described in two ways, such as happy and loving; however, unlike classification of physical objects, there may be qualifications in rules about classes—for instance, one cannot be angry and happy but one can be loving and happy. Here, Harter's (1983a) ideas about valence of feelings appear important in terms of the types of classes that are formed. It may be that the child can consider positively valenced feelings simultaneously but not feelings of opposite valences.

In response to questions about interpersonal understanding of feelings, children at Level 2 are similar to early intuitive thinkers in their level of egocentrism. They seem to know another has a different point of view but are unable to know precisely what it is. Thus, children at Level 2 recognize that they do not automatically know what their parents are feeling (that is, parents' feelings can be different from one's own feelings) but there are no rules for inferring what the feelings might be. Hence the only way to know what one's parents are feeling is to ask.

Level 3 (Ten to Thirteen Years Old). Children answering questions with Level 3 responses are primarily older children; based on my own research, no kindergarten children responded at Level 3. Children using Level 3 criteria know that feelings are internal processes rather than internal events. Feelings are viewed as being diffuse rather than based on a particular object. Children also begin to understand that they have some control over feelings. Children can hide feelings, feign them, and actively try to cause them. This aspect of control is probably the hallmark of Level 3 responses.

As children try to explain the experience and process of feelings, there is awareness that one needs to include aspects of both the internal and the external world. Something external may precipitate the internal process. This integration leads to a notion of causality that includes the relation between internal and external events; however, there is little ability to elaborate on this relation.

Children believe that multiple feelings toward a single object or event are possible. Children explain this possibility by attributing different feelings to different aspects of the same object. For example, a child might say she is happy that she gets to have a snack but sad that the snack is always fruit. This allows for feelings that are both simultaneous and directed at the same object or event.

In trying to understand how parents feel, some children will invoke a sense of familiarity or intimacy as giving one license to infer another's feelings. However, children tend to use lower levels of reasoning when inferring feelings in another than when discussing their own feelings. The difference between explanations about one's own versus another's feelings is only found when children are asked about their knowledge of feelings. When discussing causality, control, and the experience of multiple feelings, children generally use similar levels of explanations.

Discussing knowledge of another's feelings may be a more complex endeavor than discussing other issues related to other people's feelings. Knowledge of others' feelings requires not only the understanding of basic processes but also greater coordination of perspectives. That is, in answering the question "How do you know your parents are happy?" the child must assess the parents' affective state and coordinate the information with ideas about how the child comes to know any information. Answers to questions about causality, multiple feelings, and control of expression in others may merely require the application of the same principle one uses about the self. The answer to the question "How do your parents hide their happy feelings?" does not require examining one's own thought processes. It requires an application of information concerning the basic processes of feelings. Thus, there is no need to transform information from one's own perspective to that of another. Because of the greater complexity of the task of knowing what another feels, responding to questions about how others feel may develop more slowly than other areas of emotional understanding.

I: How do you know you're happy?
S: I feel it . . . I feel it all over, inside. I get real excited, I want to jump up and down, I talk a lot.
I: Could you do those things and feel sad?
S: It wouldn't make sense. I guess if I was trying to hide my sad feelings I might. That would be weird.
I: How would that work?
S: Well, like my mom, she knows me real well and knows what I do when I'm happy and stuff, so if she saw me doing those things she'd probably think I was happy . . .
I: How come if you did all those things you wouldn't be happy?
S: Well, like I can feel something way down inside but do something else . . . feelings and doing things are sometimes different . . .
I: How do you get to be happy?
S: By getting a good grade.
I: How does that work?

S: Well, like I get a good grade and that sets something off in me and I feel good inside . . .

I: When you say "sets something off," what do you think that might be?

S: I don't know.

I: How does something outside (your grade) make you feel happy inside?

S: That's a good question . . .

I: Can you be happy and angry at the same time?

S: That's harder; they don't mix. Maybe you could be happy you did well on the test but mad 'cause you thought it wasn't a fair test . . .

I: How do you know your mom is happy?

S: She tells me.

I: Any other way?

S: Oh, when she's in a good mood, and her voice is soft . . .

I: How do you know she's happy then?

S: I don't know for sure. I mean feelings are inside you and you don't really know what's inside a person. To really know she'd have to tell me. I could guess. 'Cause like I know her real well. I've seen her a lot and I know that when she is like that she's happy.

I: Would you know if I were happy?

S: I wouldn't for sure 'cause I don't know you so I don't know what you're like when you're happy.

Children's responses at Level 3 have many elements of late concrete operational thinking. Not only are feelings internal, but now they also can be intangible and without form. There are attempts to understand that feelings may be part of a larger system of knowledge, but these children do not seem able to articulate the system. In explaining the causality of feelings, children's explanations are similar to late concrete operational explanations of the origin of night. There is an appreciation for the relation between elements in the process (for night, between the sun and moon, for feelings, between the environment and internal world); however, the child still lacks the ability to formalize the relation into a theory.

At this level, children are able to coordinate their own and others' points of view so as to imagine what another might feel even though the experience is different from their own. Children also are able to separate themselves from their parents' worlds and infer what it is that would make them happy. The ability to infer another's feelings is still limited to the child and a known other, for like causality, children do not construct generalizable rules about others' feelings.

The ability to experience multiple feelings is still influenced by the critical element of the valence of the feeling. Explaining the experience of feelings of a similar valence (such as happy and loving) precedes the ability to explain the experience of feelings of opposite valences (such as happy and angry). However, children also are able to break down a single event and examine attributes or components of it, thereby allowing themselves to have multiple feelings about it. This new achievement may be similar to more difficult conservation problems (such as weight) that generally are not achieved until the stage of late concrete operational thought. Like the conservation of weight problem, thinking about the ability to hold multiple feelings may require breaking down the concept into multiple components with the added recognition that the parts can be considered both separately and as a whole.

Level 4 (Age Fourteen and Onward). Level 4 is the highest level of explanation that I encountered when interviewing children and college students about their understanding of feelings. It was used primarily by the ninth graders and college students (slightly less than half of the ninth graders and slightly more than two-thirds of the college students). Adolescents at this level view feelings as part of a complex body of scientific knowledge. Although they are not always able to articulate how feelings work, those who respond at Level 4 refer to biological, psychological, and physiological processes of emotions. Further, adolescents believe that the actual causality of feelings is a result of instigating one or more of these processes. They agree that one can try to start the process (such as try to make oneself happy) or that external events can precipitate the internal process. Unlike the younger children, adolescents at Level 4 try to explain how an external event precipitates an internal process, usually using the sensory system in their explanations.

Those responding at Level 4 also have generated some universal laws about how feelings work and what feelings can and cannot do. The question of whether one can experience multiple feelings sometimes is hedged. One never truly experiences two feelings at once: there is either a rapid and constant shift between two feelings, or the experience of two feelings is blended into a third, new feeling that actually is experienced. In explaining causality, control, and multiple feelings, adolescents use similar response levels regardless of whether they are talking about their own or others' feelings. However, in talking about how they know what another feels, these adolescents probably will give explanations invoking lower-level responses (for example, "Ask them," or "Look at their faces"). When pressed, however, many adolescents are capable of explanations invoking universal principles about feelings.

I: How do you know you feel happy?
S: Probably because you don't feel sad. You don't show signs of

sadness and you're feeling—I think it's just a stimulus [that sets off] your heart and nerves . . . It's just that your nervous system has a flow of adrenalin when you're happy and it stimulates your heart and you feel—it's like putting a pressure on your heart . . .

I: How do you get to feel happy?

S: You start by anticipating something good is going to happen. Then you get closer and closer to the reality and they [the feelings] build . . . They start in your mind and they flow throughout you . . .

I: Can you be happy and sad at the same time?

S: Yes, it's like you're confused for a minute. That's when you know you have two feelings at once—or even three . . . because you sort of feel confused. Maybe it's something that's not sad and not happy—something different from both of them, maybe like it's a new feeling and you're confused because you're not used to it.

I: How do you know your mom and dad are happy?

S: Probably 'cause they'd tell me . . . They're in a happier mood . . . posture, physical characteristics.

I: How do you know they are happy then?

S: How do I know? I don't for sure. I mean how do you ever know anyone else's experience? I could guess, but know really—you can't.

I: If you'd guess?

S: Well, it goes back to probably the same way I know about mine . . . feelings probably work the same way for everyone.

Until adolescence, formal operational thought is a rarity. The emergence of formal operational thought enables adolescents to develop a more complete, comprehensive, theoretical framework than their younger peers. Feelings follow rules and these rules apply universally, not just to particular individuals or groups. Feelings are explained within a larger body of knowledge or science; in the present example, they are linked to a biological system.

In addition, youngsters at this age are capable of coordinating multiple perspectives. As such, they are capable of recursive thought—that is, they can think about how others would know what they are feeling, and they can think about their own thoughts and feelings. Thus, adolescents who respond at Level 4 talk about being aware of their own feelings. However, when it comes to explaining how one knows what another feels, the issue becomes complicated. The difficulty may be the result of two processes. As children grow older, they develop an ability to be introspective and analyze their emotional states. In addition, as children age and formal thought processes develop, the question of knowledge about feelings becomes more of a general epistemological question concerning how one really knows anything. Although some of these adolescents will make inferences about their own experiences, they become far more cautious about what others are thinking and feeling. The cognitive advances they have made seem to lead to greater difficulties in understanding feelings because the problem has become more complex. The impact of these difficulties may be reflected in the greater self-centeredness noted in adolescent thought.

Because adolescents are involved in hypothesis generating and testing and in discovering "necessary and sufficient causes," they are apt to be precise and literal in their understanding or explanations. In the example, this is apparent in the explanation of multiple feelings. The question of whether one can feel two feelings at the same time yields such responses as "They are never really together" or "It's not really two feelings, it's a third new one."

Cognitive Links in Emotional Understanding

At the end of each section describing the levels of emotional understanding, I suggested that certain cognitive achievements are related to the particular level of emotional understanding. For example, the ability to classify according to multiple criteria seems to parallel the knowledge that a person can experience multiple feelings at the same time. The nature of the links between the development of knowledge in one domain (for example, the physical) and the development of knowledge in a second domain (for example, emotional or interpersonal) is a highly debated topic. A major issue in the debate concerns the question of whether domains of thought develop independently or in an interdependent manner. It is not my intention to engage in that debate at this time. Data that I collected demonstrate that the type of reasoning children use in discussing feelings roughly parallels the type of reasoning used when children are asked to reason about such physical problems as classification of objects or physical identity. This finding suggests an underlying similarity in reasoning across domains of knowledge. Although knowledge may develop independently for each domain, there appears to be a general framework of development that each domain follows. In noting the similarity across domains of knowledge, I make no assumption about whether the development of knowledge in one area precedes the development of knowledge in another area. Rather, my own research and that of others (Carroll and Steward, 1984; Tharinger, 1981) support the idea that there is a relation between knowledge in the physical and emotional domains.

In discussing cognitive components in emotional understanding, one also must consider the idea of stages of reasoning (Piaget, 1970;

Kohlberg, 1969). Whether emotional understanding represents a similar, orderly, and complete development of knowledge is uncertain.

Those who study several areas of emotional understanding in the same children note that there is a basic pattern that understanding of feelings follows for each area of emotion (such as causality, control of expression, and so on). This finding led some to argue for the existence of stages in emotional understanding (Selman, 1980) and others to argue for a stage-like quality to emotional understanding (Carroll and Steward, 1984). However, my own data suggest the development of emotional understanding is not a uniform process. Knowledge of feelings, in particular, appears to develop differently than does understanding causality, multiple feelings, and control of emotional expressions. Therefore, the development of emotional understanding is not uniform and as such may defy a basic premise for a stage theory—that knowledge develops as a structured whole. Resolution of whether the question of the different levels of emotional understanding represent stages will be in whether we can understand asynchronies found in the different areas of emotional knowledge.

Regardless of whether there are stages in the understanding of feelings, it is still useful to consider emotional understanding from a cognitive-developmental point of view. As mentioned earlier in this chapter, emotional understanding is one aspect of emotional development though not synonymous with it. The way in which people make inferences about their own feelings or others' feelings influences their emotional reactions. For example, if a child believes that the only way to change from sad to happy is to change environments or objects with which the child is interacting, one could predict that that child might try to change feelings by fleeing the present environment or trying to get a new toy.

Clinical Applications

Differences in levels of emotional understanding have therapeutic implications, particularly in how we speak with children about feelings, how we understand the source of their emotional difficulties or concerns, and the focus of our interventions.

Consider the vignette at the beginning of the chapter. Mark's father is trying to discipline his child and is being careful to separate his anger at Mark's behavior from his anger at Mark himself. The intention is to help Mark maintain a sense that he is worthwhile, though his behavior must change. Although the intent is positive, it is unclear whether Mark understands the message. When talking with Mark about the interchange, the therapist learns that Mark thinks his dad is mad at him because "you can't be loving and angry at the same time." Mark knows his father is angry because "he has a mad face on." Mark presumes that were he to kiss his father or do something nice, his father will stop being angry since "[my dad's happy feelings start] when I do something nice." Because Mark believes that angry feelings go away when you do something nice, it may prove distressing to Mark to discover that his father's anger does not dissipate even though Mark now has done something nice. This can be scary for Mark, leaving him to wonder if his father will ever be happy or loving again.

When Mark grows up, he will know that two feelings can coexist, particularly if directed at different objects. Despite this knowledge, Mark may still feel the need to ask his father if he still loves him when Mark is being scolded. It appears that highly charged emotional issues either undermine more advanced cognitive structures or eclipse them. (The subjugation of one domain for the other is frequently seen in pathology. In the present example a highly emotional situation results in the constriction of cognitive skills available for use. In the case of strong use of cognitive skills, for example in obsessive-compulsive disorders, emotion is highly constricted. These examples illustrate the interrelation of affect and cognition in psychopathology.) The now older Mark may ask if his father still loves him, in order to reaffirm emotional security. However, the explanation that "I am mad at you for what you did but I still love you as a person" now will make sense. In addition, Mark will know that doing something nice for his father will help to make him happy again but that it will take time for the angry feelings to wane.

A second example comes from a family therapy case. John, age five, and Beth, age fourteen, were brought to a mental health clinic by their parents. The parents were well-educated people who were getting a divorce. At the evaluation interview the family was encouraged to talk about the separation, what it meant to them, what kinds of changes it would involve, and how they felt about the changes. John burst out plaintively, "But where will my guinea pigs sleep?" Beth responded, "Who cares about your stupid guinea pigs? Don't you understand, we're going to have to choose who we want to live with!" The therapist asked Beth how she felt about that and she replied, "It stinks! If I say my mom, then my dad will get angry; if I say my dad, my mom will be upset." The therapist turned to John and asked, "What do you think about what your sister said?" John shrugged. "Beth is sad 'cause she's crying." "Are you sad?" the therapist asked. "No, I'm not crying." "I know," said the therapist, "but you have a frown on." John was quiet. The therapist added, "It must be very hard for the guinea pigs to live in two houses." John looked up and shook his head yes. "Let's draw a picture of the guinea pigs," suggested the therapist. Beth was becoming increasingly annoyed during the discussion with her brother and finally yelled, "Why are we talking about guinea pigs?"

This vignette illustrates that although both children are similarly distressed, their different cognitive levels lead to different aspects of a similar situation being internalized and becoming the source of the distress. For John, a five-year-old, the divorce is a series of concrete events with basic, concrete problems. It is a question of where his toys will be, where his guinea pigs will sleep, and where he will spend Christmas. These logistic and material concerns present the level at which John is most likely to experience the impact of the divorce. Asked about how he feels about the divorce, his feelings will probably reflect the moment. If John is thinking about having two Christmas celebrations, he might say he is happy about the divorce. If he is thinking about his guinea pigs sleeping in one house and he in another house, John will likely express being sad. A therapist attempting to help John verbalize the mass of psychological turmoil within must help John attach the different feelings to different specific events rather than attempt to help him verbalize that he has mixed feelings or even that he feels many things at once. Trying to get John to verbalize that he has mixed or different feelings may be difficult, if not impossible, until John knows he can feel two things at the same time. The therapist does not have to avoid dealing with ambivalence. Rather, by attaching the different feelings to different events instead of trying to discuss mixed feelings, the therapist is addressing the issue of ambivalence in a way that makes sense to a five-year-old child.

Finally, in helping John to talk about feelings it is important for the therapist to remember that at age five the feelings are the emotional expression—they are the event. Hence, for John it is of little use to label feelings that the therapist assumes John is experiencing if the feelings do not match the facial expression or event. To say to John that he also must be sad about his parents' separation as John is describing the joys of two Christmases likely will not make sense from John's perspective. If the therapist wants to bring out the sad feelings of the divorce, it may be better to introduce an event related to the situation that is assumed to be sad, such as sleeping in a different house than the guinea pigs.

Beth's distress, and therefore her treatment, have a different focus. She is accurate in pointing out that this discussion of guinea pigs avoids a direct discussion of the divorce. Beth is fourteen years old and her understanding of feelings—her own and others'—is more abstract, more complex. She is capable of understanding and recognizing more complex emotions, such as guilt or jealousy. For Beth, feelings are an internal process that are related, though not synonymous with, external events. Therefore, the logistics of the divorce are less important (except perhaps as they interfere with her peer support and peer interactions). What is causing Beth's pain is focused more on inner events. She may be trying to resolve confused feelings stirred up by being entangled in relationship and loyalty conflicts. She is confused by the recognition that a single event can cause her to love and hate the same people. Whereas for John it is his outer world that is out of control, for Beth it is her inner world. As a therapist with Beth, it is possible to focus the treatment on the inner feelings, whereas for John that is less meaningful since feelings are external. For Beth, one therapeutic focus becomes her relationship with others (her parents) and how those relationships will change to an eventual new emotional equilibrium.

Conclusion

Earlier in this volume, Cowan referred to the cognitive-developmental perspective as one cell in a nine-cell matrix used to conceptualize normality and pathology. In my chapter I have focused on the cognitive-developmental perspective both as a theoretical orientation in understanding normal emotional experience and as a framework for conceptualizing intervention. Regardless of the type of intervention—psychoanalysis, family therapy, social skills training—a cognitive-developmental conceptualization guides the therapist in the language and presentation of the therapeutic input. As the clinical vignette demonstrates, a cognitive-developmental perspective lets us know if we should talk about divorce in terms of feeling torn between two parents or talk about divorce in terms of where guinea pigs will sleep.

Knowing differences in how feelings are processed provides clues to therapists in terms of understanding and gaining insight into the emotional turmoil of young clients. A child who believes that the expression on another's face always reflects the feelings of the person will find it a confusing world when dealing with people who are facially unexpressive. Likewise, that same child may have difficulty reacting appropriately to others when others are purposely controlling or feigning emotional expressions in order to be socially appropriate.

Children and adolescents generally process their emotional worlds differently. What is assimilated from the same emotional experience will differ according to the cognitive capacities of those involved. What becomes internalized and forms the bedrock for further emotional experiences therefore will be different. A cognitive-developmental perspective as applied to emotional understanding provides clues to the nature of children's emotional experiences and has direct bearing on intervention. It allows us to discuss feelings with children in a way that they understand and that makes sense to them.

References

Block, J. "Assimilation, Accommodation, and the Dynamics of Personality Development." *Child Development*, 1982, 53 (2), 281–295.

Carroll, J., and Steward, M. "The Role of Cognitive Development in Children's Understanding of Their Own Feelings." *Child Development*, 1984, *55*, 1486-1492.

Cicchetti, D., and Pogge-Hesse, P. "The Relation Between Emotion and Cognition in Infant Development." In M. Lamb and L. Sherrod (eds.), *Infant Social Cognition*. Hillsdale, N.J.: Erlbaum, 1981.

Cowan, P. A. *Piaget with Feeling: Cognitive, Social, and Emotional Dimensions*. New York: Holt, Rinehart & Winston, 1978.

Cowan, P. A. "The Relationship Between Emotional and Cognitive Development." In D. Cicchetti and P. Hesse (eds.), *Emotional Development*. New Directions for Child Development, no. 16. San Francisco: Jossey-Bass, 1982.

Donaldson, S., and Westerman, M. "Development of Children's Understanding of Ambivalence and Causal Theories of Emotions." *Developmental Psychology*, 1986, *22*, 655-662.

Gnepp, J., and Gould, M. "The Development of Personalized Inferences: Understanding Other People's Emotional Reaction in Light of Their Prior Experiences." *Child Development*, 1985, *56*, 1455-1464.

Harris, P. "Children's Understanding of the Link Between Situation and Emotion." *Journal of Experimental Child Psychology*, 1983, *36*, 490-509.

Harris, P. "What Children Know About the Situations that Provoke Affect." In M. Lewis and C. Saarni (eds.), *The Socialization of Emotions*. New York: Plenum Press, 1985.

Harris, P., Olthof, T., and Terwogt, M. "Children's Knowledge of Emotion," *Journal of Child Psychiatry and Psychology*, 1981, *22*, 247-261.

Harter, S. "A Cognitive-Developmental Approach to Children's Expression of Conflicting Feelings and a Technique to Facilitate Such Expression in Play Therapy." *Journal of Consulting and Clinical Psychology*, 1977, *45*, 417-432.

Harter, S. "A Cognitive-Developmental Approach to Children's Understanding of Affect and Trait Labels." In F. Serafica (ed.), *Social Cognition and Social Relations in Context*. New York: Guilford Press, 1980.

Harter, S. "Children's Understanding of Multiple Emotions: A Cognitive-Developmental Approach." In W. Overton (ed.), *The Relationship Between Social and Cognitive Development*. Hillsdale, N.J.: Erlbaum, 1983a.

Harter, S. "Developmental Perspectives on the Self-System." In P. Mussen (ed.), *Handbook of Child Psychology*. (4th ed.) New York: Wiley, 1983b.

Harter, S., and Buddin, B. J. "Children's Understanding of the Simultaneity of Two Emotions: A Five-Stage Developmental Acquisition Sequence." *Developmental Psychology*, 1987, *23*, 388-399.

Kohlberg, L. "Stage and Sequence: The Cognitive-Developmental Approach to Socialization." In D. A. Goslin (ed.), *Handbook of Socialization: Theory and Research*. Skokie, Ill.: Rand McNally, 1969.

Nannis, E. *Structural Differences in Emotional Understanding and Their Applications to Clinical Intervention*. Paper presented at the biennial meeting of the Society for Research in Child Development, Toronto, Apr. 1985.

Nannis, E. "A Cognitive-Developmental View of Emotional Understanding and Its Applications for Child Psychotherapy." In M. Lewis and S. Shirk (eds.), *Cognitive Development and Child Psychotherapy*. N.Y.: Plenum Press, forthcoming.

Nannis, E., and Cowan, P. A. "Emotional Understanding: A Matter of Age, Dimension, and Point of View." *Journal of Applied Developmental Psychology*, 1987, *8*, 289-304.

Piaget, J. *Structuralism*. New York: Basic Books, 1970.

Piaget, J. *Intelligence and Affectivity: Their Relationship During Child Development.* Palo Alto, Calif.: Annual Reviews, 1981.

Saarni, C. "Children's Understanding of Display Rules for Expressive Behavior." *Developmental Psychology,* 1979, *15,* 424–429.

Saarni, C. "Indirect Processes in Affect Socialization." In M. Lewis and C. Saarni (eds.), *The Socialization of Affect.* New York: Plenum Press, 1985.

Selman, R., *The Growth of Interpersonal Understanding.* Orlando, Fla.: Academic Press, 1980.

Sroufe, L. A. "Socioemotional Development." In J. Osofsky (ed.), *Handbook of Infant Development.* New York: Wiley, 1979.

Taylor, D., and Harris, P. "Knowledge of the Link Between Emotion and Memory Among Normal and Maladjusted Boys." *Developmental Psychology,* 1983, *19,* 832–838.

Tharinger, D. "The Development of the Child's Psychological Understanding of Feeling." Doctoral dissertation, University of California, Berkeley, 1981.

Thompson, R., "The Development of Children's Inference of the Emotions of Others." Paper presented at the biennial meeting of the Society for Research in Child Development, Toronto, Apr. 1985.

Ellen D. Nannis is assistant professor of psychology at the University of Maryland, Baltimore County. She also is staff psychologist at the Sheppard and Enoch Pratt Hospital in Towson, Maryland.

Therapy aimed at improving adolescents' affective and interpersonal functioning should be placed within a cognitive-developmental context.

Formal Operations and Interpersonal and Affective Disturbances in Adolescents

Debra Ellen Gordon

The affective and interpersonal development of the individual does not occur in a vacuum but accompanies the cognitive development of the child. How children's developing cognitive abilities affect their interpersonal functioning at different developmental stages, however, is an issue that has been little explored. The present discussion considers the period of adolescence and describes how cognitive-developmental concerns might apply to understanding adolescent problems in interpersonal and affective adaptation. It also investigates how intervention practices with adolescents might be placed within a cognitive-developmental context.

In order to more thoroughly consider these issues, I must first review several concepts central to Piagetian developmental theory that have inspired much of this chapter. Although the subject of some criti-

The author gratefully acknowledges Daniel Weinberger for his thoughtful review of this chapter, and wishes to thank Michael Pratt for his co-leadership of the therapy groups. Names and other identifying information of all group members have been disguised in this chapter.

E. D. Nannis, P. A. Cowan (eds.). *Developmental Psychopathology and Its Treatment.*
New Directions for Child Development, no. 39. San Francisco: Jossey-Bass, Spring 1988.

cism in recent years, Piaget's model offers a relatively comprehensive description of both the stages and dynamics of cognitive acquisition and therefore lends itself to understanding the link between cognitive dysfunction and adaptational difficulties. According to Piagetian theory, optimal psychological adaptation is marked by the presence of organized cognitive acquisitions—termed structures—that vary in form according to an individual's stage of development. Advancement through Piaget's sensorimotor, preoperational, concrete operational, and formal operational developmental stages allows individuals increasingly differentiated and more complex methods of viewing the world. The preoperational child, for example, has mastered such symbolic behaviors as language and play but has difficulty with such notions as conservation and hierarchical classification. The concrete operational child understands these concepts but is unable to reason abstractly—an acquisition of the formal operational period. In sum, the structural aspect of Piaget's theory suggests that the child's ability to understand events in the outside world is qualitatively different at each developmental period.

Described in Piaget's model are not only the structural acquisitions but also the functions that theoretically represent the dynamic mechanisms behind stage acquisition. Functions are adaptive methods of interacting with the environment; they include accommodation, the modification of existing psychological structures in terms of impinging stimulation, and assimilation, the interpretation of the environment in terms of existing psychological structure. For example, an individual may interpret evidence in terms of a priori hypotheses (assimilate) but may also accommodate conclusions to fit the evidence (Cowan, 1978). The functions are believed to be innate, invariant, and occurring at every stage of development. The functional aspect of Piagetian theory suggests that a relative balance between the processes of assimilation and accommodation is required for developmental progress.

In sum, a cognitive-developmental perspective suggests that optimal growth may be characterized by the presence of developmentally appropriate acquisitions (structures) as well as adaptive patterns of interaction with the environment (functions) (Cowan, Chapter One). Promoting optimal adaptation may therefore include stimulating the construction and use of high-level cognitive structures as well as encouraging effective interaction with the outside world. Conversely, psychological dysfunction should theoretically be accompanied by retardation, fixation, or nonattainment of essential cognitive acquisitions (structural difficulties), as well as aberrant patterns of interaction with the environment (functional problems). Problems in cognitive acquisition are likely to both cause and result from adaptational problems. Once cognitive delays have occurred, however, they may have pervasive effects on an individual's ability to adapt and cope with the environment.

Research linking cognitive deficit to problems in adaptation has focused on the earlier cognitive-developmental stages in severely disturbed, psychotic children. Studies have generally revealed sensorimotor and concrete operational delays accompanying psychosis (Serafica, 1971; Rosenthal, Massie, and Wulff, 1980; de Ajuriaguerra and others, 1969; Voyat, 1980; Breslow and Cowan, 1984; Slotnick, Chapter Four), as well as difficulties with functional assimilation and accommodation mechanisms (Schmid-Kitsikis, 1976; Cowan, 1978). It is difficult to generalize such findings, however, to less severely disturbed and older individuals. Those of us with interest in nonpsychotic adolescents, for example, require clarification about whether connections between structural-functional cognitive difficulties and psychological adaptation exist for this subgroup. Because adolescence is ordinarily a time of major cognitive transition, it should theoretically represent a prime period for exploring relationships between cognitive-developmental capacities and psychological adaptation. Also, explorations of the role of adolescent cognitive dysfunction in psychological maladaptation may not only provide important suggestions for general principles of psychotherapy but may contribute to the building of clinical treatment models geared more specifically toward adolescent development.

The cognitive-developmental stage of formal operations normally occurs around adolescence and allows for such newfound cognitive capabilities as abstract thinking, the generation of all possible alternatives, evaluating alternatives via propositional logic, taking the perspective of another, and reasoning about probability and chance (Piaget and Inhelder, 1966). Not all individuals, however, have access to formal operational structures, and some do not make use of them consistently. In one study, only 30 percent of a normal adult sample exhibited complete acquisition of formal operational skills (as assessed on standard Piagetian tasks), while 55 percent exhibited incomplete acquisition, and 15 percent displayed no evidence of formal thinking (Kuhn, Langer, Kohlberg, and Haan, 1977). Given, then, that many individuals do not consistently engage in formal reasoning, it is important to discover how nonuse of formal thinking affects individuals' adaptation. From a structural standpoint, a cognitive-developmental approach hypothesizes that problems with formal operational structural acquisitions contribute to certain difficulties in affective and interpersonal functioning, while availability of formal reasoning powers may, in many situations, help individuals more effectively understand and interact with their affective, interpersonal world. From a functional standpoint, a cognitive-developmental perspective suggests that problems with assimilation and accommodation mechanisms actually underlie structural formal operational deficits, since it is these mechanisms that both create and modify cognitive structures. Although formal operations are relevant for both adolescents and adults, the following discussion is primarily concerned with the relationship of formal operations to adolescent adaptation.

Relatively little existing theoretical and empirical work has considered the connection between adolescent psychopathology (other than psychosis) and formal operational dysfunction, the importance of formal reasoning for psychological adaptation, the contribution of functional disturbance to formal operational structural delay, or the therapeutic implications of these issues (Nannis, Chapter Two). Most studies with a structural stage emphasis have focused on the cognitive-developmental level of delinquent teenagers in comparison to their nondelinquent peers. For example, delinquent adolescents have been shown to exhibit delays on standard formal operational Piagetian assessments (pendulum, balance, permutations and correlations problems, and so on), on certain tests of moral development (Hains and Miller, 1980; Jurkovic and Prentice, 1977), and on perspective-taking tasks (Chandler, 1973). There has been little examination of functional problems at adolescence.

In sum, although previous research has documented associations between cognitive dysfunction and psychological adaptation in psychotic children, much remains to be learned about the general associative and causal link between cognitive development and problems in adolescent adaptation. For those with particular clinical interests in nonpsychotic adolescents, more specific questions arise about the treatment applications of these issues. In order to broach the subject of adolescence in this relatively new research area, I have delineated three areas for further exploration. Although these are presently issues for discussion, I hope they will serve to stimulate the development of more traditional research paradigms.

The first exploratory area concerns structural aspects of cognitive development. This includes exploration of the relationship between formal operational capacities and problems in adaptation, as well as the contribution of formal reasoning to adolescents' affective and interpersonal functioning. The second exploratory area considers functional aspects of development. Because assimilation and accommodation are theoretically responsible for creating and exercising cognitive structures, problems with these mechanisms may potentially contribute to some adolescents' inability to engage in formal reasoning. In each of these two sections, implications of cognitive-developmental principles for clinical intervention with adolescents are discussed. The third exploratory area compares therapeutic issues derived from a structural-functional cognitive approach to those implied by more traditional forms of psychotherapy. This section emphasizes the unique contributions of a cognitive-developmental perspective for adolescent psychotherapy, as well as the points of overlap with existing intervention models.

Methodological Comments

In order to illustrate the importance of cognitive-developmental issues in various affective and interpersonal situations and characterize the therapeutic relevance of cognitive-developmental concerns, the ensuing discussion will be accompanied by summarized descriptions of the transactions of two adolescent therapy groups. Both of these groups took place on the premises of a middle school. In each group, seventh- to ninth-grade students were referred to group leaders by teachers and administrators, either because of problematic classroom behavior or troubles with peers. The group transactions, I believe, provide useful illustrations, in part because a wide range of affective and interpersonal difficulties were represented among the student group members. Some of the students had difficulty completing classwork and homework, others were disruptive to teachers or aggressive with peers, and still others had been described by teachers and school faculty as socially withdrawn. Further, the group medium, with its natural availability of various perspectives, offered an excellent context for observing formal operational skills, such as perspective taking and the generation of different alternatives.

Both of these groups were comparable in structure and goals of treatment. Each was comprised of seven to eight adolescents of various ethnicities who voluntarily agreed to participate after being referred. Groups were held for approximately eight weeks in an urban school setting and were led by two therapists (the author and a coleader) who had been working with the school faculty in a consultation relationship. Students were informed that the groups' goals were to help make their experiences at school and at home better for them. They were also told that the groups were a means of providing support and suggestions to fellow participants. Given the purposes specified, discussions by participants regularly dealt with both school and family concerns. Examples of topics discussed by students included arguments with teachers, fights with peers, and problems interacting with parents.

**Structural Formal Operational Difficulties and Adolescent
Affective and Interpersonal Disturbance**

The first exploratory area considers four acquisitions of the formal operational period and their implications for psychological adaptation, dysfunction, and treatment. These may be categorized as the ability to (1) use the combinatorial system, which allows the adolescent to generate alternative situations and courses of action, (2) evaluate consequences of these alternatives via propositional logic, (3) engage in perspective taking, and (4) reason about probability and chance. Each will be considered in turn, along with its therapeutic implications. Illustrations are based on the adolescent therapy groups described above.

Ability to Envision Alternatives. From the Piagetian view, formal operations open up the hypothetical world for the individual, such that reality becomes "secondary to possibility" (Inhelder and Piaget, 1958, p. 51). With the nascence of what Piaget terms the combinatorial system, the formal operator, when presented with a group of objects or events, can systematically generate all possible permutations or combinations of objects. One derivative of this capability is the formal operator's potential capacity to envision alternative ways of interacting with people and to consider how various actions or combinations of actions might differentially affect personal life events.

Difficulty generating alternatives—or a failure to invoke the combinatorial system—may well contribute to certain interpersonal and affective problems of adolescents. For example, the inability to envision alternatives may play a role in psychological difficulties such as depression, in which adolescents often experience helplessness (Seligman, 1975) or victimization, in which they remain unable to envision possibilities for change. Difficulties interacting with peers may also stem from an inability to imagine alternatives in social situations (Shure and Spivak, 1979; Weissberg, 1985). For example, impulsive and conduct-disordered youth have difficulty generating alternative methods of solving interpersonal problems (Kazdin, Esveldt-Dawson, French, and Unis, 1987; Shure and Spivak, 1979; Weissberg, 1985) and listing all possible antecedents and consequences in social dilemmas (Hains and Ryan, 1983). These studies find that social problem solving improves when individuals are provided with structured questions hinting at alternative resolutions to interpersonal dilemmas. In cases where there appear to be difficulties envisioning alternatives, then, a cognitive-developmental perspective suggests that helping adolescents generate new possibilities for action represents an important first step in the treatment process. Examples of interventions aimed at improving interpersonal functioning were found in the adolescent therapy groups described above:

> During group discussions among the middle school students, adolescents often described despair about their school situations. Many felt criticized by seemingly inflexible teachers and expressed little hope that their classroom lives would improve. Several reported receiving punishment with little opportunity to express their points of view. Andrea told us of her English teacher's continual reprimands and recounted how she often lost her temper in response. Cynthia continually received referrals for putting on makeup during class time.
>
> As an intervention strategy, the therapist asked group members to envision other possibilities for each of these

students. Suggestions for Andrea included describing her frustration to the teacher, avoiding the teacher, switching out of class, or behaving in a very subdued manner. Suggestions for Cynthia included applying makeup in various different places but also listing alternative ways to handle her frustration and boredom in the class.

A cognitive-developmental perspective thus suggests that an inability to envision alternatives may contribute to certain adolescent affective or interpersonal difficulties. Posing questions that emphasize the generation of alternatives may therefore represent an important treatment approach for the therapist.

Evaluating Alternatives. The formal operator possesses more than the ability to generate alternatives. Such a skill would be of little use without the capacity to evaluate the potential consequences. Evaluating alternatives, however, demands the use of propositional logic, deductive thinking, and the capacity to reason about hypotheses. Given a logical proposition, the formal operator is able to ascertain whether a given conclusion is true depending upon the truth of the premises. Formal reasoners thus become able to formulate events or situations in propositional terms and to generate hypotheses about how their actions affect situations. Implicated in this process is a growing capacity for planfulness, where the consequences of behavioral alternatives are carefully considered and assessed. Also, by reasoning about cause-effect relationships, formal operators can deduce which are reasonable courses of action to adopt and which situations they are capable (or not capable) of influencing. The importance of such consequential thinking for adaptive interpersonal functioning also has been emphasized by researchers interested in cognitive-behaviorally oriented social problem-solving techniques (Weissberg, 1985; Shure and Spivak, 1979).

Formulating hypotheses about interpersonal interactions, systematically varying behavior, and logically evaluating the effect of actions can help adolescents make the first steps toward developing theories about how past actions (of self and others) have influenced life events and how future actions might alter them. This active modification of a personal theory not only may contribute to adolescents' cognitive development but also to a more differentiated understanding of their emotional and interpersonal lives.

It was our impression that many adolescent group members did not regularly consider the consequences of their actions or reason about how their behavior influenced life situations. As a therapeutic intervention, the group members therefore were asked not only to generate alternative courses of action but to discuss what each of the direct consequences of their behavior might be. The therapist thus helped the adolescents construe the situation in terms of a logical proposition: "If Cynthia puts on makeup in the classroom, what will happen?" or "If Andrea reconciles with the teacher after class, then she will probably not be suspended." In this way, the therapist also was stimulating the use of other formal skills, such as reasoning on hypotheses. By considering these interpersonal situations in an evaluative light, the adolescents in essence were helped to step back from the immediacy of the situation and develop a theory of their difficulties with teachers. In trying out some of the alternatives suggested, they not only were modifying their behavior but reconstructing personal theories about the reasons for their actions and the resulting interpersonal consequences.

Eventually, Cynthia tried putting on her makeup before school and found that she did not receive referrals from her teacher. She also told her teacher that class assignments were too difficult for her and consequently was given tasks on which she could better maintain her attention. Andrea attempted to speak with the teacher after class, but the latter reportedly refused to listen. Andrea then tried out several other methods of approaching her teacher, but she was unsuccessful (in part because the teacher had become discouraged by many previous negative interactions with Andrea). The group therefore discussed what it was like for Andrea to be in a situation where she had little influence over interpersonal events.

The above example illustrates the importance of developing the power to evaluate consequences and to theorize about life situations. Working on the ability to evaluate alternative courses of action may help those who have chronic difficulty interacting with peers and adults accept greater responsibility for behavior, as they realize that their actions indeed have interpersonal consequences. In contrast, the ability to identify causes and consequences may aid adolescents who adopt too much responsibility for life circumstances (for example, those who blame themselves for parental separations) to discriminate which incidents are beyond personal control.

Perspective-Taking Abilities. Inhelder and Piaget (1958, p. 345) write that "objectivity presupposes a decentering—i.e., a continual refocusing of perspective." This ability to decenter—or adopt the point of view of another—may be extremely important for effective interpersonal functioning, in that it allows for optimal engagement in close relationships. It is almost certainly a prerequisite for true empathy. Decentration is not only a requirement for mutuality but also for maintaining a clear perspective of one's own as opposed to other's view of the world (that is, self-other differentiation). Ability to decenter also includes a capacity for distancing from the self. In this way, the individual's behavior and reactions become objects of study. This helps initiate personal theory building.

> Students in our middle school groups frequently had difficulty adopting others' viewpoints. They often did not understand why teachers became angry with them, or how peers responded to their aggressivity. Robert, for example, had particular trouble monitoring his angry outbursts at school. These often escalated, interfered with classroom routines, and led to eventual expulsion from the classroom. Therapeutic intervention first involved having Robert role-play himself (other group members played his teacher and classmates), and then his teacher. After each role-play, Robert was asked about his enacted character's feelings and thoughts. Not surprisingly, Robert was able to acknowledge that as the teacher he felt angry and became worried that his class was getting out of control.

The importance of perspective taking for adaption and intervention has been acknowledged by many researchers and clinicians who concern themselves with adolescent difficulty. Studies cited by Chandler (1973) described deficits in perspective taking among delinquent teenagers and supported the use of role-playing as a technique for enhancing perspective-taking abilities. Further, those concerned with the prevention of teenage pregnancy have advocated role-playing exercises that simulate marriage, divorce, birth, and motherhood (Black and DeBlassie, 1985) as a means of helping adolescents more fully comprehend the various roles such situations demand. Attention to perspective taking within the therapeutic context may thus represent an important change ingredient for a range of adolescent interpersonal difficulties.

Reasoning About Chance and Probability. The ability to effectively reason about chance and probability represents a significant acquisition of the formal operational period. When given appropriate information, formal operators are better capable of estimating the odds of an event's occurring. Certain adolescents, however, seem to have difficulty understanding these notions. Young adolescent delinquents, for example, were shown to be poor determiners of the likelihood of consequences in social problem-solving tasks (Hains and Ryan, 1983). Similarly, teenagers who became pregnant were demonstrated to be poor estimators of the probabilistic relationship between intercourse and pregnancy (Cvetkovich, Grote, Bjorseth, and Sarkissian, 1975; Zelnik and Kantner, 1979). Helping such adolescents estimate the likelihood of consequences may thus be relevant therapeutically. Examples of intervention geared toward reasoning about probability and chance could be found in our middle school therapy groups:

> Andrea, the student described earlier, had begun to make plans for approaching her teacher about problems in their relationship. The therapist asked Andrea how her teacher was likely to respond. Group members then engaged in some discussion and arrived at several formulations regarding the teacher's habitual reactions to students. In this way, Andrea was able to calculate her own probable responses. Similarly, the therapist encouraged Robert to evaluate the likelihood of fellow students' responding aggressively to some of his more provocative actions.

The ability to calculate the probability of events occurring may thus render adolescents' worlds more predictable and manageable, allowing them to plan for appropriate action in a variety of interpersonal situations.

Structural Dysfunction at Adolescence: Further Considerations and Therapeutic Implications. The preceding paragraphs have emphasized how formal operational acquisitions such as the ability to generate all possible alternatives, evaluate alternatives via propositional logic, engage in perspective taking, and reason about probability and chance are relevant for making adaptive life decisions, for experiencing true mutuality and empathy, for understanding feelings and interpersonal situations, and for adaptively altering affective and behavioral reactions through realistic appraisal of life events. They also have explored how unavailability of formal reasoning powers may place adolescents at a disadvantage in dealing with many affective and interpersonal issues. Two central considerations, however, remain concerning the therapeutic implications of these statements. The first deals with potential reasons behind some adolescents' seeming inability to reason formally. The second considers whether formal operations are either necessary or sufficient for positive adaptation.

In order to derive therapeutic suggestions from a cognitive-developmental perspective, it is first important to consider potential reasons behind some adolescents' seeming inability to make use of formal operational skills. With regard to structural aspects of cognitive development, two possibilities merit further discussion. These may be conceptualized as global nonattainment of formal operational structures, where the adolescent appears not yet able to reason formally in all areas of knowledge (including interpersonal and general, nonsocial knowledge), and asynchrony of formal structural development, where the adolescent appears able to reason formally only in specified domains (for example, about nonsocial topics, but not about interpersonal situations). Each of these possibilities calls for somewhat different therapeutic strategies.

Since the time of transition from concrete to formal reasoning varies in adolescents, it is likely that many teenagers do not yet have formal reasoning capacities available (that is, they exhibit global nonattainment of formal operational skills). Findings suggesting that a significant proportion of normal adults make little use of formal thinking (Kuhn, Langer, Kohlberg, and Haan, 1977) support the idea that many adolescents also do not reason formally. Some of our middle school therapy group participants, for example, were experiencing major difficulties in the more abstract, academic subjects that generally require formal reasoning. It is conceivable that a substantial number of these students were not yet capable of formal thought. In fact, the inability to meet academic demands for formal reasoning may well have contributed to some of these teenagers' frustration at school. The work of Cowan (1978) and Turiel (1966) suggests that challenging adolescents to reason just one step above existing cognitive capacities creates an "optimal mismatch" between existing cognitive structures and task demands, and thereby promotes development. For example, adolescents who do not yet reason formally might profit from perspective-taking exercises (such as role-plays) but might be unable to answer abstract questions regarding significant others' feelings and thoughts. In other words, actually enacting different roles and life situations might demand perspective-taking skills that are optimally discrepant from existing cognitive capacities. Also, when there is global nonattainment of formal reasoning, it is relevant for therapists to pose questions that challenge cognitive structures in interpersonal (for example, concerning friends, family, significant others) as well as noninterpersonal areas.

Asynchronicity of formal thinking (where the adolescent reasons formally in only specified domains) may be a relatively common phenomenon. Research cited earlier suggests that a sizable portion of normal adults exhibit incomplete acquisition for formal operational skills (Kuhn, Langer, Kohlberg, and Haan, 1977). Thus, it would not be unusual for an adolescent to exhibit formal reasoning on a more nonsocial task (for example, a standard Piagetian probability or combination of liquids assessment) but reason more concretely about interpersonal relationships (or vice versa). Understanding why asynchrony occurs has posed complex problems for developmental theorists. Turiel and Davidson (1986) suggest that since nonsocial knowledge is gained through subject-object interactions and interpersonal knowledge is derived from subject-subject interactions, asynchrony between social and nonsocial reasoning may be inevitable. This suggestion is supported by J. H. Block's (1983) observation that knowledge attained through subject-subject interaction is more inconsistent, complex and fractious, and therefore causes reasoning about interpersonal situations to often lag behind structural acquisition in the nonsocial realm.

> Examples of asynchrony were common among certain therapy group members. These students performed well in academic subjects requiring formal thinking (such as algebra and geometry) but had considerable trouble adopting others' perspectives in interpersonal role-taking tasks. For these adolescents, intervention specifically emphasized applying formal reasoning to affective and interpersonal areas, via discussion and role-plays involving peers, teachers, and family members.

The second central therapeutic issue is whether formal operational thinking is both necessary and sufficient for positive changes in adaptation. This is a thorny question, in that some individuals may function quite well without using formal reasoning on a day-to-day basis. Given findings that many adults do not consistently engage in formal thinking (Kuhn, Langer, Kohlberg, and Haan, 1977), it seems reasonable to conclude that formal operations are not always prerequisites for adequate interpersonal interactions. Although formal reasoning may not be necessary for positive adaptation under all conditions, formal thinking may be of special importance in those situations requiring empathy, social problem solving, and resolution of interpersonal conflict. This is because these contexts draw upon acquisitions such as perspective taking, generating and evaluating alternatives, and reasoning about probability and chance. I also have described how formal operations can help individuals suffering from affective difficulties such as depression arrive at more realistic personal theories and more adaptive appraisals of life events.

This leads to another concern: It is unclear whether the presence of formal reasoning guarantees—that is, is sufficient for—positive adaptation. One counterargument to such a supposition is that some adolescents' newly acquired formal capacities for self-critique may play a role in initiating depression. For example, becoming overly preoccupied with possibilities such as real versus ideal discrepancies may lead to various forms of psychological discomfort (Higgins, 1987), while considering too many alternatives can become obsessional. This line of thinking suggests that formal operational skills must be adaptively applied to the outside world. In other words, adaptive application of cognitive structures implies an experimental, nonperseverative attitude, where new possibilities for life are attempted and explored. But the process of experimentation is functional and therefore relies upon the proper working of assimilation and accommodation mechanisms. These are considered more closely in the following section.

Functional Considerations in Adolescent Disturbance and Their Therapeutic Implications

The second area to be explored in this chapter concerns functional aspects of development and their role in adolescent adaptation, psychopathology, and therapy. Although the present discussion deals with formal reasoning at adolescence, consideration of the functions transcends the formal operational period. This is because mechanisms such as assimilation and accommodation are thought to operate at all developmental stages. In theory, then, functions are responsible for the creation and modification of structures, and problems with these dynamic mechanisms may therefore contribute to structural nonattainment and asynchrony at adolescence or other developmental periods. Here, I will consider three functional disturbances and their therapeutic implications. These may be described as (1) lack of opportunity for assimilation and accommodation either globally or within a specific domain; (2) functional imbalance, or a strong and nonadaptive predominance of either assimilation or accommodation; and (3) difficulty intercoordinating reasoning across different domains of knowledge.

An individual may have limited occasion to encounter others' perspectives and therefore to adaptively modify personal perspectives when confronted with different views (accommodation). Alternatively, a person may have little occasion to apply attitudes or ideas to new realms of knowledge (assimilation). In both these cases, cognitive-developmental progress may be hindered. This problem may be characterized as a lack of opportunity for assimilation and accommodation, which in turn may lead to global structural delay or developmental asynchrony. (The latter may result when there is opportunity for assimilation and accommodation only within specified domains of knowledge.) When adolescents have little chance to discuss their personal relationships, for example, opportunities for assimilation and accommodation in the interpersonal realm are significantly decreased. Thus, because of their frequent isolation from peers, teachers, and parents, several of our middle school therapy group participants had little occasion to exchange ideas about interpersonal events. These teenagers therefore missed important opportunities for assimilating or accommodating around topics such as their personal relationships at home and at school. Hains and Miller (1980) similarly suggested that a tendency toward social clustering may limit delinquents' encountering of varying viewpoints, thereby reducing opportunities for accommodation to differing perspectives about interpersonal subjects. Encouraging discussion around previously unconsidered or forbidden topics may be one way in which therapeutic encounters can stimulate functional mechanisms and consequently promote adaptation.

Structural deficit may result not only from a lack of opportunity to exercise functional processes but from a strong and maladaptive predominance of either the assimilation or accommodation mechanisms (Cowan, 1978; Schmid-Kitsikis, 1979). Overassimilation, or a perseverative stance toward the environment, prevents adaptation to reality (Block, 1982) and impedes the development of psychological structures. Overaccommodation, involving either blatant conformity to the environment or a negation of personal interpretations of events, may also prevent the creative modification of structures (Cowan, 1978; Schmid-Kitsikis, 1979). Examples of overassimilation and overaccommodation could be found among our adolescent therapy group participants:

> Many of our therapy group members adopted an overly assimilative stance to reality, by insisting on the accuracy of their own interpretations of interpersonal problems. Several group participants, for example, tended to blame their teachers for problems occurring in their classrooms. It was difficult for these teenagers to modify impressions of themselves or of others by considering different viewpoints (such as those of the teachers). To counteract overassimilation, therapy became largely accommodative and stressed adaptation to reality after careful observation and consideration of significant others' perspectives. This was often accomplished through techniques that emphasized accommodation to different perspectives, such as role-playing. Here, students who had chronic classroom difficulties were asked to adopt the role of teacher in their dramatizations. By elaborating the teacher role, these students were helped to modify their perspectives about why teachers became angry with them. For a very withdrawn adolescent who had trouble asserting himself, however (that is, an overaccommodator), intervention involved a predominantly assimilative therapeutic stance. In this case, therapy focused on the elaboration of personal feelings and perspectives. Role-playing was once again used in therapy; however, this time, the adolescent was asked to play himself in dramatizations. In this way, the student was helped to elaborate his own reactions to situations involving family and peers.

The above example suggests that counteracting functional imbalance first involves encouraging clients to engage in activities that elicit the nondominant functional mechanism. This calls for a highly active therapist, who possesses the willingness to actually introduce activities into the therapeutic situation and the flexibility to adopt either an assimilative or accommodative emphasis.

The ability to coordinate judgments from different domains of knowledge (Turiel and Davidson, 1986) is also a functional issue, primarily because this process involves combining separate information (via the functional mechanisms of assimilation and accommodation) in order to generate new psychological structures. The process is complex, in that judgments that draw upon different areas of knowledge often conflict around a single decision or event.

Teenage pregnancy provides a striking example of this phenomenon, because many pregnant adolescents are unavoidably confronted with conflicting judgments arising from the areas of intrapersonal, social/conventional, and moral reasoning (see Turiel and Davidson, 1986). Imagine, for example, a pregnant teenager who reasons formally about her psychological state (thus drawing from intrapersonal or psychological knowledge). This adolescent may envision the difficult psychological consequences of teen motherhood, leading to a judgment favoring either having the baby but giving it up for adoption, keeping the baby, or having an abortion. A conflicting judgment may arise from reasoning in the social/conventional realm, however, when the adolescent considers which option is accepted within her peer group and community. Some communities or peer groups provide supports for teen parenting, while others regard it an unacceptable. Also, when considering moral issues, the teenager may arrive at some overarching moral principle about the ethics of abortion versus adoption versus teen parenting. It is easy to see that reasoning arising from these three realms may not always lead to the same judgment about an appropriate course of action. Gilligan's (1982) work, in fact, suggests that high-level moral decision making for females—such as decision making about an unexpected pregnancy—involves joint consideration of the needs of self (intrapersonal), needs of significant others (interpersonal), and societal expectations (social/conventional). Her formulations thus reinforce the importance—and the difficulty—of coordinating reasoning across domains.

Turiel and Davidson (1986) believe that when reasoning across different domains conflicts, salience often becomes the basis for making final judgments. Making decisions based on salience is a common developmental phenomenon and often signals a failure to intercoordinate several important dimensions of a cognitive problem. One familiar example is preoperational children's tendency to base conservation judgments on a salient physical dimension: For example, they sometimes judge an amount of liquid by the height of its container without consideration for the width (or vice versa). With respect to salience and teenage pregnancy, social/

conventional norms (encompassing consideration of the peer group) and interpersonal needs (encompassing the desires of significant others, such as a boyfriend and girlfriend) are naturally predominant at adolescence and may therefore become the issues on which many teenagers base their decisions around sexuality and pregnancy. Gilligan (1982), in fact, describes the reasoning of several pregnant females who make abortion decisions based primarily upon one domain—interpersonal considerations (that is, what others expect). It is only later in their development that these individuals become able to integrate or intercoordinate judgments based upon consideration of personal needs along with the needs of others.

In cases where intercoordination is an issue, therapeutic intervention might attempt to diminish salience effects. This would first necessitate helping adolescents consider the various domains of reasoning involved in a particular problem (for example, psychological, social/ conventional, moral, and so on), then decide on the most relevant domains from which to base decisions, and finally facilitate coordination of judgments from each relevant area of reasoning. In the case of pregnant adolescents, for example, the therapist might pose questions that provoke consideration of issues around personal feelings and values, as well as those of peers and family. In adolescent therapy groups, participants might be encouraged to discuss how peer group pressure (social/ conventional reasoning), values (moral reasoning), and personal emotional issues (psychological reasoning) impinge on behavior during interpersonal conflicts. In this way, the therapist helps adolescents clarify which issues are most important for making personal judgments, as well as which issues they may have neglected to consider.

In conclusion, assessing the nature of the adolescent's functional difficulties (that is, assimilation and accommodation imbalance, lack of opportunity for assimilation and accommodation, or difficulty coordinating reasoning across domains) has implications for both assessment and intervention. The therapist must be a careful observer of the adolescent's approach to interpersonal and other problems: Does he or she tend to elaborate personal feelings without considering alternative perspectives (that is, overassimilate), or, alternatively, conform to others' opinions while failing to consider personal interpretations of events (that is overaccommodate)? Does the adolescent have and make use of occasions for exchanging ideas with other individuals around particular subjects (that is, have sufficient opportunity for assimilation and accommodation)? Finally, is the adolescent faced with a dilemma that necessitates coordinating information from different domains of knowledge? Attention to these issues may highlight the presence of functional problems, and in turn suggest an appropriate therapeutic orientation. The optimal treatment approach may thus incorporate either the encouraging, balancing, or coordinating of functioning assimilation and accommodation mechanisms. Further, the above illustrations suggest that these three processes may occur when adolescents are encouraged to reason about abstract, hypothetical situations. Thus, assimilation and accommodation may take place before direct action is actually taken.

Contributions and Comparisons to Other Therapies

Thus far, this chapter has highlighted how the development of formal operational structures may be enhanced through therapeutic intervention and has offered suggestions about possibilities for therapeutic change. Now I will consider both the unique therapeutic contributions of a cognitive-developmental approach as well as the areas of overlap with other common forms of psychotherapy. Because specific adolescent intervention theories are sparse, discussion centers on common forms of adult treatment that are often applied in work with adolescents. Both structural and functional issues are considered.

Many existing treatment models incorporate goals that are consistent with the elaboration of formal operational structures for both adolescents and adults. Most obvious are the cognitive-behavioral therapies (Young and Beck, 1982; Ellis, 1973), which advocate a scientific approach to problem solving and regularly use such techniques as "hypothesis testing, setting up an experiment, . . . generating alternatives, . . . weighing advantages and disadvantages, . . . [and] role-playing" (Young and Beck, 1982, pp. 190, 193). Similarly, those cognitive-behavioral techniques geared specifically for children (for example, social problem solving and interpersonal cognitive problem solving approaches) stress alternative solution thinking and consequential thinking (Shure and Spivak, 1979; Weissberg, 1985). Other forms of therapy less explicitly emphasize formal operational acquisition but nonetheless regularly incorporate them in their treatment strategies. For example, psychoanalytic therapies, in emphasizing insight and interpretation, draw on formal operational skills such as theory building and hypothetico-deductive reasoning. Similarly, client-centered therapy theoretically enhances such formal skills as decentration and perspective taking by developing clients' abilities to differentiate their own values from those of others (see Rogers, 1951). One important contribution of a cognitive-developmental emphasis, then, is that it suggests new ways of conceptualizing what many therapists already do (Nannis, Chapter Two). That is, many forms of therapy enhance the cognitive and the emotional development of the individual, although they do not formally acknowledge the cognitive-developmental aspect of the change process.

Neglect of this cognitive-developmental component, however, has theoretical and practical consequences. For example, cognitive-behavioral therapies attempt to modify specific cognitions, assumptions, or interpretations of events, without attention to developing cognitive structures, or the overall organization of patients' thinking. Interpersonal cognitive problem-solving training approaches, for example, often uniformly apply prestructured interventions, regardless of the developmental level of the child. Studies evaluating these techniques often employ subjects ranging from elementary school age to adolescence, without analyzing differential developmental effects (Kazdin, Esveldt-Dawson, French, and Unis, 1987).

In contrast, a Piagetian perspective suggests that changing an individual's way of thinking is facilitated by optimal mismatch (Cowan, 1978) between the individual's existing level of cognitive functioning and the cognitive structures required for solving a particular interpersonal problem. Achieving this state of mismatch requires that the therapist be attuned to the patient's current level of cognitive functioning. In other words, altering a cognition (advocated by cognitive-behavioral methods), providing an interpretation (advocated by psychoanalytic methods), or helping clients differentiate their own from others' perspectives (advocated by client-centered therapies) may be difficult tasks without knowledge of the patient's current cognitive structural level. And without this diagnostic sensitivity to cognitive-developmental structural issues, the therapist may not succeed in posing questions, offering interpretations, or provoking new methods of problem consideration that are adequately understood by his or her patients. Knowing about cognitive-developmental level in different knowledge domains therefore provides an essential beginning for intervention with children, adolescents, and adults.

The cognitive-developmental approach I have described also offers several unique functional intervention contributions. First, the cognitive-developmental stance proposed emphasizes the importance of therapist flexibility in introducing either assimilation or accommodation into the therapy situation. This contrasts the functional orientation of many existing intervention methods, which often emphasize either one or the other of the functional change processes. Cognitive-behavioral therapies, for example, largely emphasize accommodation, since they attempt to have clients engage in more scientific and reality-based thinking. Client-centered therapy is largely assimilative, since the therapist helps clients develop their world view by mirroring their personal feelings and perceptions. The psychoanalytic techniques of free association also stress assimilation, since clients repeatedly exercise their personal schemes and interpretations of the environment. Thus, many therapies favor either one or the other of the functional processes, and do not recognize the importance of equilibration of functional mechanisms (that is, use of both assimilation and accommodation) in development.

Another contribution of the functional assimilation and accommodation model is that it emphasizes the activity of the individual. In essence, cognitive structures develop only by the individual's making his or her own discoveries about the objective and interpersonal world. This stance cautions against overuse of techniques such as interpretation, where the therapist essentially makes discoveries for the client. It also guards against strategies such as training individuals to make effective problem-solving statements. These prestructured phrases that children are taught to recite (for example, "I should plan ahead") (Kendall and Bemis, 1983) do not result from the activity or discoveries of the individual and may therefore not stimulate the creative and permanent modification of cognitive structures. This may be one reason, in fact, why such cognitive-behavioral training methods sometimes report short-term, but not long-term, effects (Kendall and Bemis, 1983).

Finally, many cognitive-behavioral therapies hold that modification of patients' internal language—either by altering negative self-verbalizations (Ellis, 1973) or by progressively internalizing adaptive problem-solving statements (Kendall and Bemis, 1983)—can induce cognitive change. This Vygotskyesque notion that language mediates cognition contrasts the Piagetian view that language itself cannot modify cognitive structures. The Piagetian viewpoint holds that active discovery involving assimilation, accommodation, and the intercoordination of reasoning across domains is the road to promoting changes in patients' thinking.

Summary and Conclusions

This chapter has described how the development of formal operational structures can contribute to effective interpersonal functioning at adolescence and how the therapeutic context may be adapted to stimulate formal reasoning. Specifically, it has been suggested that developing the abilities to envision alternatives, evaluate alternatives, engage in perspective taking, and reason on chance and probability may be important for optimal adaptation at adolescence, and that enhancement of formal operational abilities may be directly addressed within the therapeutic context. Promoting the development of cognitive structures and stages, however, demands clinical attention to the functions of assimilation and accommodation, which theoretically represent the dynamics of change. At all developmental periods including adolescence, enhancing reasoning powers involves stimulating and balancing these two functional processes across different domains of knowledge. Also, promoting the functional ability to coordinate judgments from different domains of reasoning can facilitate adolescents' making more adaptive life decisions. Of course, research is necessary to validate many of the specific links between structural and functional aspects of cognition and adaptation that I have suggested.

The approach outlined here indicates that therapeutic intervention must incorporate several cognitive-developmental strategies. First, initial evaluations should include assessment of the adolescent's current level of reasoning. Second, the process of therapy should involve developing cognitive structures by creating optimal mismatch between existing capacities and new demands for reasoning. This should be accompanied by the stimulation, equilibration, and intercoordination of assimilation and accommodation within and across domains of knowledge. Although adolescent and adult intervention models often incorporate some of these goals, they frequently neglect to acknowledge cognitive-developmental therapeutic issues. This lack of attention to adolescents' cognitive-developmental level may dilute the effectiveness of treatment, in that clients may be less able to effectively process or use interventions that are either too cognitively sophisticated or that fail to sufficiently challenge existing cognitive structures. Further, the case illustrations provided suggest that group therapy with adolescents most markedly facilitates the enhancement of structural and functional aspects of cognition. This is because the group medium encourages perspective taking, optimal mismatch (when existing structures are challenged by other individuals), and active experimentation with assimilative and accommodative processes.

I do not believe that we are at the point of recommending specialized cognitive-developmental techniques for the treatment of specific diagnostic categories in adolescence. The goal of this chapter was to more broadly suggest how a cognitive-developmental perspective might be incorporated into various intervention approaches and conceptualizations of nonpsychotic adolescent psychopathology. The clinical vignettes presented illustrate that cognitive-developmental treatment strategies may be relevant for a wide range of adolescent difficulties. Examples have emphasized general problems in interpersonal and affective functioning, including those related to delinquency and depression. Further, cognitive-developmental issues have been suggested relevant for pregnancy and birth control counseling, as teenagers who become pregnant often have difficulties with such formal operational skills as perspective taking (Emans, 1983; D'Augelli and D'Augelli, 1977), reasoning on chance and probability (Cvetkovich and others, 1975), envisioning and evaluating alternatives (Steinlauf, 1979; Dembo and Lundell, 1979), and coordinating reasoning across knowledge domains. In sum, treatment methods that incorporate a cognitive-developmental viewpoint may prove applicable for adolescents with a wide range of psychological difficulties and for therapists with a broad range of theoretical backgrounds. Cowan's point (Chapter One) that intervention strategies may be independent of etiology is relevant here. Attention to the child's stage level or functional style may be important, no matter which theoretical view of psychological dysfunction is adopted.

It is important to review the relative roles of emotional and cognitive issues in psychotherapy. The purpose of the present discussion was not to suggest that cognitive-developmental issues be the sole or even primary thrust of treatment, or that they replace affective and interpersonal explanations for psychological difficulty. Therapy most certainly provides a context for emotional exploration but also represents a medium for enhancing cognitive growth. Here, I have stressed that development of formal operational structures may help with interpretation of emotional and interpersonal events and that adaptive functional mechanisms may enhance interpersonal interactions. Such a view does not propose inflation of the cognitive at the expense of the emotional but instead underscores an essential interdependence between the affective and cognitive worlds.

References

Black, C., and DeBlassie, R. "Adolescent Pregnancy: Contributing Factors, Consequences, Treatment, and Plausible Solutions." *Adolescence*, 1985, *20* (78), 281–290.

Block, J. "Assimilation, Accommodation, and the Dynamics of Personality Development." *Child Development*, 1982, *53* (2), 281–295.

Block, J. H. "Differential Premises Arising from Differential Socialization of the Sexes: Some Conjectures." *Child Development*, 1983, *54*, 1335–1354.

Breslow, L., and Cowan, P. "Structural and Functional Perspectives on Classification and Seriation in Psychotic and Normal Children." *Child Development*, 1984, *55* (1), 226–235.

Chandler, M. J. "Egocentrism and Antisocial Behavior: The Assessment and Training of Social Perspective-Taking Skills." *Developmental Psychology*, 1973, *9* (3), 326–333.

Cowan, P. *Piaget with Feeling: Cognitive, Social, and Emotional Dimensions*. New York: Holt, Rinehart & Winston, 1978.

Cvetkovich, G., Grote, B., Bjorseth, A., and Sarkissian, J. "On the Psychology of Adolescents' Use of Contraception." *Journal of Sexual Research*, 1975, *11*, 256–270.

D'Augelli, J. F., and D'Augelli, A. R. "Moral Reasoning and Premarital Sexual Behavior: Toward Reasoning About Relationships." *Journal of Social Issues*, 1977, *33* (2), 46–66.

de Ajuriaguerra, J., Inhelder, B., Jaeggi, A., Roth, S., and Stirlin, M. "Les Troubles de l'Organisation et la Désorganization Intellectuelle chez les Enfants Psychotiques [Problems of intellectual organization and disorganization in psychotic children]." *La Psychiatrie de l'Enfant*, 1969, *12*, 309–412.

Dembo, M. H., and Lundell, B. "Factors Affecting Adolescent Contraceptive Practices: Implications for Sex Education." *Adolescence*, 1979, *9* (56), 657–664.

Ellis, A. *Humanistic Psychotherapy*. New York: McGraw-Hill, 1973.

Emans, S. J. "The Sexually Active Teenager." *Developmental and Behavioral Pediatrics*, 1983, *4* (1), 37–42.

Gilligan, C. *In a Different Voice: Psychological Theory and Women's Development*. Cambridge, Mass.: Harvard University Press, 1982.

Hains, A., and Miller, D. "Moral and Cognitive Development in Delinquent and Nondelinquent Children and Adolescents." *Journal of Genetic Psychology*, 1980, *137*, 21–35.

Hains, A., and Ryan, E. "The Development of Social Cognitive Processes Among Juvenile Delinquents and Nondelinquent Peers." *Child Development*, 1983, *54*, 1536–1544.

Higgins, E. T. "Self-Discrepancy: A Theory Relating Self and Affect." *Psychological Review*, 1987, *94* (3), 319–340.

Inhelder, B., and Piaget, J. *The Growth of Logical Thinking from Childhood to Adolescence*. New York: Basic Books, 1958.

Jurkovic, G., and Prentice, N. "Relations of Moral and Cognitive Development to Dimensions of Juvenile Delinquency." *Journal of Abnormal Psychology*, 1977, *86* (4), 414–420.

Kazdin, A. E., Esveldt-Dawson, K., French, N. H., and Unis, A. S. "Problem-Solving Skills Training and Relationship Therapy in the Treatment of Antisocial Child Behavior." *Journal of Consulting and Clinical Psychology*, 1987, *55* (1), 76–85.

Kendall, P., and Bemis, K. "Thought and Action in Psychotherapy: The Cognitive-Behavioral Approaches." In M. Hersen, A. Kazdin, and A. Bellack (eds.), *Clinical Psychology Handbook*. Elmsford, N.Y.: Pergamon Press, 1983.

Kuhn, D., Langer, J., Kohlberg, L., and Haan, N. "The Development of Formal Operations in Logical Moral Judgment." *Genetic Psychology Monographs*, 1977, *95* (1), 97–188.

Piaget, J. *Structuralism*. New York: Basic Books, 1970.

Piaget, J. *Le Jugement Moral Chez l'Enfant* [Moral judgment of the child]. Paris: Presses Universitaires de France, 1978. (Originally published 1932.)

Piaget, J. *Intelligence and Affectivity*. Palo Alto, Calif.: Annual Review, 1981.

Piaget, J., and Inhelder, B. *Psychologie de l'Enfant* [The psychology of the child]. Paris: Presses Universitaires de France, 1966.

Rogers, C. *Client-Centered Therapy*. Boston: Houghton Mifflin, 1951.

Rosenthal, J., Massie, H., and Wulff, K. "A Comparison of Cognitive Development in Normal and Psychotic Children in the First Two Years of Life from Home Movies." *Journal of Autism and Developmental Disorders*, 1980, *(10)* (4), 433–444.

Schmid-Kitsikis, E. "The Cognitive Mechanisms Underlying Problem-Solving in Psychotic and Mentally Retarded Children." In B. Inhelder and H. Chapman (eds.), *Piaget and His School*. New York: Springer-Verlag, 1976.

Schmid-Kitsikis, E. "Modes de Fonctionnement Mental et Modèles du Développment Psychologique [Types of mental functioning and models of psychological development]." *Cahiers de Psychologie*, 1979, *22*, 43–58.

Seligman. M.E.P. *Helplessness: On Depression, Development, and Death*. San Francisco: Freeman, 1975.

Serafica, F. C. "Object Concept in Deviant Children." *American Journal of Orthopsychiatry*, 1971, *41*, 473–482.

Shure, M., and Spivak, G. "Interpersonal Problem-Solving Thinking and Adjustment in the Mother-Child Dyad." In M. Kent and K. Rolf (eds.), *Primary Prevention of Psychopathology*. Vol. 3: *Social Competence in Children*. Hanover, N.H.: University Press of New England, 1979.

Steinlauf, B. "Problem-Solving Skills, Locus of Control, and the Contraceptive Effectiveness of Young Women." *Child Development*, 1979, *50*, 268–271.

Turiel, E. "An Experimental Test of the Sequentiality of Developmental Stages in the Child's Moral Judgment." *Journal of Personality and Social Psychology*, 1966, *3*, 611–618.

Turiel, E., and Davidson, P. "Heterogeneity, Inconsistency, and Asynchrony in the Development of Cognitive Structures." In I. Levin (ed.), *Stage and Structure*. Norwood, N.J.: Ablex, 1986.

Voyat, G. "Piaget on Schizophrenia." *Journal of the American Academy of Psychoanalysis*, 1980, *8* (1), 93–113.

Weissberg, R. P. "Designing Effective Social Problem-Solving Programs for the Classroom." In B. H. Schneider, K. H. Rubin, and J. H. Ledingham (eds.), *Children's Peer Relations: Issues in Assessment and Intervention*. New York: Springer-Verlag, 1985.

Young, J. E., and Beck, A. T. "Cognitive Therapy: Clinical Applications." In J. A. Rush (ed.), *Short-Term Psychotherapies for Depression*. New York: Guilford Press, 1982.

Zelnik, M., and Kantner, J. "Reasons for Nonuse of Contraception by Sexually Active Women Aged 15–19." *Family Planning Perspectives*, 1979, *11* (5), 289–296.

Debra Ellen Gordon spent two years studying Piagetian theory at the University of Geneva, Switzerland. As a visiting scholar at Stanford University, she is engaged in research on adolescent psychopathology. She is also assistant professor at Pacific Graduate School of Psychology, where she teaches courses in child and adolescent therapy. She practices clinically with adolescents at the Division of Behavioral Sciences, Stanford Medical Center.

Is the cognitive development of developmentally delayed autistic children the same as younger, normal children or does it differ in significant ways that have implications for the clinical assessment and treatment of these children?

Cognitive Differences in Classification Tasks Among Autistic Children

Carol Fisher Slotnick

A cognitive-developmental comparison of autistic and normal children's cognition raises central issues about the nature of autism. These issues have implications both for developmental theory and clinical practice. Do autistic children have a central cognitive deficit? If so, are they developmentally delayed, resembling younger, normal children or do they demonstrate an unusual pattern of development? Do they also have social disturbances, which interact with the cognitive deficits? What are the implications of these cognitive and social disturbances for clinical assessment and intervention with these children?

In this chapter, I will demonstrate that a cognitive-developmental assessment of autistic children provided unique information about their functioning. The following study (Slotnick, 1984) was designed to assess both structural and functional aspects of autistic children's cognitive

Appreciation is due to Professors Jonas Langer and Leonard Breslow for their helpful comments on earlier drafts of this paper. This research was supported in part by NICHD predoctoral training grants 5 TOL HD00153-10 and 1T32 HD07181-01.

E. D. Nannis, P. A. Cowan (eds.). *Developmental Psychopathology and Its Treatment.*
New Directions for Child Development, no. 39. San Francisco: Jossey-Bass, Spring 1988.

development. Social interactions that had a negative feedback effect upon their cognitive development also were investigated. I will discuss these findings and their implications for the clinical assessment and treatment of autistic children.

Description of Autism

Many mental health workers and educators have been intrigued with the assessment and treatment of autistic children, even though autism constitutes a small percentage of the clinical childhood population (4 or 5 out of 10,000). DSM-III R (American Psychiatric Association, 1987) provides a behavioral description of autism. Autistic children are isolated socially and have impaired relations to the world around them. They prefer objects to people, are resistant to change, have restricted activities, and often engage in unusual behaviors, such as hand flapping and twirling objects. Many sources of brain dysfunction are thought to predispose children to autism, and most of these children also have other neurological deficits. Most autistic children are delayed in cognitive development, functioning years below their age level. Only a small percentage appear to have normal intellectual abilities. Autistic children also have impaired communication abilities and imaginal activities. The age of onset is during infancy or childhood. Because of their social isolation and delayed development, autistic children are difficult to establish rapport with and present a challenge to professionals working with them.

Theories about the etiology of autism have changed over the years. Autism was initially defined by Kanner (1943) as a disturbance of social and emotional relationships among young children. Consequently, the characteristics of autistic children's parents, their parental skills, and the parent-child relationship were considered appropriate targets for intervention. Current studies have shifted the focus of concern away from the autistic child's parents and their nurturing style, and have described the central deficit of autism as cognitive (Morgan, 1986; Rutter, 1978b, 1983, 1986). The focus now is on the nature of the autistic child's perceptions of and understanding of the environment, and how these perceptions influence social interactions. I will present a brief review of the major research findings that address these issues.

Selective Review of Research

Intelligence, sensory, and perceptual tests have described a range of cognitive deficits in autistic children. Preliminary research by Rutter (Rutter, 1968; Lockyer and Rutter, 1970) identified a language disability in autistic children. Rutter's (1983) subsequent research described a broader-based cognitive deficit that included difficulties with symbolization, coding, abstract abilities, logic, and sequencing. Another series of studies of autistic children described cognitive deficits in coding and categorizing processes (Hermelin and O'Connor, 1970), difficulties extracting patterns from stimulus materials (Hermelin and Frith, 1971), problems with nonlinguistic representation (Hermelin, 1978), and difficulties using psychological and intentional criteria when sorting pictures (Baron-Cohen, Leslie, and Frith, 1986). In studies of perception, autistic children have been described as overselective (that is, attending to only one cue) when attending to multiple stimulus cues (Lovaas, 1977) and as having tunnel vision (Rincover, Feldman, and Eason, 1986; Rincover and Ducharme, 1987).

Many researchers have conducted cognitive-developmental studies of psychotic and retarded children in order to describe their cognitive abilities. Cognitive-developmental tasks have been used less frequently with autistic children because of their social isolation and limited language skills. Studies have been limited to the evaluation of sensorimotor behavior characteristic of infants from birth to two years of age or have contained tasks that required receptive language skills.

Researchers using the Uzgiris and Hunt sensorimotor scales have described developmental delays among autistic children. Autistic children were deficient in symbol formation and imitation skills (Curcio, 1978; Ertel and Voyat, 1982; Sigman and Ungerer, 1981; Ungerer and Sigman, 1981) and were developmentally delayed in their concept of object permanence (Ertel and Voyat, 1982; Sigman and Ungerer, 1981). Some of these studies reported that the autistic children's performances on other subtests on these scales were more delayed than their object concept (Curcio, 1978; Ertel and Voyat, 1982; Thatcher, 1977). However, results on these other subtests differed from study to study.

Autistic children also have been described as rigid in manipulating internal images because they did not imitate symbolic gestures or anticipate the movements of objects (Hammes and Langdell, 1981). These deficits were thought to interfere with social relationships. They have also been found deficient in symbolic play (Doherty and Rosenfeld, 1984; Gould, 1986). Symbolic play has either been absent or narrow and repetitive.

Finally, James (1978) described autistic children as delayed in classification matching tasks. He reported that although autistic children demonstrated the same developmental pattern as normal children matched for IQ in classification matching tasks, the autistic children had a lower rate of categorical matching (objects with the same name but different functions) than the normal children.

Only two studies addressed deficient cognitive processes rather than structural delays among autistic children. Thatcher (1977) described autistic children as failing to accommodate (that is, adapt) to environmental feedback. Instead they repeated familiar schemes, demonstrating a lack of flexibility and a failure to progress intellectually. In contrast, another study described attentional and linguistic problems as central in explaining autistic children's delayed development (Lancy and Goldstein, 1982).

A recent review argued that the defining criterion for autism is deficient social and communicative behaviors (Denckla, 1986). Some research findings support this contention. In classification studies, Cowan, Hoddinott, and Wright (1965) found that autistic children made intentional classification errors, suggesting that the delays found were due to social resistance. Hobsen (1983) found that autistic children had difficulty classifying the age-related characteristics of social items but not of physical items. Additionally, recent studies identified deficits in non-verbal indicating behaviors—for example, pointing and looking (Mundy, Sigman, Ungerer, and Sherman, 1986; Sigman, Mundy, Sherman, and Congerer, 1986).

Thus both the nature of the developmental delay and the underlying mechanisms that may account for it require further investigation among autistic children. The nature of the cognitive deficit is one area of inquiry. The issue of deficient social and communicative behaviors and the feedback relationships between the cognitive and social domains also require investigation.

Cognitive-Developmental Study of Autism

The following study was designed to address these issues. Autistic children who were functioning above the sensorimotor period of development and who had limited expressive language skills were evaluated. I used a nonverbal, microanalytic method (Langer, 1980, 1986) originally designed for use with infants and young children up to five years of age. This provided a cognitive assessment for autistic children with poor receptive language skills who were difficult to assess using standardized tests.

Twelve autistic children, ages five to eight years, were selected to be in this study through a process that included direct observation, the review of previous testing and reports, and the evaluations of school administrators. When this study was conducted, the diagnostic criteria for autism from DSM III (American Psychiatric Association, 1980) were utilized. They included (1) onset before thirty months of age, (2) a pervasive lack of social responsiveness, (3) gross language deficits, (4) language abnormalities, such as pronoun reversals and echolalia, (5) a bizarre response to the environment, such as resisting change and being attached to objects, and (6) a lack of delusions, hallucinations, and loose associations. (Changes in the DSM III-R [American Psychiatric Association,

1987] definition of autism include reclassifying autism as a Developmental Disorder on Axis II, combining Infantile Autism and Childhood Onset Pervasive Developmental Disorder under the rubric Autistic Disorder because the age of onset is no longer used as a criterion for differential diagnosis, and providing a more detailed list of clinical symptoms.) The developmental delay of the autistic children was assumed and built into the research design. Therefore, the autistic children were matched to a control group of younger, normal children, ages twenty-two to thirty months. I will describe the procedure for matching the two groups of children after describing the tasks they were given.

Classification tasks were administered for two reasons. Classification is a central cognitive ability. Additionally, normative data using a similar methodology are available for comparative purposes (Langer, 1980, 1986; Sugarman, 1983).

The children were given two classification tasks. In one task, the objects varied along one dimension (objects differed by form) and in the other task, the objects varied along two dimensions (objects differed by form and color). In both tasks, the children were presented with a total of twelve objects. The type of object varied so that children received both geometric objects (for example, cylinders) and realistic objects (for example, cups). Both the task order and the object types were balanced across the subject groups.

Each task began with a two-and-a-half minute free-play condition. The experimenter intervened only to pick up fallen objects. A provoked sorting condition followed in which the experimenter began sorting the classes either spatially on the table or into separate opened containers. Additional objects were handed to the child in random order. If a child placed similar objects together, it was considered a correct placement. However, if dissimilar objects were placed together, it was considered a placement error. These errors were corrected as they occurred. The sorting condition elicited sorting by form in the form sorting task and sorting by (1) form, (2) color, and (3) form and color into a matrix in the form and color task.

This study evaluated both the structural and functional components of the children's activities. In general, structural analyses assess children's acquisition of knowledge through stages of development. In this study, the children's structural organization of the blocks was analyzed. In particular, this involved classification measures. Functional analyses pertain to developmental processes underlying children's acquisition of knowledge. In this study, functional analyses focused upon the children's regulatory activity. The regulations studied pertained to how the children monitored their actions and corrected their errors.

The subject groups were matched on one classification measure in the free-play condition of the form sorting task and then compared on other classification measures in this task and on the form and color sorting task. The measure used for matching the children assessed whether classes were sorted successively or simultaneously. This measure was used for matching the groups because the normative pattern of development was well researched. The children usually sorted one class at a time spatially on the table. When two classes did overlap, they were not constructed simultaneously as assessed by the children's order of handling the objects. In other words, they grouped one class at a time rather than switching back and forth between the classes (for example, they grouped four cylinders, then grouped four squares, rather than switching back and forth between cylinders and squares when making two groupings). This failure to coordinate the construction of spatial groupings was the criterion used to match the autistic and normal children. This successive sorting is characteristic of two-year-old children (Denney, 1972; Langer, 1986; Nelson, 1973; Ricciuti, 1965; Sugarman, 1983) and has been described as a perceptually bound procedure (Sugarman, 1983). It represented a vast developmental delay for the five- to eight-year-old autistic children in this study. The autistic children, therefore, were matched to younger, normal children around two to two-and-a-half years of age.

Thus, the subject groups were matched on one classification measure in the two tasks presented and then were compared on other classification measures in these tasks. This approach enabled comparisons of classificatory abilities and processes underlying these abilities within one cognitive domain. Thus, we avoided the problems encountered when subject groups are matched on tasks not highly correlated with the cognitive domain (for example, IQ, mental age, or chronological age) or are matched on tasks in cognitive domains that are not directly related to the domain being studied (Breslow and Cowan, 1984).

The results will be presented in two sections. First, the central cognitive findings and their implications will be summarized. Then, the social and interpersonal disturbances that had a feedback effect upon the autistic children's cognitive development will be described.

Central Cognitive Deficits in Autism

Structural Similarities. The older autistic children and younger, normal children were similar in many aspects of their block play. Recall that they were matched on the basis of their successive sorting procedure—that is, sorting one class at a time. They also produced similar sized groupings, similar activity rates, as measured by the number of block groupings produced per minute, and similar end products. At best, children constructed two classes overlapping in time. However, they did not construct two classes with full membership (for example, only two cylinders and two square-columns were grouped rather than four of each).

Similarly, when ordering classes within a grouping, the second class did not contain full membership (for example, cylinder, cylinder, cylinder, cylinder, square-column). Furthermore, in the form and color sorting task, inconsistent sorting criteria were used (for example, one collection was grouped on the basis of form and the other was grouped by color). Children did not use a consistent sorting criterion across the two groups.

The similarity between the younger, normal children and the developmentally delayed autistic children reflected the latter's difficulty coordinating preoperations in which the part and whole are considered simultaneously (Inhelder and Piaget, 1964). The autistic children were only organizing parts of classes and were not taking into account the whole class. The simultaneous consideration of a part of a class to the whole class is a necessary component in logical classification. It is essential to the development of the concept of class inclusion (that is, understanding the quantitative relationship between a subset and a set). Simultaneity is considered a prerequisite to both logical development (Inhelder and Piaget, 1964) and symbol formation (Langer, 1980), areas in which autistic children have been found deficient (James, 1978; Lockyer and Rutter, 1970; Sigman and Ungerer, 1981, 1984; Ungerer and Sigman, 1981). The autistic children's limitations in coordinating preoperations may be one factor contributing to their delay in both of these areas.

The autistic children's failure to coordinate classes may also have broader implications for their general cognitive development. Unlike younger, normal children who progress to coordinate classes and operations (Inhelder and Piaget, 1964), the autistic children may be arrested at the preoperational level. Longitudinal research is necessary to determine whether they have reached a developmental ceiling. If indeed, autistic children organize their interactions with the environment in a successive fashion, the coordinations underlying advances in social cognition (Turiel, 1983) also may be lacking. This failure to coordinate social events may be one factor underlying the inappropriate social interactions characteristic of these children.

Structural and Functional Differences. Despite many similarities in performance, the older autistic children's block play differed functionally and structurally from the younger, normal children in many important ways. Thus, their cognitive development was similar to but not the same as the younger, normal children's cognitive development. They were not just delayed but were different.

The autistic children's perceptual dominance exceeded that of the younger, normal children in two ways. The autistic children's perseveration in the class of objects they chose to manipulate was notable (for example, they always chose objects from the same class when making object substitutions). This perseveration prevented the autistic children from experimenting with different combinations of blocks in order to obtain different end results. Autistic children also demonstrated either an exclusive or very strong preference for sorting by a particular object dimension in the form and color sorting task (for example, always sorting by form or always sorting by color), significantly more than the normal children. This failure to switch back and forth between the object features may have been one factor impeding the autistic children's coordination of form required in sorting matrices.

This excessive perceptual dominance among the autistic children was a symptom of cognitive rigidity. Such rigidity has been described among pathological adults (Werner, 1948), mental retardates (Inhelder, 1968; Stephens, Manhaney, and McLaughlin, 1972), and psychotic children (Inhelder, 1971; Schmid-Kitsikis, 1973).

Regulatory differences between the autistic and normal children also were found. Transformational actions or operations are called regulations when they are applied to the correction of a disturbance. These self-correction regulations were divided into two groups. Repeating a previous action was considered a rigid regulation; engaging in a new action was considered a more flexible regulation. Contrary to what was expected functionally, the autistic children produced significantly more flexible corrections than the younger, normal children. For example, when trying to stabilize a tower that was not balancing, an autistic child would engage in a new action (for example, take off the block and substitute a new block for it). A younger, normal child would repeat a previous action (for example, remove and then replace the same block that was not balancing).

Contrary to what was expected structurally, the autistic children's flexible regulations were more detached than the normal children's rigid regulations. The regulations were detached because the autistic children's actions and object use were independent (that is, they repeated an action with a new object). Thus, their procedural means and end products were not fused and had the potential for being differentiated. Producing flexible regulations such as substitutions provided the opportunity for switching between classes and this allowed for some reorganization of the end product. In contrast, children engaging in rigid regulations such as replacements did not create an opportunity to change the end products; they merely repeated what they had already constructed.

The autistic children's production of more detached regulations was an advance over the younger, normal children. The nascent independence of actions and objects enabled the beginning detachment of operations from their application onto objects. This is one of the necessary prerequisites for the abstraction of logical and mathematical operations (Langer, 1986).

Why, then, did the autistic children function at a developmentally delayed level if they produced more flexible, detached regulations than the normal children? Neither the means-ends differentiation nor the reorganization of the end product were realized by the autistic children due to functional interference from their rigid perceptual system. Because of the autistic children's perceptual dominance they engaged in perseverative object choices, substituting objects from the same class (for example, cylinder 1 for cylinder 2). This substitution strategy had the same end result as the replacement of the same object by the normal children. Thus, the autistic children's self-regulations were more advanced structurally and the prerequisites for developmental progress were present. However, due to the interference of the autistic children's rigid perceptual system, the regulations were of limited effectiveness and the potential for developmental progress was not realized. Thus, their procedures appeared repetitive (Hermelin and Frith, 1971) and impeded their development of representational thought.

Social Disturbances in Autism

The autistic children in this study also demonstrated social disturbances that were reflected primarily in their differential responses to components of the provoked sorting conditions. The provoked sorting phase differed from the spontaneous sorting phase in two significant ways. First, the provoked phase was more structured in that either containers or spatial groupings were placed on the table to suggest classification. Second, the experimenter played a more active, structuring role, by correcting placement errors made by the children. In comparison to the spontaneous phase, the provoked phase pulled for the classification of the objects more directly, using both physical and social prompts.

In a previous study (Thatcher, 1977), autistic children were described as unable to accommodate (that is, adapt to the environment). In the provoked sorting phase of this study, the autistic children were found to accommodate differentially depending upon the source of the stimuli or disturbance. The autistic children accommodated less to the socially structured aspects of the task but more to the physical aspects of the task than the normal children.

The autistic children's social avoidance was evident (Cowan, Hoddinott, and Wright, 1965). They resisted the sorting task by making significantly more irrelevant placements than the normal children (for example, building towers next to the containers or making minor adjustments of the objects in the containers, rather than placing additional objects in the containers). Additionally, the autistic children imitated the experimenter's corrections of their sorting placements less frequently, matching their actions to the experimenter's actions significantly less often than the normal children.

However, when they were not resisting the experimenter and were making relevant sorting placements, the autistic children produced a higher percentage of correct sorting placements than the normal children. This indicated that when the autistic children were cooperating, they accommodated more to the physical positions of the sorted objects than the normal children. Additionally, more autistic children than normal children increased the number of classes sorted from the free-play to provoked sorting conditions. This suggested that the autistic children's increased accommodation to physical objects occurred in the more structured task. Thus, the autistic children accommodated more to the physical positions of the sorted objects but accommodated less to the socially structured aspects of the task than did the normal children.

This limited social accommodation had implications for the autistic children's cognitive development. The autistic children's social resistance reduced their exposure to disequilibrating experiences considered necessary for cognitive development, particularly in the area of social imitation. Imitation (Piaget, 1962) and social interaction (Bruner, 1975; Werner and Kaplan, 1963) are considered central to the development of symbol formation. The autistic children's paucity of social imitation may be related to their reported deficiencies in symbol formation. The function of social interaction as a general source of information and feedback also appeared limited in these children. Some theorists (Bruner, 1975; Vygotsky, 1978) have emphasized the central role of social relationships in the development of cognition. It is likely that the autistic children's social avoidance has impeded their cognitive development in all areas.

In contrast, the autistic children's accommodation exceeded that of the normal children when the structure was provided by the arrangement of the objects themselves. This suggests that the autistic children are capable of receiving feedback and accommodating in response to feedback in a more limited capacity. This provides a more positive view of their accommodation abilities than has previously been cited (Thatcher, 1977).

Implications of the Findings for Clinical Assessment and Intervention

Cowan (1978) discussed some implications of structural and functional differences between psychotic and normal children for clinical assessment and treatment. Schizophrenic children's cognitive development was described as structurally retarded and characterized by a functional imbalance between assimilatory and accommodatory functions. Their cognition was characterized by a figurative dominance and structural-functional asynchronies. Cowan suggested that a therapist should act as a disequilibrator, presenting the child with slightly more advanced concepts from the next stage of development to stimulate disequilibrium and help stimulate development. The therapist should also move the child away from the extremes of the assimilation-accommodation imbalance.

These implications and suggestions apply in a general sense to autistic children as well. The cognitive-developmental approach provides unique information about autistic children's cognitive and social functioning. This method evaluates the organization of the child's abilities in terms of a stage or level of development. It also analyzes actions closely, allowing the identification of flexible components in seemingly repetitive behaviors.

This study points to the importance of evaluating a child's stage of cognitive development when carrying out an assessment or planning a treatment program. The five- to eight-year-old autistic children in this study were found to be delayed many years on classification tasks and were characterized at the two-year-old level. This identification of their cognitive level provided valuable information about their current abilities. Most notably, they failed to coordinate the construction of classes. This failure provided information that could be generalized to other cognitive domains (that is, that coordinating preoperations in general was difficult). It may indicate that autistic children are arrested at the preoperational stage of development.

These cognitive limitations may spill over into the social realm and characterize social interactions as well. In particular, the children's failure to flexibly alternate between classes may constitute a more general inability to flexibly alternate between events. Social communication and social interaction both require sharing a focus and taking turns. Autistic children's characteristic assimilatory interactive style may reflect their difficulty switching back and forth between speakers and events. Additionally, their difficulty coordinating preoperations indicates that they may have difficulty coordinating social interactions and developing social knowledge. This paucity of social knowledge may interfere significantly with their social functioning.

The cognitive-developmental assessment provided both the identification of potential areas for development and areas that were inhibiting development. This provided a more differentiated view of autistic children's abilities. Rather than just being considered perseverative (for example, Black, Freeman, and Montgomery, 1975; Rutter, 1978a), a distinction was made between perseverative and flexible components of their cognition. Autistic children were found to have potential for development in regard to using detached operations and flexible means. This potential separation of means and ends provided one of the prerequisites for abstracting operations. However, the autistic children were found to have a perceptual or figurative dominance. This resulted in a structural rigidity or lack of flexibility that characterized all of their actions and interactions and rendered their flexible means ineffective. Rather than being considered nonregulatory, these children appeared to be ineffective regulators and therefore nonprogressive in their development. Recognizing cognitive potential for growth provided a more positive view of these children. It suggests that research about clinical intervention needs to address the means for actualizing this potential while circumventing the cognitive rigidity that obstructs it.

This rigidity is manifested clinically in two symptoms characteristic of autistic children: perseveration and insistence on sameness. Their inflexibility, often referred to as social resistance to change, has a strong cognitive component and must be addressed from this perspective. This awareness of autistic children's perceptual dominance and cognitive rigidity is central to clinical assessment and treatment.

The cognitive assessment also provided an evaluation of social disturbances that had a negative feedback effect on the autistic children's cognitive development. The autistic children were found to accommodate well when the classification structure was provided by the organization of objects. However, they did not accommodate very well to the structure provided by the experimenter. Socially, then, they were very assimilative (that is, structuring the environment to fit their understanding). This social resistance pointed to the importance of differentiating between relevant and irrelevant activity prior to assessing the autistic children's cognitive skills. Irrelevant activity produced to resist the experimenter should be discounted.

Although this study was not focused on intervention, some implications for intervention with these children can be hypothesized. The assessment demonstrated that a social approach had a negative effect and a structured approach using the objects had a more positive effect in regard to moving the autistic children away from their highly assimilative functioning. Because of the autistic children's low level of social accommodation, the task of therapeutic intervention is very difficult. The autistic children avoided social sources of disequilibration, which is precisely the role of teachers and therapists working with these children. This might suggest the usefulness of psychoanalytic play because therapists reflect the child's play rather than guide it. However, psychoanalytic play therapy may be inappropriate for autistic children due to their poor symbol formation and symbolic play (Wulff, 1985). The present research findings suggest the development of an active, but indirect, structured approach. A therapist needs to be active in regard to preventing perseveration and provoking disequilibrating experiences. The latter is crucial to providing opportunities for both cognitive and emotional growth. Ironically, this must be done indirectly, through the manipulation and structuring of a physical medium. For example, one could structure the physical environment so as to limit the opportunity for perseveration across objects by providing only one toy of each kind. This type of indirect provocation is necessary to circumvent the autistic children's avoidance of socially instigated disequilibrium.

A cognitive-developmental approach also may be useful in formulating specific interventions. By evaluating the child's cognitive level, the next developmental step to be taken also can be identified. The therapist as disequilibrator can present the child with logical and social concepts one step above the child's level, disequilibrate the child, and help stimulate development. For example, the autistic children in this study had difficulty coordinating classes simultaneously. They could not consider the relationship of subsets to sets and therefore did not always construct classes with full class membership. This indicates that provoking the simultaneous consideration of classes or part-to-whole relationships would be an appropriate intervention to stimulate preoperational coordinations in both the logical domain and other related domains of development. In a practical setting, a therapist could provoke the child to move back and forth between toys, actions, or communications in order to stimulate taking two things into account simultaneously.

In sum, a cognitive-developmental approach provided information not obtained through traditional assessment methods that pertained to assessment and therapeutic intervention with autistic children. It identified the current cognitive level, the next step in development, the flexible and inflexible components of the child's cognition, social disturbances, and approaches that may be effective in working with these children. An active, but indirect approach of structuring the physical environment was suggested to disequilibrate the autistic children and stimulate them to coordinate preoperations and become less assimilative, both cognitively and socially.

References

American Psychiatric Association. *Diagnostic and Statistical Manual of Mental Disorders.* (3rd ed.) Washington, D.C.: American Psychiatric Association, 1980.

American Psychiatric Association. *Diagnostic and Statistical Manual of Mental Disorders* (3rd ed., rev.) Washington, D.C.: American Psychiatric Association, 1987.

Baron-Cohen, S., Leslie, A., and Frith, U. "Mechanical, Behavioral, and Intentional Understanding of Picture Sorting in Autistic Children." *British Journal of Developmental Psychology,* 1986, *4,* 113–125.

Black, M., Freeman, B., and Montgomery, J. "Systematic Observation of Play Behavior in Autistic Children." *Journal of Autism and Childhood Schizophrenia,* 1975, *5,* 363–371.

Breslow, L., and Cowan, P. "Structural and Functional Perspectives on Classification and Seriation in Psychotic and Normal Children." *Child Development,* 1984, *55,* 226–235.

Bruner, J. "From Communication to Language—A Psychological Perspective." *Cognition,* 1975, *3,* 255-287.

Cowan, P. *Piaget with Feeling: Cognitive, Social, and Emotional Dimensions.* New York: Holt, Rinehart & Winston, 1978.

Cowan, P., Hoddinott, B., and Wright, B. "Compliance and Resistance in the Conditioning of Autistic Children: An Exploratory Study." *Child Development,* 1965, *36,* 913-923.

Curcio, F. "Sensorimotor Functioning and Communication in Mute Autistic Children." *Journal of Autism and Childhood Schizophrenia,* 1978, *8,* 281-292.

Denckla, M. "New Diagnostic Criteria for Autism and Related Behavioral Disorders: Guidelines for Research Protocols." *Journal of the American Academy of Child Psychiatry,* 1986, *25,* 221-224.

Denney, N. "Free Classification in Preschool Children." *Child Development,* 1972, *43,* 1161-1170.

Doherty, M., and Rosenfeld, A. "Play Assessment in the Differential Diagnosis of Autism and Other Causes of Severe Language Disorder." *Journal of Developmental and Behavioral Pediatrics,* 1984, *5,* 26-29

Ertel, D., and Voyat, G. "Sensorimotor Analysis of Early Onset Childhood Psychosis." *Teachers College Record,* 1982, *84,* 423-451.

Gould, J. "The Lowe and Costello Symbolic Play Test in Socially Impaired Children." *Journal of Autism and Developmental Disorders,* 1986, *16,* 199-213.

Hammes, J., and Langdell, T. "Precursors of Symbol Formation and Childhood Autism." *Journal of Autism and Developmental Disorders,* 1981, *11,* 331-346.

Hermelin, B. "Images and Language." In M. Rutter and E. Schopler (eds.), *Autism: A Reappraisal of Concepts and Treatment.* New York: Plenum Press, 1978.

Hermelin, B., and Frith, U. "Psychological Studies of Childhood Autism: Can Autistic Children Make Sense of What They See and Hear?" *Journal of Special Education,* 1971, *5,* 107-117.

Hermelin, B., and O'Connor, N. *Psychological Experiments with Autistic Children.* Elmsford, N.Y.: Pergamon Press, 1970.

Hobsen, P. R. "The Autistic Child's Recognition of Age-Related Features of People, Animals, and Things." *British Journal of Developmental Psychology,* 1983, *1,* 343-352.

Inhelder, B. *The Diagnosis of Reasoning in the Mentally Retarded.* New York: Chandler, 1968.

Inhelder, B. "Developmental Theory and Diagnostic Procedures." In D. Green, M. Ford, and G. Flamer (eds.), *Measurement and Piaget.* New York: McGraw-Hill, 1971.

Inhelder, B., and Piaget, J. *The Early Growth of Logic in the Child.* Boston: Routledge & Kegan Paul, 1964.

James, W. "Effect of Level of Classification Skill on Matching Performance for Autistic and Nonautistic Children Ages 12-21." *Dissertation Abstracts International,* 1978, *38,* 7270B.

Kanner, L. "Autistic Disturbances of Affective Contact." *Nervous Child,* 1943, *2,* 217-250.

Lancy, D., and Goldstein, G. "The Use of Nonverbal Piagetian Tasks to Assess the Cognitive Development of Autistic Children." *Child Development,* 1982, *53,* 1233-1241.

Langer, J. *The Origins of Logic: 6 to 12 Months.* New York: Academic Press, 1980.

Langer, J. *The Origins of Logic: One to Two Years.* New York: Academic Press, 1986.

Lockyer, L., and Rutter, M. "A Five-to-Fifteen-Year Follow-Up Study of Infantile Psychosis: IV. Patterns of Cognitive Ability." *British Journal of Social and Clinical Psychology*, 1970, *9*, 152–163.

Lovaas, O. I. *The Autistic Child*. New York: Irvington, 1977.

Morgan, S. "Early Childhood Autism: Changing Perspectives." *Journal of Child and Adolescent Psychotherapy*, 1986, *3*, 3–9.

Mundy, P., Sigman, M., Ungerer, J., and Sherman, T. "Defining the Social Deficits of Autism: The Contribution of Non-Verbal Communication Measures." *Journal of Child Psychology and Psychiatry*, 1986, *27*, 657–669.

Nelson, K. "Some Evidence for the Cognitive Primacy of Categorization and Its Functional Basis." *Merrill-Palmer Quarterly*, 1973, *19*, 21–39.

Piaget, J. *Plays, Dreams, and Imitation in Childhood*. New York: Norton, 1962.

Ricciuti, H. "Object Grouping and Selective Ordering Behavior in Infants 12–24 Months Old." *Merrill-Palmer Quarterly*, 1965, *11*, 129–148.

Rincover, A., and Ducharme, J. "Variables Influencing Stimulus Overselectivity and 'Tunnel Vision' in Developmentally Delayed Children." *American Journal of Mental Deficiency*, 1987, *91*, 422–430.

Rincover, A., Feldman, M., and Eason, L. "Tunnel Vision: A Possible Keystone Stimulus Control Deficit in Autistic Children." *Analysis and Intervention in Developmental Disabilities*, 1986, *6*, 283–304.

Rutter, M. "Concepts of Autism: A Review of Research." *Journal of Child Psychology and Psychiatry and Allied Disciplines*, 1968, *9*, 1–25.

Rutter, M. "Diagnosis and Definition." In M. Rutter and E. Schopler (eds.), *Autism: A Reappraisal of Concepts and Treatment*. New York: Plenum Press, 1978a.

Rutter, M. "Language Disorder and Infantile Autism." In M. Rutter and E. Schopler (eds.), *Autism: A Reappraisal of Concepts and Treatment*. New York: Plenum Press, 1978b.

Rutter, M. "Cognitive Deficits in the Pathogenesis of Autism." *Journal of Child Psychology and Psychiatry and Allied Disciplines*, 1983, *24*, 513–531.

Rutter, M. "Child Psychiatry: The Interface Between Clinical and Developmental Research." *Psychological Medicine*, 1986, *16*, 151–169.

Schmid-Kitsikis, E. "Piagetian Theory and Its Approach to Psychopathology." *American Journal of Mental Deficiency*, 1973, *77*, 694–705.

Sigman, M., Mundy, P., Sherman, T., and Congerer, J. "Social Interactions of Autistic, Mentally Retarded, and Normal Children and Their Caregivers." *Journal of Child Psychology and Psychiatry*, 1986, *27*, 647–656.

Sigman, M., and Ungerer, J. "Sensorimotor Skills and Language Comprehension in Autistic Children." *Journal of Abnormal Child Psychology*, 1981, *9*, 149–165.

Sigman, M., and Ungerer, J. "Cognitive and Language Skills in Autistic, Mentally Retarded, and Normal Children." *Developmental Psychology*, 1984, *20*, 293–302.

Slotnick, C. F. "The Organization and Regulation of Block Constructions: A Comparison of Autistic and Normal Children's Cognitive Development." Unpublished doctoral dissertation, University of California, Berkeley, 1984.

Stephens, B., Manhaney, E. J., and McLaughlin, J. A. "Mental Ages for Achievement of Piagetian Reasoning Assessments." *Education and Training of the Mentally Retarded*, 1972, *7*, 124–128.

Sugarman, S. *Children's Early Thought: Developments in Classification*. Cambridge, England: Cambridge University Press, 1983.

Thatcher, M. "An Application of Piaget's Theory to Autistic Children." *Dissertation Abstracts International*, 1977, *38*, 919B.

Turiel, E. *The Development of Social Knowledge.* Cambridge, England: Cambridge University Press, 1983.

Ungerer, J., and Sigman, M. "Symbolic Play and Language Comprehension in Autistic Children." *Journal of the American Academy of Child Psychiatry,* 1981, *20*, 318-337.

Vygotsky, I. *Mind in Society: The Development of the Higher Psychological Processes.* Cambridge, Mass.: Harvard University Press, 1978.

Werner, H. *Comparative Psychology of Mental Development.* New York: International Universities Press, 1948.

Werner, H., and Kaplan, B. *Symbol Formation: An Organismic-Developmental Approach to Language and the Expression of Thought.* New York: Wiley, 1963.

Wulff, S. B. "The Symbolic and Objective Play of Children with Autism." *Journal of Autism and Developmental Disorders,* 1985, *15*, 139-148.

Carol Fisher Slotnick is a licensed clinical psychologist. She is a staff psychologist at the Children's Health Council in Palo Alto, California, specializing in the evaluation and treatment of infants and young children. She is also in private practice in Palo Alto, California.

*A social-development theory of self is introduced as a
framework for developmental psychopathology. Psychodynamic
and Piagetian principles are viewed as building blocks within
a broadened frame where both traditions are transformed.*

A Constructivist Approach
to Developmental
Psychopathology

Gil G. Noam

Few people have influenced developmental psychology more than Jean
Piaget. A productive philosopher, biologist, and psychologist, he introduced what we now call cognitive-developmental psychology. But
although Piaget had considerable knowledge about psychoanalysis and
psychopathology, neither he nor most of his coworkers in Geneva dedicated much energy to understanding atypical development. This is not
surprising for a man who devoted his life to the study of universal
structures of rationality and thought.

Change has been considerable. In the last decade a significant
number of cognitive-developmental psychologists have joined other developmentalists in studying emotions, interpersonal relationships, and psychopathology. These exciting research endeavors have given momentum
to the emerging fields of developmental psychopathology and clinical-
developmental psychology.

I would like to thank Barbara Anderson and Nadine Bozek for editorial
suggestions and manuscript preparation. Discussions with Sophie Borst on the
case of Rachel were very helpful and are acknowledged with appreciation. The
work was supported by a grant from the Isabel Benton Trust.

E. D. Nannis, P. A. Cowan (eds.). *Developmental Psychopathology and Its Treatment.*
New Directions for Child Development, no. 39. San Francisco: Jossey-Bass, Spring 1988.

While developmental psychopathology is dedicated to the systematic research of psychological disorders from a developmental—especially longitudinal—vantage point, clinical-developmental psychology focuses on developmentally-based interventions to alleviate or prevent psychological problems (for detailed definitions see Sroufe and Rutter, 1984; Noam, 1985b, and Chapters One and Six, this volume). One can argue that throughout this century psychoanalysis has been comprised of both a developmental psychopathology and a clinical-developmental practice. But the recent advances in developmental psychology have given these fields a new emphasis. If some researchers are hostile toward psychoanalytic principles, a variety of Freud's ideas have nevertheless been transformed and introduced into the developmental psychopathology literature. For example, object relations psychoanalysis has been given an ethological reformulation by Bowlby (1969), and the resultant attachment theory has had a strong impact on developmental psychology and psychopathology (Sroufe and Waters, 1977). Another example can be found in theory and research on adolescent development, which has been strongly influenced by Erikson's psychoanalytic reformulations. More recently, researchers have turned to the systematic study of defense mechanisms to help explain development and pathology in adulthood (Vaillant, 1977).

While psychodynamic principles have provided a resource for studying developmental psychopathology, the most important insights have come from longitudinal empirical investigations into the natural history of psychological disorders, into patterns of resilience of at-risk populations, and into the later onset of psychopathology in groups that do not show earlier signs of behavioral problems. An impressive body of literature now exists that includes studies on depression, hyperactivity, delinquency, and many other disorders of affect, thought, and behavior (for a review see Rutter and Garmezy, 1983). Most of these studies demonstrate the complex relationship between development and psychopathology and question the possibility of predicting adult outcome from childhood disorders (Kohlberg, LaCross, and Rick, 1972).

Most prospective developmental psychopathology studies have used chronological age or social timetables (for example, going to college, marriage, and so on) as key developmental variables (Achenbach, 1982). Cognitive-developmental psychology introduces a different developmental marker: a structural organization or stage that is defined independently of age. For example, a typical fourteen-year-old functions at the cognitive stage of early formal operational thought, but her fourteen-year-old classmate may organize reality at the concrete or full formal operational stages. For this reason, cognitive-developmental psychologists assume that it is crucial to study the developmental course organized around the concept of stages (for a fuller discussion about the relationship between stage and age models, see Noam, Kohlberg, and Snarey,

1983; Noam, 1985a). Although the cognitive approach has been widely recognized for normal developmental psychology, like psychoanalysis it has had only a small direct influence on developmental psychopathology.

In clinical theory and practice, too, cognitive-developmental psychology has had a minimal impact. Some psychoanalysts have dealt seriously with the potential contribution of Piaget (Anthony, 1976; Greenspan, 1979; Wolff, 1960) but, by and large, clinicians have not altered their practices based on these writings. This is true even for behavioral psychologists who have embraced a cognitive approach (Beck, 1976). They have not used the many developmental ideas found in Piaget's work. Recently, though, the rigid boundaries of the different psychotherapy schools have become more permeable, and as a consequence, a variety of syntheses are being proposed. Interestingly, they all involve some principles from the cognitive-developmental tradition. Ciompi (1982), for example, suggests an integration of family systems theory and Piaget's genetic epistemology. A Rome-based group (Guidano and Liotti, 1983) has introduced cognitive theory that simultaneously makes use of attachment theory. Within the psychoanalytic school, Atwood and Stolorow (1984) have formulated a theory of subjectivity that builds on Kohut and cognitive-epistemological principles. In my own work (Noam, 1986a, 1986b), I have argued against the eclectic use of different and unrelated theory pieces and have instead suggested a developmental synthesis that builds on social-cognitive theory as well as on Eriksonian and object-relations principles.

However, it is too easy to take the position that advanced knowledge in cognition should be imported into the "underdeveloped territories" of the clinician's consulting room or the developmental psychopathologist's research laboratory. Nothing could be less appropriate. Both settings have a great deal to teach the cognitive-developmentalist who is traditionally a researcher with little experience in pathology or an applied developmental psychologist with an educational focus. Furthermore, the variety of integrative approaches has been introduced because cognitivists were faced with the limitations of a pure transfer of cognitive-developmental principles to psychological disorders and their treatments. This is understandable since psychopathology is not based solely on cognitive processes. Patients usually demonstrate a complex combination of behavioral, cognitive, and emotional issues. The road to recovery usually entails an intense interpersonal experience between therapist (or setting) and patient.

This chapter, then, introduces a new theory in discussing the difficult relationship between cognitive theory and developmental psychopathology. While building on some of the principles introduced by Piaget, this perspective simultaneously attempts to overcome limitations of cognitive-developmental theory, such as the overly strong emphasis on thought over emotion. Referred to as a constructive-developmental theory (rather than a narrowly defined cognitive approach), it is taken into the social domain and used to define the movements of self and important others throughout life. Such a broad structural perspective focuses primarily on what I term the transformational and biographical activities of the self and their systematic relationships.

The transformational side of the self refers to the continued development of the self throughout life. New interactions between the self and others create opportunities for restructuring self-understandings, including reconstructing the past and reorienting in the present. This activity leads to more advanced developmental organizations that are not, as they are in psychoanalysis, interpreted as a set of separate ego functions (such as stress tolerance or defensive style) but as a structure that the self creates to give coherence to its internal and interpersonal reality. The structuring concept, which builds on Piaget and Kohlberg, does not differ greatly from a variety of other stage theories of social-cognition and self that I will address in a later section of this paper (for example, see Broughton, 1978; Kegan, 1982; Loevinger, 1976; and many others).

The overall theory of self, however, differs from these earlier stage theories significantly. While creative in their scope, they have reduced the social construction of self to a current balance between person and world and have lost sight of the fact that the self, in fact, can continuously fluctuate between different developmental levels. Because of this misconception, a central aspect of human development, the experience of and knowledge about the self's history, has been screened out and consequently impoverished our view on development. Biography has been reduced to nothing more than a content, which in Piagetian circles has always been treated with some disdain, since it supposedly does not contribute much on the royal road toward uncovering the structure of mind. Even Kohlberg, who had been at the forefront of the cognitive revolution, has acknowledged that the Piagetian perspective has a serious limitation in its neglect of life history.

Given the importance of life history in psychopathology, I asked myself whether there was a way to integrate structural-developmental concepts into a larger theoretical frame that would hold simultaneously the evolutionary history of the person and the present-day developmental organization. I considered this program not only the central meeting point of Werner (1948), Piaget, and psychoanalytic thinking but also, more importantly, the starting point for an encompassing theory of self and a new conception of psychopathology.

In the theory of biography and transformation, the biographic component of the self refers to the history of important relationships and their internalizations. The theory assumes that these internalized relationships can continue to shape a person's experience long after the self has developed more complex meaning frames. Each developmental transformation provides the opportunity for a new self-synthesis yet can also occur while the person remains under the influence of aspects of an old structure (less differentiated and integrated). Under ideal circumstances, the earlier structures become transformed. But frequently, this integration does not occur and leads to what I have termed encapsulations, a form of living biography through which earlier self-systems coexist with later ones.

This conception of biography is not viewed as a composite of the real events in a person's life but has two more complex meanings. First, the history of structural transformations is reflected in the present-day shape of the self. If the earlier transformations were all-encompassing, the self will be integrated and there will be little pull to earlier self positions. If, however, there have been problems in transformation, it is quite likely that the self will be pulled to earlier self positions. Embedded in this idea is a new conceptualization about the strength and fragility of the self, which I will address later in the chapter. Second, biography is also created through organizing meanings about the self that have an enduring character. I term these continuities in the relationship between self and other *core life themes* and view them as central bridges between the mature self positions and the encapsulations. The struggle over the self's development and regression is not fought in the relatively safe world of Piagetian experiments, but around these biographical themes of separation and connection, self-continuity and discontinuity.

Through these concepts, the theory of biography and transformation has moved beyond describing different self components and toward the explanation of their systematic relationships. We can now uncover the forces of self-integration and disintegration. They are at the heart of the basic striving toward a unified view of self, but also at the root of the typical returns to earlier self constructions. This comprehensive view, which requires a new understanding of psychological structure and its developmental course, is applicable to both psychopathology and normal development. In fact, the study of psychopathology has served as a microscope to highlight typical processes relevant also to the development of the self and personality. We will now turn to the cognitive-developmental tradition in self theory and psychopathology. The need for a new model will be explained by focusing on problems in existing theory.

Social Development: Limitations of Stage Theory and the Need for New Direction

At an early stage of his work, Piaget already had profound insights into the social dimensions of child development. His path-breaking book, *The Moral Judgment of the Child* (Piaget, 1932), guided many psychologists in their understanding of social development. But Piaget's emphasis shifted when he turned to the child's intellectual development and the universal logico-mathematical structures. While Piaget drew heavily from the social theories of the Chicago school (Baldwin, 1897; Mead, 1934), it was Kohlberg's synthesis of symbolic interactionism (as the Chicago school became known) and Piaget's genetic epistemology that created new possibilities for a social theory based on cognitive-developmental principles. Kohlberg's papers on the cognitive-developmental approach to morality (Kohlberg, 1969, 1976) inspired many of the psychologists who have become known as social cognitivists. Clearly, others building on Piaget's ideas also greatly influenced developmental and personality psychology (Flavell, 1977; Loevinger, 1976), but the organizing principles for a cognitive-developmental social theory were introduced through Kohlberg's work on moral judgment.

Many clinical disorders involve intellectual and moral issues, domains studied so carefully by both Piaget and Kohlberg. With his focus on psychoses and mental retardation, Piaget's contribution to developmental psychopathology relates most closely to the function of intelligence (for a review see Cowan, 1978). In the study of psychoses he and his coworkers (Schmid-Kitsikis, 1973) explored the breakdown of intelligence. Their work with mentally retarded children helped to answer whether atypical populations still progressed through the same universal stages of intelligence, albeit at a different rate and with a low ceiling. Kohlberg and his coworkers focused on the disorder that directly related to the theory of moral development: delinquency. They were able to demonstrate that delinquency is most commonly associated with early stages of moral development. But the broad spectrum of psychiatric disorders, including those studied by Piaget and Kohlberg, involves a variety of other relevant social and self processes (self-integration, self-esteem, interpersonal relationships, to mention but a few).

The cognitive approach has been taken into some of these domains. In his creative work on the developmental line of epistemology, for example, Broughton (1978) demonstrated structural growth in understanding mind, body, and knowledge. And research on children's conceptions of friendships (Selman, 1980; Keller, 1984), authority relationships (Youniss, 1980), and faith (Fowler, 1981; Oser and others, 1980) demonstrated the strength of a constructive-developmental orientation to social development. It is striking how similar the stage descriptions have been even across a wide variety of cognitive and personality areas.

Partly inspired by these similarities and by Loevinger's stage theory of ego development (Loevinger, 1976), a variety of social-cognitive self theories have been introduced (Blasi, 1983; Damon and Hart, 1982; Kegan, 1982; Noam, 1985b). These theories examine the self in terms of an underlying logic of self-understanding, self-representation, or self-other differentiation. They differ in their definitions of the self and in their approach to the question of whether the self is a unitary process or is comprised of a number of subdomains (for example, physical, psychological, social self, and so on). But again, the descriptions of the sequences are strikingly similar, even when the methodologies differ greatly.

As conceptions of self became more established, the insight slowly ripened that important clinical questions could be addressed with these new theoretical tools. Since so much of what concerns both the psychopathology researcher and the practicing clinician involves processes of self-reflection and interpersonal relationships, it could be assumed that central concepts of social-developmental theory could become useful clinically. A beginning cross-fertilization between clinical and developmental theories occurred that was facilitated by a number of earlier conceptualizations that had emerged in psychoanalysis and psychiatry (Erikson, 1950; Sullivan, 1953).

It is my view that the initial excitement about new possibilities in understanding and working with psychopathology from a Piagetian perspective has given way to a more realistic evaluation of the cognitivist's contribution in developing clinical theories and interventions. As mentioned above, we require an evaluation of the strengths and weaknesses of a structural approach in psychopathology. This discussion poses difficulties since it involves a critical account of the work of esteemed colleagues and friends. But clarifying these positions is a way to give them deserved respect and is also the only way to give appropriate direction to theory and method in the new and growing field of developmental psychopathology. Thus, I will now turn to three main points that address the unrecognized problems inherent in structural-development theory of self and psychopathology.

Underlying Logic of a Constructivist Theory of Self. Although I will present a developmental stage model in describing the self, I differ from other structural-developmentalists in the status ascribed to the development, stages, and transformation. From my perspective, Piaget's theory of intellectual development is as yet the only theory that has been able to describe the underlying logic, or so-called structural operations of a developmental sequence. For this reason, Kohlberg (1984) defined Piaget's stages as *hard*. According to Kohlberg, a theory is hard when a clear distinction is made both between structure and content and between competence and performance. Furthermore, the structures have to form an invariant sequence, independent of cultural influences; the stages have to represent hierarchical integrations that are increasingly differentiated and integrated. Kohlberg was convinced that his theory of moral judgment was also organized by hard-stage criteria (justice structures). Doebert (1987), however, has recently argued quite convincingly that the stages of moral judgment are defined in structural terms, but that without a variety of contents the structures would be rather empty. He shows, for example, how the notions of trust and affiliation so relevant to Kohlberg's stage three are simultaneously structure and content dimensions.

According to Kohlberg, *soft-stage* theories deal more with the content and function of personality than with the structure of cognitive operations. They refer to the individual's reflections upon the self's psychology rather than to structural forms of reasoning and are self-constructed individual theories (Perry, 1968; Fowler, 1981; Loevinger, 1976; Kegan, 1982). It is not clear as yet whether it will be possible to develop some criteria for the underlying structures, the operative structures that organize the course of social development, but a successful attempt would be a great contribution to the field. Kegan (1982) has introduced stages of the self that parallel the descriptions of Loevinger ego stages but that take the step of defining an underlying structural system at each position. This step has provided important information regarding the organization and reorganization of the self. Kegan claims to have found the underlying logic for all structural development, including Piaget's logical development and Kohlberg's moral development sequence. Because of this claim, it is necessary to address the work in greater detail. Each of his stages is considered in terms of the relationship between a current subjective experience and that which had been subjective in the previous stage and has become objective. The *object* refers to those feelings, thoughts, and relationships that are held consciously, that are observed and thus available for coordination and mediation. The *subject* side of this balance refers to those aspects of the self of which a self-observing person has no current awareness—those in which the person is embedded and from which he has no distance. For example, impulses define Stage 1, needs define Stage 2, and an interpersonal orientation defines Stage 3. It is unclear, however, what these different biological and personality dimensions have in common that make them part of one developmental sequence. Impulsivity, needs, and interpersonality are not tied to a single function that gets reorganized at each new stage. It is also not apparent why they should comprise the underlying logic of the development of the self. Could one not argue that a developmental line of impulses or needs exists that can be described for all stages? It is even more difficult to understand why, for example, the subject-object relationship between "being one's relationships" (Stage 3) and "having one's relationship" (Stage 4) should be the underlying organization for Piaget's formal operational stages or any of the stages of moral and social development.

Much future energy will have to be focused on uncovering the underlying logic of the self and social cognition. In the meantime, Kohlberg's (1969, 1976, 1984) and Selman's (1980) proposal for viewing social perspective-taking as the underlying developmental principle for moral and social development can guide our work. The stages of social perspective avoid mixing biological and social metaphors and provide a unitary function (the understanding of the relationship between self and other) in development. I will return to the social perspectives when I introduce the stages of self.

Soft Stages and the Reification of Structural Principles. A second problem of a variety of social-developmental theories is that hard-stage principles of structural wholeness, sequentiality, and hierarchical integration have been applied to the social domain as if they were dealing with the development of cognitive operations. It is my view that soft-stage theorists directly applied the principles of logical operations to self and life without noticing the analogical nature (cognitive stages and the rules of transformation translate into theories dealing with very different topics like personality, faith, and so on) of the procedure. I had at first taken a similar approach (Noam and Kegan, 1983) and have only gradually discovered the emerging contradictions in part through in-depth developmental psychopathology research. Piaget himself did not believe in this kind of a stage sequence but rather viewed personality dimensions as multiple and contradictory processes. The broadening radius of structural interpretations (from intellectual functions to moral judgment, to epistemology, to self and faith) casts a shadow on clear structural categories. What was for Kohlberg a focus on moral judgment has mushroomed into views on thinking and feeling, judging and acting, being in relationship with a concrete person and an ultimate being, and so on. What began as a circumscribed sequence has been transformed into a developmental metaphor—a notion of evolution and growth that somehow relates to self, life, and religion.

No doubt, these metaphors have strength but the analogical nature of the models was not taken into consideration. It was quite literally assumed that a stage transformation was reorganizing all the categories of self, personality, or faith into a new and structured whole. But since more and more soft contents have been included in the models, it is incorrect to assume that a stage change will reorganize and transform all the aspects of self and personality as these theorists claim. Evidence for this skepticism comes from the narrower cognitive realm. There are more and more findings that show that some cognitive capacities can develop while others do not undergo transformation (Fischer, 1980).

This is not to say that there has not been important empirical evidence for the developmental nature of the concept of ego (Loevinger, 1976) or faith (Fowler, 1981). In many cases, however, it requires mathematical techniques rather than hermeneutic ones to arrive at a single stage. Considerable stage scatter is not infrequent on Loevinger tests or even on structured interviews that pull for consistency. Structural interviewing does not make it a point to listen for those self-descriptions that do not fit the overall frame. If such material emerges in an interview, it is often viewed as unscorable. Clinicians often listen for breaks in an interview sequence and try to understand a person's explicit and hidden meanings. Similarly, developmental psychopathology researchers could ask questions that explore less differentiated and integrated thoughts and feelings that coexist with the more mature forms. These questions could be made part of the usual semistructured interview technique but require, first, a rethinking of the theories themselves. Such questions could include, for example, "Have you experienced a moment when you realized 'I've been here before, I don't want to be here, and I can't do anything about it'?" or "Give me an example of something about yourself that does not make sense to you."

Clear structural distinctions for social development will make it possible to give up trying to press more and more content into a stage hierarchy while losing sight of the dynamic interplay between different developmental positions so typical for the domains of self and faith. If the analogical nature of the models is realized, the strict application of Piaget's principles can be given up and a freer and more appropriate view on social development can emerge.

Necessary Distinctions: Self-Complexity and Self-Cohesion. Another issue emerges here, relevant to any theory of development. Social-cognitive theories fail to provide a theory of ego strength. In fact, there is so much conceptual imprecision around this issue that the development of the self is implicitly viewed as identical to its strengthening in that the higher stages are defined as more adequate, comprehensive, and adaptive. In Kohlberg's scheme, "higher stages are better stages." For example, stage five is the morally stronger position about issues of justice and fairness than all preceding stages. In his and Piaget's models, development of cognitive structures always means moving toward greater equilibrium, which provides the individual with an expanded capacity for knowledge and adaptation.

Some Piagetian theorists (Kegan, 1982; Loevinger, 1976) have adapted this orientation to self and personality development. Again, we have to review whether such a general transfer of principles to this psychological domain is appropriate. Are higher self stages better than earlier ones?

An individual in Loevinger's Stage 5 is described as able to cope with inner feelings, has tolerance of ambigiuty, a focus on self-fulfillment, and so on. The stage description reads much like a statement of positive mental health. Furthermore, this stage as compared to all earlier stages is a better, more encompassing, more complex, and stronger stage. I have frequently observed serious weaknesses of self (fragmentation under stress, inability to act willfully, difficulty tolerating ambiguity, and so on) associated not only with the lower stages of ego and self-development but also with the more complex ones. These cases show us that higher stages are not necessarily better stages if the criterion is adaptation. Were we to speak of a more complex self, without any interest in the quality of adaptation, we could understand higher stages as better stages. But then it is difficult to understand how individuals who have reached mature stages of the self can in fact be considerably less organized and possess less knowledge about themselves than some people at earlier stages.

One could argue that the domain of psychopathology is responsible for "noise" in the system and that psychopathology is independent of development. There is, however, a significant body of empirical work that demonstrates associations between ego development and psychopathology (for a review see Noam and others, 1984). In addition, Kegan (1982) has explicitly woven into his stage positions typical psychological disorders. But simultaneously, he describes the higher stages as more adaptive and "truer." This creates a perspective from which it is no more possible to explain the difference and the relationship between the normal course of development and the pathological one. How is it that if we take two people at Stage 3, one can be a model of strength and integration and the other is a sad example of psychological disorganization, and both are described with the same conceptual tool of developmental stage? I have found it necessary to introduce the distinction between self-complexity and self-cohesion in order to end this theoretical confusion. Self-complexity refers to the most mature structural self stage achieved, while self-cohesion addresses the status of structural integration. These distinctions will be described in greater detail later.

The problems stated above require detailed theoretical exploration. I will now turn to a short case example from a large developmental psychopathology study in order to provide some life to the otherwise all too abstract principles of a theory of self and psychopathology. Space limitations and the goal of laying a foundation make it necessary to abbreviate descriptions and definitions. Even with these shortcomings, it is my hope that the dynamic nature of this theory will come to life.

A Case from Developmental Psychopathology Research

After completing a collaborative longitudinal study on adolescent and family development three years ago (Hauser and others, 1984), I began a new set of studies that were geared toward uncovering important relationships between development and psychopathology. For this purpose, I founded a developmental psychopathology research setting located at Harvard Medical School and one of its teaching centers, the McLean Hospital. Each year approximately one hundred children and adolescents (consecutive admissions to a psychiatric inpatient setting) are included in the studies and are given an extensive battery of tests, including developmental instruments (cognitive, moral, and ego measures), diagnostic symptom inventories (structured diagnostic interview schedule and behavior checklists for children and their parents), and assessments of their coping and defense styles. In addition, we include a number of family, neurological, and biological assessments. The patients are followed during the course of hospitalization through a repeated-measures design. A longitudinal one- and three-year posthospitalization, follow-up is at present being piloted with the goal of systematically following the children and adolescents into adulthood.

At present 370 children and their families have been included in this large-scale developmental psychopathology research program. The majority of patients has received the diagnoses of affective disorder and conduct disorder, but the sample also includes patients diagnosed with attention deficit, anxiety, and pervasive developmental disorder. My colleagues and I are presently reporting on a variety of aspects of the project. For the purpose of this more theoretical expose, I will only briefly describe one of our subjects, whom I will call Rachel.

Rachel is a thirteen-year-old girl who was admitted to a child and adolescent unit because of a serious depression. For about one year she exhibited strong mood swings, attempted suicide, and isolated herself from her family. In addition to the depressive symptoms, she was also quite impulsive and aggressive. Her parents reported that she lied, stole, was truant, and experimented a great deal with drugs and alcohol. But while the aggression was limited to the family (threatening her mother and brother with a knife), many of the other behaviors became more pronounced within a delinquent peer group. Although Rachel reported that she never felt close to her parents and was viewed by them as an "unhappy child," she was able to function quite well before adolescence.

Upon hospitalization, Rachel was viewed by the treatment staff as "developmentally extremely delayed and cognitively quite limited." She was seen as intelligent, but the staff complained that she showed little insight into her problems. Her depression in combination with her impulsivity made her a great suicidal risk in the eyes of her therapist. Our research diagnoses based on a structured interview were conduct disorder, socialized aggression, and major depression. On our symptom checklist she also scored high both on the internalizing scale (which includes symptoms such as perfectionism, sadness, anxiety) and on the externalizing scale (which includes symptoms like destroying property, aggressiveness toward people, and so on).

A standard psychological test battery, which included the Rorschach, Thematic Apperception Test, Wechsler Intelligence Scale for Children (WISC), and a variety of other cognitive and personality tests, provided a detailed description of the inner world of the child. The psychologist writes: "When tasks are relatively unstructured or when elaborated social reasoning is involved, personal concerns intrude and performance worsens. There is a marked reluctance to involve the self with others and mistrust of others is so profound that virtually no sharing of personal information occurs. There is even an avoidance of the examination of personal feelings and reactions when alone. Although Rachel can present herself as social and related, her real disconnectedness from others cannot be overemphasized." A senior consultant known for his thoughtful clinical assessments viewed her as "infantile," suspected a "developmental arrest at the age of six," and was concerned about an "absence of abstract thinking" that manifested itself in concreteness, denial, and a lack of introspection.

But while our diagnostic and symptom instruments were similar to the judgments of the psychological tester and the clinical team, our developmental interviews and tests did not correspond with their views. On Kohlberg's Moral Judgment Interview (for a description see Kohlberg, 1984) and Loevinger's Washington University Sentence Completion Test (for a description see Loevinger, 1976) Rachel scored higher than the great majority of her hospitalized age-mates. On both tests she functioned at the conformist-conventional levels demonstrating a great deal of complex thought, empathy, and an ability to view herself through the perspective of others.

How are we then to understand the discrepancy in view between the skillful staff who viewed this adolescent as developmentally extremely immature and the testing results that placed her on a relatively mature developmental stage? We are faced with the paradoxical situation where the treatment staff's insistence on Rachel's primitive functioning omits the more mature social-developmental abilities, while a structural-developmental account does not capture the immature cognitive and affective processes. Rachel is quite typical in the display of fluctuation of thought, feeling, and behavior. The theory of biography and transformation is a response to those psychological theories that tend to interpret psychopathology as an early developmental arrest. It is also a response to the social-developmental theories that would confuse the most mature self-position with the overall organization of the self. Only when we relate the mature and the immature parts of the self can we have a chance to capture the full strength of a developmental psychopathology perspective that can enlighten our work with Rachel.

I will now return to our theoretical discussion and will return to Rachel twice during the text to exemplify the theory.

The Transformational Self: Its Internal and Interpersonal System

I have earlier mentioned that we continue to search for the underlying logic of the social-cognitive self and that the concept of social perspective provides us with an acceptable construct. This theoretical concept was first introduced in the self theories of the symbolic-interactionist school of Chicago during the early part of this century (Mead, 1934; Baldwin, 1897, and so on). Selman (1980) has empirically operationalized this construct and conducted a variety of important developmental studies on the evolution of perspective taking in childhood and adolescence. He, as well as others who have employed a perspective-taking analysis (Chandler, 1973; Flavell, 1977), have not, however, taken the necessary step of developing an explicit theory of self based on the "deep structure" of social perspective taking.

The theory of biography and transformation takes this step. It assumes that the activities of the self always involve role taking—that is, an understanding that the other is in some way both like and unlike the self and that the other knows or is responsive to the self in a system of complementary expectations. This notion makes the interpersonal nature of the self a fundamental notion, an idea also found in the important psychological theories of Sullivan (1953) and Vygotsky (1986). For example, Vygotsky (1979) states: "We are aware of ourselves, for we are aware of others, and in the same way as we know others; and this is as it is because in relation to ourselves we are in the same position as others are to us" (p. 29). Vygotsky viewed the intrapersonal processes as internalized interpersonal relationships. He states, "Each function in the child's cultural development appears twice: first on the social level, and later on the individual level; first between people (interpsychological), and then inside the child (intrapsychological)" (Vygotsky, 1978, p. 30). These ideas bring him into close proximity to the symbolic interactionists such as Mead and Baldwin. For Baldwin (1897), what once was attributed to others becomes part of the self: "By imitating the other he [the child] has brought them [significant others] over to the opposite pole, and found them applicable, with a richer meaning and a modified value, as true predicates of himself also" (p. 8).

The fact that the genesis of the interpersonal and intrapersonal worlds has the same origin does not mean, however, that they can be viewed as identical. The process of internalization produces many opportunities for modifications, distortions, and reorganizations. For this reason, I have found it necessary to develop the category of internal perspective, the intrapsychic counterpart to the interpersonal perspective of social development. The concept refers to the internalized life of interpersonal relationships and their manifestations of self-observation, self-reflection, and the experience of internal dialogue.

I will briefly summarize my stages of the developing self. Due to space considerations I will not describe the two most mature stages (5 and 6), which are dealt with in detail in other publications.

Stage 1: Subjective-Physical Self. At the subjective-physical stage there is no consideration of the other's interests and desires as different from the self's. There is an emerging awareness of the distinction of physical and psychological characteristics in people, but mostly actions are evaluated in terms of physical consequences. Impulsive responses are typical and feelings are expressed in action language. Strength is the ability to distinguish between fantasy and reality, to show strong will and to demonstrate an independent curiosity. These strengths are in part based on at least a partial achievement of object constancy. The weakness is an emphasis on wish fulfillment, seeing others as suppliers and being very dependent on them. The concrete perspective on the self leads to a dichotomous view of being good or bad. In the process, the self hides from or submits to powerful authority figures that can inflict physical harm.

Stage 2: The Reciprocal-Instrumental Self. At the reciprocal-instrumental stage there is the possibility of understanding self-interests and goals as separate from the intent of others. Conflicting interests between self and other are usually resolved through instrumental exchange. The person can step out of the concrete bounds of the self, thus creating reciprocity. This perspective also changes the internal perspective-taking ability. There is now the conceptual distinction between the outer appearance of the public self and the inner, hidden self. This creates the possibility of planned deception through which the self can impose its boundaries. Conflict usually does not lead to submission or impulsive action, but to self-protective assertion of control. The negative outcome is opportunism, exploitation, and manipulation. The positive outcome is the mastery of the tool world, the ability to control feelings and to concentrate on tasks. The limitation of the reciprocal-instrumental stage is the isolation of two exchange-partners whose relationship is not primarily guided by trust and altruism but rather by interest.

Stage 3: The Mutual-Inclusive Self. At the mutual-inclusive self-other perspective, the person understands others in relationship coordinated through a generalized perspective. The person experiences different points of view through the Golden Rule of seeing reality through the eyes of another person. This perspective creates the context for altruistic actions and for surpassing the bounds of self-interest. Attitudes and values are seen as persisting over time, often leading to stereotypes like "I am that kind of person." These self-traits, in addition to the new internal perspective, lead to more complex self-observational capacities. The limitations of this stage, however, are an overidentification with the views of the other and the dangers of conformist social behavior. It is crucial for the self to be liked and appreciated in order to feel a sense of self-esteem. Typical feelings of low self-esteem and a proneness to experienced depression and anxiety are linked to a sense of abandonment and feeling lost in the world.

Stage 4: The Systemic-Organizational Self. At the systemic-organizational stage, the societal point of view is distinguished from the interpersonal one. Multiple mutual perspectives can be integrated into a broader systems view. When the self takes a systemic perspective on relationships, the communication between people is seen as existing on a number of levels simultaneously. Individual relations are interpreted in terms of their place within a larger system of consciously defined roles and rules. System maintenance of the self becomes the hallmark of this stage. The person views the self as having control over his or her destiny. It is also the point, however, at which the person realizes the existence of parts of the self not easily managed by the system's control—that is, the discovery of unconscious motivations. The societal perspective also brings out strong motivations of achievement, duty, and competition. The limitations of systemic self-other perspective are the attempt to over-control self and other, to reflect on social relations too much in terms of power, role, and status, and to take so many perspectives on self and other that obsessive-compulsive indecision can result. These contradictions are reintegrated into a new whole at the integrated (5) universal and (6) self-other perspectives.

Elsewhere, my colleagues and I have described a method of empirically evaluating the various self positions based on a clinical research interview (Noam, Powers, Kilkenny, and Beedy, in press). This semistructured instrument is called Stage, Phase, and Style Interview. Note, however, that the self in this framework is broader than its most mature position. The most mature self-system is only one side in a dynamic interplay within the self.

I will now briefly return to Rachel, our thirteen-year-old. What concerns me here is how we can understand her most mature developmental position. The moral judgment dilemma (should Heinz steal a drug for his dying wife?) reveals a great deal of concern for others in need. Rachel states that the drug should be stolen, but is in considerable conflict over the question whether Heinz should steal for someone he does not love. After much deliberation, she decides that Heinz should steal the drug even for strangers, since "it's wrong to watch someone die, if you know you can help them." The completion of sentence stems on Loevinger's test reveals a great deal of complex thought. Rachel writes, for example, "A good mother . . . is listening to your child, giving advice, and trusting them to make the right decision. And knowing how to let go" and "What gets me into trouble . . . is my attitude that I want to be a troublemaker."

The profile shows a great deal of variation in stage response (responses range from low stage delta to a very high stage 4/5). As mentioned before, however, the final result is a single stage score that is derived mathematically and that has systematically screened out the interesting scatter observable on the test.

Our knowledge of Rachel's most mature developmental capacities is not an esoteric cognitive-developmental concern but has important implications for understanding her and the problems she is facing. Rachel has developmental capacities typical for the mutual-inclusive stage of self-development. For example, she demonstrates a concern for others even when she does not receive a direct benefit in return. The sentence quoted above from the Loevinger test reveals an ability to take some perspective on her acting-out behavior, since she states that she chooses to create trouble and that it is her attitude (rather than other people or outside events) that gets her into trouble. Her statement about her mother repeated in a variety of other sentence stems demonstrates a complex view on self and relationships (the notion of listening, trust, letting go at the appropriate time, and so on).

Very typically, patients in our sample who function at this developmental position experience a great deal of depression, are fearful of separation, and frequently discuss their low self-esteem. The fact that they are capable of experiencing self and other from the perspective of the important relationships in their lives makes them especially vulnerable to the rejections from others. It is much less frequent, however, that adolescents at the mutual-inclusive stage are as aggressive as Rachel (attacking mother with a knife, having delinquent friends, threatening the parents). I will address this issue at a later point.

The data forces us to reject the interpretation of the consultant and some of the treatment team that the adolescent is developmentally fixated at an early stage. We have to acknowledge, however, that the observations of the clinicians (not all of them psychoanalytic in orientation) acknowledged that Rachel was in many important ways immature and underdeveloped. The consultant summarized the clinicians' apprehensions by stating that Rachel "had a lack of ego and identity substance." It is this issue, the relationship between a more mature self position and a missing substance, that we will take up when we return to Rachel later.

An expanded view on the self requires more than stage descriptions. What is necessary is an analysis of developmental process. Dimensions of process are found in Piaget's work on equilibration but require significant expansion to appropriately address the development of self and psychopathology.

Developmental Processes of the Self: Assimilation, Accommodation, and Encapsulation

As is widely known, a schema is a cognitive or mental structure by which individuals intellectually adapt to and organize the environment. By means of these structures, events are organized into groups according to common characteristics. Perhaps Piaget's greatest contribution was to describe the developmental nature of schemas from birth to maturity.

Each new life situation creates the opportunity for a developmental spurt, a reorganization of a cognitive (and affective) schema. This change is what Piagest refers to as accommodation—that is, the organism's ability to adapt to the world by changing its internal structure or schema. Important events in a person's life hold the potential for such critical, qualitative changes. It is, however, possible even for dramatic experiences to be integrated into the existing developmental schemes. Piaget describes this integration as assimilation—the incorporation of an object into the existing structure.

The nature of the relationship between assimilation and accommodation, what Piaget terms equilibration, is the description of process in development. Equilibrium is the stage of balance between assimilation and accommodation; disequilibrium is the state of imbalance between these two processes. Piaget states that equilibrium is a condition toward which the organisms strives. When disequilibrium occurs, it provides an individual the motivation to further assimilation and accommodation and to achieve equilibrium. These processes are based on the idea that the organism finds new equilibrium after a state of disequilibrium (transition) in which all earlier self-structures are synthesized into a new structure (stage). Such a perspective on development has influenced many of the more recent social-developmental theories described above.

For this reason, I have developed an analysis that can account for those aspects of development that remain unaccommodated even when overall transformation occurs. Such an analysis, I believe, best accounts for what Piaget referred to as the "multiple, divided, and contradictory" nature of self and personality, and is central to what I am calling the theory of biography and transformation. This theory emphasizes how particular experiences resist integration into a higher-order system—a process I term overassimilation (incorporating experiences into an earlier structure when a more developed structure exists). The consequences or products of these overassimilations are encapsulations. This term refers to pockets of old meaning systems that are guided by the cognitive and affective logic (Ciompi, 1982) that governed at the time the encapsulation occurred.

The reader might have the impression that encapsulations refer to internal time capsules. This view of development, which had been quite prevalent in psychoanalysis, has been criticized in a variety of psychoanalytic papers (Schafer, 1976; Kohut, 1977). I too, view the overassimilative activity as a process that does not return us to a real past but rather to a living biography. This living biography implies that even with a great deal of continued interaction with the environment old meaning systems (in Werner's sense of less differentiated and less integrated) continue to be applied.

Overassimilation and encapsulations are concepts less concerned with momentary regressions but convey systematic ways of viewing self and world. These earlier views I term belief systems. Used in this context, a belief is a meaning system that is not truly tested against an external reality but follows some internal logic. In therapy, testing, or in-depth, open-ended interviews, it usually becomes quite apparent that even though certain beliefs do not hold up to close scrutiny, they still exert a strong hold over the person. Continued development and the present-day experiences will influence these basic beliefs, but the point is that a great deal of the energy to maintain these less differentiated thought and feeling states emerges from this living biography and cannot be subsumed under the most mature aspect of the self.

Depending on the developmental level the beliefs are associated with, they can be more physical (based on magical thinking, focused on the body-self and images of bodily survival during physical separations), concrete-action oriented (based on a view of the self as an agent that acts on the world or needs to manipulate the world deceptively to achieve need gratification), or psychological (a state where needs are expressed in symbolic form around identifications with others). I will now turn to two consequences of overassimilation, horizontal and vertical encapsulation.

First, I will give an example that will illustrate the type of encapsulation that I term vertical. We have often observed that young children can perceive themselves as responsible for their parents' divorce. What begins as one area of developmentally appropriate, egocentric thinking in children can be arrested to become a strong, primitive, living part in an otherwise evolving self-system. Vertical encapsulations result from early belief systems that are also a main source of unintegrated affective states. Since these developmental pockets are also connected to strong feelings and vulnerabilities about important primary relationships, much energy is expended to preserve their separateness from the most mature self-structure.

The second type of encapsulations are horizontal. They are camouflaged discrepancies and appear under the governance of the most advanced developmental position. In reality, the earlier belief systems are very much involved but have led not so much to an arrest as to a specific, sophisticated-appearing derailment. The early experience continues to shape an aspect of the person's world view but appears differently (that is, more complex) at each point in development. By adulthood, the person has usually attained a full formal-operational system that can observe the self and develop an ideology and theory of relationships. It will appear, therefore, that the most mature developmental position dominates. In fact, however, the early derailment has caused a separate developmental line in the self, which has transformed an early state along the developmental positions of the rest of the self. Although the integration of horizontal encapsulations into the overall self-system might seem simpler because there has been continued development in that realm, the dissolution of the horizontal split clinically is very difficult. The person often experiences the split as a matter solely of the present, which makes the critical return to the earlier, yet living source of the derailment a matter of particular difficulty.

Self-Complexity and Self-Integration

We have seen that accommodation does not provide a guarantee that all aspects of the self will undergo transformation. Often, the loss involved in detachment from old and known interpersonal constructions is greater than the broadened perspective and freedom that can be the result of development. The personality and developmental psychologist Jack Block (1982) once captured this conservative aspect of human beings by stating that we assimilate if we can and accommodate if we must. Where we deal with strong and affectively anchored interpersonal relationships inside and outside the self, we can assume that his statement holds even more truth than in the strict cognitive domain.

The idea that individuals can develop in only some areas and as a consequence function at multiple developmental levels is in line with some of the findings of recent Piagetian research (Fischer, 1980). As mentioned earlier, this research found considerable discrepancies in developmental levels achieved across domains. Most explanations of developmental asynchrony focus on limited generalizations to all domains due to a lack of opportunity to try and apply new skills. From the perspective of the self, I am suggesting an interpersonal interpretation for discrepancies in the relationship between competence and performance. The interpersonal ties, ties that have been internalized, keep the person from experimenting with possible new responses. This shying away creates a protective foil against an application of newly found abilities from other domains and can occur each time a developmental transformation occurs.

As mentioned earlier, schema representing interactions with meaningful others become part of the inner world. Internalization is both a cognitive and affective process. According to the conceptual framework presented here, at each developmental stage the self internalizes important relationships with effects on both self-esteem and internal conflict. While the parental relationships are crucial, there are many other relationships that provide the building blocks for inner life: siblings, grandparents, teachers, peers, and romantic relationships.

The process of internalization is always a constructivist activity, not built solely on the reality of the other but transformed by the meanings attributed to the relationship. These meanings are guided in part, by the inner logic of the developmental level achieved. Prone to significant distortions, internalized others often become tied to strong emotions and a sense of loyalty. Often the loss involved in detachment from the old interpersonal constructions exceeds the gains anticipated in development. Yet the present interpersonal world provides the opportunities for transformation. When we are forced to accommodate, there are, as we have seen in the previous section, ways to protect certain aspects of the self from joining the overall thrust of development. What tends to occur in such a situation is a partial transformation, one that does not generalize to all aspects of the self and is at the source of encapsulations.

When we pursue this line of theory construction, we find that a basic developmental dimension can now be introduced and receive new importance. The strength of the self, a construct without tradition in Piagetian psychology and central to the theory of biography and transformation, is tied to the principles of integration and to the origins of encapsulations. The strong self has integrated and synthesized earlier experiences each time a developmental transformation has occurred. While there are other nonstructural contributors to the strength of the self (temperament, attention, will), I have observed that integration is a central component of such strength. By integration I mean how encompassing earlier transformations have been or conversely, how much of the earlier organizations have been encapsulated. If encapsulations have occurred, the person will have to expend a great deal of energy on making sense of multiple constructions that pull the person in different directions. Thus, by giving up the idea imported from cognitive development that each self-transformation synthesizes and reorganizes all earlier forms of making meaning, we not only have brought theory closer to the data, we have created the possibility to develop a theory of strength from within the overall architecture of a structural-developmental framework. The strength of the self does not need to be imported as an alien category (for example, in some of Kohlberg's research measured on a subscale of an intelligence test), nor is it necessary to locate it solely within a given stage sequence (for example, higher stage is stronger self).

The idea of self-integration is so important for a developmental psychopathology because most psychological disorders are related to a lack of strength, a fragility of the self. One of the most extreme examples of nonintegration is given to us by patients who are diagnosed as multiple personality. Their very basic function of integration is impaired, leading to a major weakness of the self: The different parts of the self are separated and laid out without much knowledge or control over the two other selves. But also in the personality disorders such as borderline and narcissistic psychopathology we can observe a lack of self-integration and considerable fluctuations between more mature and less mature cognitive and affective states. Cognitive-behavioral therapists have made similar observations with patients suffering from depression.

A theory of self-integration can contribute in areas where the two most important psychological theories of ego and self-strength, Erikson's principles of ego virtues and Kohut's theory of cohesion and fragmentation, have remained limited. For Erikson, the strengths and weaknesses of the ego always arise out of a present crisis that consists of psychological conflict, age-specific tasks, and the historical moment. Each new stage has a positive, strengthening outcome or a negative, weakening one. His theory of the stages of ego development and virtues is widely known and has helped broadened the scope of psychoanalysis considerably. But even though Erikson points to the importance of relating earlier strengths and weaknesses to later ones, he himself noted the difficulty of this endeavor and left it to future contributors to develop relevant methodologies.

Another important theory of strength in development is found in Kohut's concepts (Kohut, 1977) of self-cohesion and fragmentation. His complex developmental theory not only describes the process of cohesion and fragmentation in psychoanalysis but simultaneously offers an explanation about the causality of the strong and the weakened (narcissistic) self. As is widely known, he viewed disturbed self-object relationships between the child and the parents as the core of the weak (fragmented) self. Much like Erikson, Kohut offers an interpersonal rather than a traditional drive explanation by viewing the evolution of self-weakness as a break in empathy in the early phases of development. From my perspective, however, Kohut overemphasizes the earliest conflicts in their relationship to self-strength. Most of Kohut's case examples depict adults in treatment. It is unlikely that the healing interactions (transmuting internalizations) arc solely based on a return to childhood and parental images rather than on experiences that strengthen the self in the course of its continued evolution in adulthood. If this assumption is correct, what is required is a theory of self-cohesion that traces the important transformations through all the stages and ages of the human life-cycle.

Kohut's theory of early self-development and Erikson's life span approach complement each other well. However, there is a need for a theory of the development of strength that systematically relates earlier and later stages of development. By viewing the strength of the self as emerging from a sense of integration of early and later constructions, I attempt to build a bridge between the most mature developmental positions and the encapsulation. An important insight into the relationship between development and psychological strength has to do with the fact that structural development is no guarantee for better mental health. At each developmental point, problem areas can be transformed rather than disappear and create greater damage in the self. Because each stage transition is a form of internalization, there is the possibility of a paradox outcome: From the perspective of self-development, the person can have achieved more complexity and a broader self-awareness, while from the perspective of self-strength, the person can be more alienated from the original problems (that is, vertical encapsulation) or have a more complex false self (horizontal encapsulation).

This phenomenon can often be observed when we compare an adult at the mutual-inclusive and the systemic-organizational stages. Because at Stage 3 the self is strongly tied to identifications with significant others, often the vitality and strength of the self can be restored through more appropriate interpersonal relationships. At Stage 4 the problems of self-esteem and fragmentation have become part of the inner organization of the self. Often people feel more isolated, less able to reach out to others. The alienation potentially turns into hatred of the self with suicide becoming one aspect of the theory of the self (that is, the only power people have is to control their self-chosen time of death). It is thus possible that structural development of the self not only creates mental health or strengthening of the self but can lead to worse outcome on these dimensions. We will now turn to the bridge between encapsulations and transformations of the self: the core life themes.

Core Life Themes: The Biographical Bridge Between Equilibration and Encapsulation

Each person holds core themes that are central reference points throughout life. These themes organize a multitude of life experiences into key interpersonal and intrapsychic forms. Some refer to these gestalts as a narrative, story line, or script. In the study of the self, we need to be attentive to the major images and metaphors that not only are elaborated and changed throughout the course of development but that also show a great deal of consistency. Life themes are based on continuous relationships with the environment, instructions about the relationships in the world, and past experiences filtered through memory. They are a biography of meanings. Similar to a symphony with its numerous movements, each developmental step has its own internal organizations, rhythm, and mood. However, the more general themes that span across the entire piece, continuously undergoing elaborations, are part of each separate movement. What sounds at first like a repetition often ends up being a reworking with important changes. As with a symphony, in the study of the self one can focus on the new movements and their differences of tempo and tone or on the continuity of an overarching musical project.

The study of evolving lives is most frequently guided by one of two approaches; one deals primarily with the continuous elaboration of personality traits, temperament, or cognitive styles. The other approach focuses on the discontinuous psychological organizations. Life is viewed as consisting of major points of reorganization—new narratives and styles get created as a consequence of these transformations. In a musical piece or a novel one would have little difficulty embracing both perspectives at once or receiving pleasure and excitement from the tension. This dynamic interplay is difficult to capture in psychological theory and research. But life themes and their relationship to mature self-processes and encapsulations put this interplay at center stage. While the stages of self-transformation focus our view on discontinuous constructions about life, core themes speak to an unfolding of biographical continuities.

The methodology of extracting core themes does not have to rely solely on clinical and intuitive material. Preferably, one works from the individual's detailed descriptions of relationships, scenes, and locations of past and present. Clinical research interviews, diaries, or more standardized stimuli such as the Thematic Apperception Test (TAT) are data sources that can provide the necessary information to generate specific life themes. Csikszentmihalyi and Beattie (1979) have outlined systematic research in the area of life themes. They have defined *theme* as a hierarchical affective-cognitive system that is composed of a central existential problem. The problem is surrounded by interpretations of its supposed causes and by strategies to be used for solving it.

Given the transformational aspect of the theory of biography and transformation, the core themes are used to reveal the bridge between the most mature aspect of the self and the encapsulations. They are filtered through the present point of view and through the less differentiated, earlier perspectives. First we turn to the transformational side of the self. For example, when the individual is at the mutual-inclusive stage, we expect to see themes of self-definition through group membership. We expect biographical content that reflects concern about other's acceptance of us. In contrast, at the reciprocal-instrumental stage, we can expect to find themes that reveal a need for concrete control and mastery. Biographical preoccupations are with behaving in consonance or discordance with other's rules placed on the self. There is generally an orientation toward people as either "being on my side or curtailing my freedom." But core themes must not be understood as a function of the continued evolution of the self alone.

In the example of a person at the mutual-inclusive stage, it is important to determine whether the concern for acceptance by others is fueled by an earlier belief system that the self will be abandoned and is not worthy of love. Similarly, it is necessary to explore whether the person at the reciprocal-instrumental stage believes that there is no possibility for intimate relationships because all earlier experiences have been hurtful. In that case, the need for concrete control is linked to a belief that giving up control will lead to abandonment. What has been viewed as themes emerging from a stage perspective (Kegan, 1982; Loevinger, 1976) now becomes part of a larger configuration, housing early and later images.

It would be a mistake to view the categories of equilibration, integration, and core theme analysis as separate functions. Rather, I view them as being intricately intertwined. Much like photography, which builds on the relationship between light, speed, and distance, the self entails numerous, complex functions. It is impossible and ultimately fruitless to discuss the many functions, because without a strong theory one gets lost in a multitude of influencing variables. It is also unnecessary to reduce the study of the self to only one principle. We must focus on a few basic and well-defined functions and their interrelationships when we study the self.

Thus, structural activity, so brilliantly outlined by Piaget and the social-cognitive school, must be placed within the larger theoretical construct of the developing self. The core themes are continuously elaborated and reorganized through the process of accommodation, yet each reorganization requires a return to those parts of the self that are encapsulated in order to foster integration. This self-integration is important at all ages of life, but adulthood provides special opportunities to broaden its scope. As the person deals with the conflict of intimacy, the care for the next generation, and the anxieties about mortality, the self's radius is frequently expanded. Developmental transformations hold a special opportunity for returning to the encapsulations and overcoming the negative aspects of recapitulation. It is easier to generalize the process of accommodation to previously nonaccommodated parts of the self during times of transition than to do so during times of stability when assimilation prevails. However, any student of personality knows that even when rapid developments occur, the forces associated with encapsulations are very powerful and resist integration. As mentioned earlier, encapsulations are infused with strong affects and are connected to internalized primary relationships. The consequences of ignoring the encapsulations and focusing only on the present transformation has also been discussed earlier and will also be addressed as we return, for a last time, to Rachel.

Rachel described a world in which people she cared about were unreliable and hurtful. She continuously felt rejected, a state she can remember from early on in her life. Interestingly, the parents' report of their relationship with Rachel as an unwanted child corresponds to her feelings and recollections. Rachel's core life themes, including a pervasive sense of rejection (rejection theme), were based on the experience that important people in her life were untrustworthy (distrust theme). As a consequence, Rachel had become very self-protective (isolation theme) and vindictive (retaliation theme). It is not possible to describe the core themes in detail as they emerge in a variety of treatment reports and from our developmental psychopathology research material.

As mentioned above, the life themes have their most mature expressions, in Rachel's case, at the mutual-inclusive stage. Her self-esteem rests on group affiliations and her needs for affirmation in intimate relationships is heightened, as it always is, at this developmental position. For that reason, the rejection theme is more intense and consciously experienced. The distrust and the related isolation create more conflict than at the previous reciprocal-instrumental stage, since the motivation for closeness and intimate sharing usually becomes quite pronounced. In fact, trust in relationships is one of the hallmarks of this stage and the theme of not being able to trust becomes especially painful. While the aggressive themes could be viewed as a response to unfulfilled need for closeness, it is interesting that Rachel chose a delinquent group, less for the concrete benefits (stolen goods) but more to protest against the parents and to find one setting where she can feel accepted.

This most mature perspective has not been generalized to all aspects of the self. The core themes also house developmentally less mature cognitions and feeling states. While Rachel was able to go through a number of developmental transformations, the degree of synthesis at each developmental point seems to have been rather weak. We cannot reconstruct the actual transformations, but we know that her level of integration demonstrates aspects of a living biography where earlier forms of thinking and feeling continue to coexist with later ones. This resultant self-fragility might be a more hopeful idea than the consultant's notion of *lack in ego and identity substance,* a term that indicates a more fundamental deficiency. Rachel has a very basic and undifferentiated belief that she is bad and does not deserve to live. The rejection and isolation themes are also forms of primitive self-hate and demonstrate a lack of ability to soothe herself. Encapsulated beliefs are also evidenced in her view of the parents as possessing overwhelming powers and that she is unable to negotiate with them since they will take over her thinking. As a consequence, she has to isolate herself in order to preserve her fragile sense of self. Thus, boundary maintenance has to occur in ways that do not match her most mature developmental position, through physical action or by trying to do away with the mother. Paradoxically, it could be the new ability to experience the world through the eyes of the other that creates also the added need for distance and reverting to concrete boundary setting.

Any clinical intervention would have to be extremely cognizant of the fact that this adolescent is fighting for her life. Her new relatively mature developmental capacities have not been put to very productive use to secure a new and enlarged integration for the self. There is very little possibility to engage the more mature observational capacities to challenge some of the basic beliefs about herself. It requires very concrete containment of her impulses to kill herself or others in order to make use of her potential developmental insight. Without a very firm holding environment, a therapeutic relationship can create more momentum toward destructive action, since the negative belief system combines with a renewed yearning for closeness. Well managed, the new motivation for closeness, trust, and intimacy can be an invaluable ally in creating development and strength in the self.

Outlook: Implications for Clinical-Developmental Practice— Development as the Aim of Therapy?

The cognitive-development contribution to education has provided great inspiration to educators and has led to many innovations in school settings. This is not surprising since the theory of intellectual development is relevant to learning and to the educational process. Kohlberg viewed cognitive development so much a part of education that he, in the tradition of John Dewey, claimed that the educational aim is development.

Few cognitive-developmental applications have been proposed for clinical settings (see Chapters Two, Three, and Four). This chapter has proposed a constructivist extension of cognitive theory to the self and to psychopathology. Specific suggestions regarding clinical techniques cannot be introduced here (for more detailed discussions see Noam, 1986b), but I will end by raising some broad questions about the aims of therapy from the perspective of developmental psychopathology. Can we state, in the tradition of progressive education, that development is the aim of therapy?

An answer to this question is more complex than one first imagines, since good arguments can be made in favor and against this claim. Many therapy schools subscribe to the view that much of what occurs in therapy is developmental in nature. The client who experiences himself in new ways, who challenges old conceptions and experiments with new behaviors can be viewed as developing. In many cases, this psychological reorganization goes hand in hand with a structural-cognitive and self-transformation, an observation I have consistently made in my clinical work. The developmental psychopathology research mentioned earlier is now addressing, among other things, the issue of structural change and clinical outcome systematically. But we also have discussed in this chapter the limitations of those approaches that directly import constructive-developmental principles to the clinical setting. Structural transformation does not necessarily produce more mental health, better adaptation, and strength for the self (see Chapters Two and Seven). Furthermore, therapeutic work that produces more self-complexity but not mental health can hardly be viewed as successful treatment.

This is the problem we face when we define development solely in structural-developmental terms. Not only health develops in a person, but also vulnerabilities have their developmental line. As the person develops structurally, the disorder can become more entrenched and complex. An impulsive externalized stance against others can be expressed at later stages of development as internalized aggression against the self. Or the more advanced intellectual and social capacities are used by the person to develop a consistent theory of self, but rigidly and with a great deal of self-hate. Of course, no therapist would be insensitive enough to apply developmental principles to produce more complex psychopathology. However, a premature and rapid cognitively oriented reorganization—especially in short-term interventions—can have that effect even when not intended.

If development in a structural tradition can create more complex forms of pathology rather than expanded mental health, one would be inclined to dismiss the hypothesis that the aim of therapy is development. If we broaden our view on development, however, we do not have to abandon this important idea. For this reason, the constructivist theory of biography and transformation introduces a more encompassing developmental perspective. Both self-complexity and self-integration are defined in developmental terms and in their interrelationship are viewed to produce a sense of wellness. The resultant vitality gives a person freedom to explore intimate relationships and to pursue new experiences in work and love. This, in turn, can provide a new sense of integration and a greater readiness toward development.

From this broadened developmental perspective, clinical-developmental practice can make use of the knowledge about social development to support a new, stronger sense of integration. This approach requires a serious interest in the biography of the person and a knowledge about the possibility to weave in aspects of the self that remained unintegrated. Each structural-developmental reorganization provides the opportunity for this process of weaving-in, but it is also possible for the development to occur without a greater sense of integration. Fortunately, it is often the person in need of help who will guide us, if we are willing to listen. The client will lead us to the points of vulnerability in the self. This provides the opportunity for the therapist to attend to the fragility of the self. This in turn supports the person's growth toward more encompassing ways of understanding the world. But if our clients teach us what our clinical sensitivities also tell us, why should we not create appropriate theories? Cognitive-developmental models, even when applied to ego and self, have not been able to address these central clinical dimensions.

Freed from the confusion of viewing self-complexity as psychological health, we can now propose a radical aim for clinical developmental psychology: that the ultimate definition of mental health is not the person who can love and work, but the person who can continue to develop throughout life. The ability to function in love and in work is a necessary-but-not-sufficient condition for developmental maturity. The aim of therapy is the person who can create ever new meanings in work and love by taking constructively the hurdles and opportunities, as well as disappointments, created by life. The enemy of development is stagnation and disintegration. To help understand the different forms of stagnation and disintegration and to uncover the healing and strengthening developmental forces will give clinical developmental psychology and developmental psychopathology important challenges for the decades to come.

References

Achenbach, T. *Developmental Psychopathology*. New York: Wiley, 1982.

Anthony, E. J. "Freud, Piaget and Human Knowledge: Some Comparisons and Contrasts." *Annual of Psychoanalysis*, 1976, *4*, 253–277.

Atwood, G. E., and Stolorow, R. D. *Structures of Subjectivity: Explorations in Psychoanalytic Phenomenology*. Hillsdale, N.J.: Erlbaum, 1984.

Baldwin, J. M. *Social and Ethical Interpretations in Mental Development*. New York: Macmillan, 1897.

Beck, A. T. *Cognitive Therapy and Emotional Disorders*. New York: International Universities Press, 1976.

Blasi, A. "The Self and Cognition." In B. Lee and G. Noam (eds.), *Developmental Approaches to the Self*. New York: Plenum Press, 1983.

Block, J. "Assimilation, Accommodation, and the Dynamics of Personality Development." *Child Development*, 1982, *53* (2), 281–295.

Bowlby, J. *Attachment and Loss*. Vol. 1: *Attachment*. New York: Basic Books, 1969.

Broughton, J. "Development of Concepts of Self, Mind, Reality, and Knowledge." In W. Damon (ed.), *Social Cognition*. New Directions for Child Development, no. 1. San Francisco: Jossey-Bass, 1978.

Chandler, M. "Egocentrism and Antisocial Behavior: The Assessment and Training of Social Perspective-Taking Skills." *Developmental Psychology*, 1973, *9*, 326–332.

Ciompi, S. *Affektlogik* [Affective logic]. Stuttgart: Klett-Cotra, 1982.

Cowan, P. *Piaget with Feeling: Cognitive, Social, and Emotional Dimensions*. New York: Holt, Rinehart & Winston, 1978.

Csikszentmihalyi, M., and Beattie, O. V. "Life Themes: A Theoretical and Empirical Exploration of Their Origins and Effects." *Journal of Humanistic Psychology*, 1979, *19*, 45–63.

Damon, W., and Hart, D. "The Development of Self-Understanding from Infancy Through Adolescence." *Child Development*, 1982, *53*, 841–864.

Doebert, R. "Wider die Vernachlaessigung des 'Inhalts' in den Moraltheorien von Kohlberg und Habermas: Implikationen fuer die Relativismus/Universalismus Kontroverse [Against the neglect of content in the moral theories of Kohlberg and Habermas: Implications for the relativity/universality controversy]." In W. Edelstein and G. Nunner-Winkler (eds.), *Zur Bestimmung der Moral*. Frankfurt: Suhrkamp, 1987.

Erikson, E. *Childhood and Society*. New York: Norton, 1950.

Fischer, K. W. "A Theory of Cognitive Development: The Control and Construction of Hierarchies of Skills." *Psychological Review*, 1980, *87*, 477–531.

Flavell, J. H. *Cognitive Development*. Englewood Cliffs, N.J.: Prentice-Hall, 1977.

Fowler, J. R. *Stages of Faith*. New York: Harper & Row, 1981.

Gilligan, C. *In a Different Voice*. Cambridge, Mass.: Harvard University Press, 1982.

Greenspan, S. I. "Intelligence and Adaptation: An Integration of Psychoanalytic and Piagetian Developmental Psychology." In *Psychological Issues Monographs*. New York: International Universities Press, 1979.

Guidano, V. F., and Liotti, G. *Cognitive Processes and Emotional Disorders: A Structural Approach to Psychotherapy*. New York: Guilford Press, 1983.

Hauser, S., Powers, S., Jacobson, A., Noam, G., Weiss, B., and Follansbee, D. "Familial Contexts of Adolescent Ego Development." *Child Development*, 1984, *55*, 195–213.

Kegan, R. *The Evolving Self*. Cambridge, Mass.: Harvard University Press, 1982.

Keller, M. "Resolving Conflicts in Friendship: The Development of Moral Understanding in Everyday Life." In W. Kurtines and J. Gewirtz (eds.), *Morality, Moral Behavior, and Moral Development*. New York: Wiley, 1984.

Kohlberg, L. "Stage and Sequence: The Cognitive-Developmental Approach to Socialization." In D. Goslin (ed.), *Handbook of Socialization: Theory and Research*. Skokie, Ill.: Rand McNally, 1969.

Kohlberg, L. "Moral Stages and Moralization." In T. Lickona (ed.), *Moral Development and Behavior*. New York: Holt, Rinehart & Winston, 1976.

Kohlberg, L. *The Psychology of Moral Development*. San Francisco: Harper & Row, 1984.

Kohlberg, L., LaCross, J., and Rick, D. F. "The Predictability of Adult Mental Health from Childhood Behavior." In B. A. Wolman (ed.), *Manual of Child Psychopathology*. New York: McGraw-Hill, 1972.

Kohut, H. *The Restoration of the Self*. New York: International Universities Press, 1977.

Loevinger, J. *Ego Development: Conceptions and Theories*. San Francisco: Jossey-Bass, 1976.

Mead, G. H. *Mind, Self, and Society*. Chicago: University of Chicago Press, 1934.

Noam, G. "Developmental Psychopathology: An Introduction." *McLean Hospital Journal*, 1985a, *10* (1), 12–14.

Noam, G. "Stage, Phase, and Style: The Developmental Dynamics of the Self." In M. Berkowitz and F. Oser (eds.), *Moral Education: Theory and Application*. Hillsdale, N.J.: Erlbaum 1985b.

Noam, G. "Borderline Personality Disorders and the Theory of Biography and Transformation." *McLean Hospital Journal*, 1986a, *11*, 19–43.

Noam, G. "The Theory of Biography and Transformation and the Borderline Personality Disorders: A Developmental Typology." *McLean Hospital Journal*, 1986b, *11*, 79–105.

Noam, G. "Marking Time in the Hardest Movement: Borderline Psychopathology in Lifespan Perspective." In K. Field, G. Wool, and B. Cohler (eds.), *Psychoanalytic Perspectives on Learning and Education*. New York: International Universities Press, 1987.

Noam, G. "The Self, Adult Development, and the Theory of Biography and Transformation." In D. Laplsey and C. Power (eds.), *Ego, Self, and Identity*. New York: Springer, in press.

Noam, G., Hauser, S., Santostefano, S., Garrison, R., Jacobson, A., Powers, S., and Mead, M. "Ego Development and Psychopathology: A Study of Hospitalized Adolescents." *Child Development*, 1984, *55*, 184–194.

Noam, G., and Kegan, R. "Social Cognition and Psychodynamics: Towards a Clinical-Developmental Psychology." In W. Edelstein, and M. Keller (eds.), *Perspektivität und Interpretation [Perspective and interpretation]*. Frankfurt: Suhrkamp, 1983.

Noam, G., Kohlberg, L., and Snarey, J. "Steps Toward a Model of the Self." In B.

Lee and G. Noam (eds.), *Developmental Approaches to the Self.* New York: Plenum Press, 1983.

Noam, G., Powers, S., Kilkenny, R., and Beedy, J. "The Interpersonal Self in Lifespan Perspective." In R. Lerner, P. Baltes, and D. Featherman (eds.), *Lifespan Development and Behavior.* Vol. 10. Hillsdale, N.J.: Erlbaum, in press.

Oser, F., Power, C., Gmeunder, P., Fritzsche, U., and Widmer, K. "Stages of Religious Judgment." In J. Fowler (ed.), *Inward Moral and Religious Maturity.* Morristown, N.J.: Silver Burdett, 1980.

Perry, W. *Intellectual and Ethical Development in the College Years.* New York: Holt, Rinehart & Winston, 1968.

Piaget, J. *The Moral Judgment of the Child.* San Diego, Calif.: Harcourt Brace Jovanovich, 1932.

Rutter, M., and Garmezy, N. "Developmental Psychopathology." In P. Mussen, *Handbook of Child Psychology.* Vol. 4: *Socialization.* New York: Wiley, 1983.

Schafer, R. *A New Language for Psychoanalysis.* New Haven, Conn.: Yale University Press, 1976.

Schmid-Kitsikis, E. "Piagetian Theory and Its Approach to Psychopathology." *American Journal of Mental Deficiency,* 1973, *77,* 694–705.

Selman, R. L. *The Growth of Interpersonal Understanding: Developmental and Clinical Analyses.* Orlando, Fla.: Academic Press, 1980.

Sroufe, L. A., and Rutter, M. "The Domain of Developmental Psychopathology." *Child Development,* 1984, *55,* 17–29.

Sroufe, L. A., and Waters, E. "Attachment as an Organizational Construct." *Child Development,* 1977, *48,* 1184–1199.

Sullivan, H. S. *The Interpersonal Theory of Psychiatry.* New York: Norton, 1953.

Vaillant, G. *Adaptation to Life.* Boston: Little Brown, 1977.

Vygotsky, L. *Mind in Society: The Development of the Higher Psychological Processes.* Cambridge, Mass.: Harvard University Press, 1978.

Vygotsky, L. "Conciousness as a Problem of Psychology of Behavior." *Soviet Psychology,* 1979, *170,* 29–30.

Vygotsky, L. *Thought and Language.* Cambridge, Mass.: MIT Press, 1986.

Werner, H. *Comparative Psychology of Mental Development.* New York: International Universities Press, 1948.

Wolff, P. H. "The Developmental Psychologies of Jean Piaget and Psychoanalysis." *Psychological Issues.* Vol. 5. New York: International Universities Press, 1960.

Youniss, J. *Parents and Peers in Social Development.* Chicago: University of Chicago Press, 1980.

Gil G. Noam received degrees in clinical psychology at the Free University, Berlin, and in human development at Harvard University. He directs a research department at Harvard Medical School and the Hall-Mercer Children's Center of McLean Hospital. He is also codirector of the Clinical-Developmental Institute in Belmont, Massachusetts. His research interests include developmental psychopathology, borderline and narcissistic disorders and their treatment, as well as socioemotional and self-development in adolescence and through the life span.

*A developmental framework emphasizing stage-salient issues
in infancy and toddlerhood can be applied toward the
implementation of a transactional model of intervention.*

Stage-Salient Issues:
A Transactional Model
of Intervention

*Dante Cicchetti, Sheree L. Toth, Marcy A. Bush,
Janet F. Gillespie*

In recent years, an increasing number of researchers have directed their
attention toward elucidating the organization of development in at-risk
children and on uncovering the relation between the quality of early
adaptation and later developmental outcomes (Lewis, Feiring, McGuffog,
and Jaskir, 1984; Main, Kaplan, and Cassidy, 1985; Sroufe, 1979a, 1983).
By explaining abnormal ontogenetic processes in the social, emotional,
cognitive, and linguistic domains, contributions can be made to theories
of normal development. In addition, the developmental perspective
broadens our understanding of the deviations and distortions that occur
in psychopathological conditions (Cicchetti, 1984, in press; Rutter and
Garmezy, 1983).

The organizational perspective on development, which conceptu-
alizes development as a series of reorganizations around stage-salient

The writing of this chapter was supported, in part, by a grant from the
National Institute of Mental Health (R01-MH37960). We would like to thank
Bonnie Gangadean and Victoria Gill for typing this manuscript.

E. D. Nannis, P. A. Cowan (eds.). *Developmental Psychopathology and Its Treatment.*
New Directions for Child Development, no. 39. San Francisco: Jossey-Bass, Spring 1988.

tasks, has been a guiding framework for research in the area of developmental psychopathology (Cicchetti and Schneider-Rosen, 1986; Cicchetti and Sroufe, 1978; Sroufe, 1979a). According to the organizational perspective, competence results from successful resolution of the tasks most salient for a given developmental period. A hierarchical depiction of adaptation follows, in that successful resolution of a stage-salient issue increases the likelihood of subsequent successful task resolution (Sroufe and Rutter, 1984). Because early structures often are incorporated into later structures, an early deviation or perturbation in functioning may ultimately cause much larger disturbances to emerge subsequently.

In addition, the organizational perspective, by virtue of its emphasis on the interrelation among ontogenetic domains (for example, cognitive, linguistic, social, emotional, and biological development), necessitates a multisystem approach to the assessment of children, parents, and environments (A. Freud, 1965). Historically, most organismic theories focused either on cognition or emotion (Cicchetti, in press; Cicchetti and Pogge-Hesse, 1981; Kaplan, 1967). However, since the 1970s there has been a burgeoning interest in the nature of affect-cognition relations (Cicchetti and White, in press; Izard, 1977; Sroufe, 1979b). Moreover, several organismic theorists who have been viewed as ignoring the emotional domain also have been shown, upon careful inspection of the content of their works, to address the emotional aspects of development (Cicchetti and Hesse, 1983; Cowan, 1982; Piaget, 1981). Our focus upon stage-salient developmental issues, tasks that require the child to coordinate cognition, affect, and behavior, causes us to search for interventions that include, yet are much broader than, single developmental domains such as cognition.

In this chapter, instead of comparing developmental dysfunctions among various groups of pathology, we examine development within pathological or high-risk conditions. Rather than focusing on chronological age to guide intervention, the child's level of development on a number of stage-salient tasks and domains must be considered when designing interventions. Therefore, we see development and the associated areas of competence/incompetence as the defining variables of intervention.

Transactional Model

Inherent in the organizational perspective on development is the recognition of the importance of transacting genetic, constitutional, neurobiological, biochemical, psychological, and social factors in the determination of behavior (Sameroff, 1983). Throughout time, most etiological models of psychopathology have been main effect or linear in nature. According to the main-effect model, psychopathology is the direct and inevitable result of some specific early pathogenic experience or inherent biological/biochemical dysfunction that exerts a profound impact on the individual throughout the life span. Although the past two decades witnessed the emergence of more interactional models (for example, the argument that both genes and a poor environment are necessary and sufficient for schizophrenia—Gottesman and Shields, 1972), there still exists great dissatisfaction with prevalent conceptualizations of psychopathology (Engel, 1977).

Proponents of the transactional model contend that the various factors that operate in normal or pathological conditions do not occur in isolation but together affect the developmental process through a hierarchy of dispositions (Cicchetti and Aber, 1986). According to Sameroff and Chandler (1975), the multiple transactions among parental, child, and environmental characteristics contribute to the outcomes of child development in a reciprocal, dynamic fashion. Accordingly, if a child manifests pathological development over time, it is presumed that the child has been involved in a continuous maladaptive transactional process. The long-standing manifestation of child maladaptation is shaped by parental and environmental support, while the child's characteristics help to determine the nature of the environment. Because the child and the environment are seen as reciprocally influencing each other, it follows that development at a later point reflects not only the quality of earlier adaptation but also the effect of intervening environmental inputs.

Illustrative Conditions Involving Disorders of Development

In this chapter, we demonstrate how a transactional developmental psychopathology perspective that focuses on the young child's resolution of stage-salient issues can be applied to the identification and treatment of nascent and incipient psychopathology in early childhood. Through early diagnosis and intervention, disruptive impacts of new developmental tasks on future maladaptation may be ameliorated. We have chosen to focus on four illustrative problematic conditions: (1) Down syndrome, (2) nonorganic failure-to-thrive syndrome (failure-to-thrive), (3) offspring of parents with a major depressive disorder, and (4) child maltreatment. These conditions were chosen for several reasons. They occur with sufficient frequency to warrant clinical and research attention. Together they define a continuum in terms of the hypothesized relative contribution to psychopathology of reproductive (genetic and constitutional) and caretaking (parental and environmental) casualty factors (Sameroff and Chandler, 1975). That is, they vary with regard to the relative significance that child-specific versus parent-specific influences play on the course of development. Finally, they all possess compelling characteristics that enable us to expand, affirm, and challenge our understanding of normal developmental theory.

Down Syndrome. Since Down syndrome is a genetically determined condition that is identifiable at birth, child-specific constitutional factors are extremely significant. Transactional processes are set in motion when the reproductive casualties (the constitutional disabilities) of children with Down syndrome pose problems for the parents of these children, presenting unique challenges to the caretaking system (Cicchetti and Sroufe, 1978; Sorce and Emde, 1982). In the past decade, a more broadly based developmental perspective has begun to replace earlier emphases on the cognitive deficits of children with Down syndrome (Cicchetti and Pogge-Hesse, 1982). Despite delays in development, children with Down syndrome exhibit developmental patterns and sequences that are remarkably similar to those observed in normal children (Cicchetti and Beeghly, in press).

Nonorganic Failure to Thrive. Although it is not clearly genetically linked, infants evidencing nonorganic failure-to-thrive also can be identified very early in life through the assessment of their growth patterns and through comprehensive physical and psychosocial diagnostic batteries (Drotar, 1985). Deceleration in rate of weight gain in the absence of primary organic disease is the fundamental defining characteristic of failure-to-thrive. Additional commonly associated characteristics include dysfunctional caregiver-infant interaction (Lieberman and Birch, 1985), lack of developmentally appropriate signs of infant social responsivity and relatedness (American Psychiatric Association Committee on Nomenclature, 1987), and developmental delay (Drotar, in press). Finally, infants with failure-to-thrive generally exhibit physical and psychosocial gains following institution of adequate caretaking or hospitalization.

Failure-to-thrive provides an important illustration of how psychological factors affect biological functioning and of how caretaking casualties may contribute to the emergence of neuroendocrine and other biological system complications. However, the mechanisms underlying the interplay among altered caretaker child-interaction, medical illness, infection, and biological system alterations have yet to be clearly elucidated.

Offspring of Depressed Parents. Children with depressed parents have been shown to be genetically and environmentally at risk for developing a future affective disorder and other types of psychopathology (Beardslee, Bemporad, Keller, and Klerman, 1983). If the depressed parent is the primary caregiver, then the child's environment is likely to reflect the symptomatic behaviors of depression (Radke-Yarrow, Cummings, Kuczynski, and Chapman, 1985). Even in the absence of possible genetically determined predispositions, this environment may result in difficulty for the child in stage-salient task resolution and future maladaptation. For example, dysphoric maternal affect may lead to subsequent difficulties with self-regulation (Cohn and Tronick, 1983). In fact, negative transactions between the caregiver and child may instigate and perpetuate disturbances in both members of the dyad (Cicchetti and Schneider-Rosen, 1986).

Child Maltreatment. Of the four conditions of infancy and toddlerhood chosen to illustrate the transactional developmental psychopathology perspective, child maltreatment loads highest on the continuum of caretaking casualty. Although the impact of maltreatment on various aspects of developmental functioning has become the focus of systematic study only in the past two decades (Aber and Cicchetti, 1984), the deleterious effects of maltreatment experiences have been documented in every developmental domain. Additionally, the role of maltreatment as a predisposing cause of future psychopathology has been articulated (Cicchetti and Olsen, in press).

Despite their etiologic heterogeneity, all of these conditions can be understood and their respective problem areas addressed through the use of a transactional model of intervention. Furthermore, we wish to underscore that these particular conditions were chosen as illustrative of a transactional developmental psychopathology approach in which child dysfunction emerges in a process of biological and psychosocial transactions. Many other maladaptations can be conceptualized within this framework.

Stage-Salient Issues of Early Development

There is a great deal of agreement concerning the presence of a series of stage-salient issues that are characteristic of the early years of life (Erikson, 1950; Greenspan, 1981; Sander, 1962; Sroufe, 1979a). Rather than construing the ontogenetic process as a series of unfolding tasks that must be accomplished and then decrease in importance, we perceive development as consisting of a number of important age- and stage-appropriate tasks that, upon emergence, remain critical to the child's continual adaptation. As new tasks emerge, old issues may decrease in relative salience. Consequently, each issue represents a life-span developmental task that requires ongoing coordination and integration in the individual's adaptation to the environment and to the stage-salient developmental issue of the period. Furthermore, there are corresponding roles for caregivers that increase the probability that their children will successfully resolve each stage-salient issue (see Sroufe, 1979a).

These stage-salient issues, which include (1) homeostatic regulation and the development of a reliable signaling system, (2) management of tension and the differentiation of affect, (3) development of attachment, (4) development of an autonomous self, and (5) symbolic representation and self-other differentiation, are described in the next section.

In this section we will review the empirical literature as it pertains to stage-salient task resolution in the four dysfunctional conditions of infancy and toddlerhood that we have chosen. Our discussion will be somewhat circumscribed in that we will focus on research findings and not clinical observation. Since empirical data are not available for all conditions, each high-risk group will not be represented for every stage-salient issue.

Homeostatic Regulation and the Development of a Reliable Signaling System (Birth to Three Months). An initial task of infancy is to develop a simultaneous interest in the self and in the external world in order to achieve homeostatic regulation and the emergence of a reliable signaling system. Achievement of homeostatic regulation is facilitated by a protective, predictable, and engaging environment. A chaotic, arbitrary, hypo/hyperstimulating environment contributes to problems in the successful resolution of the tasks associated with this stage-salient issue.

Infants with Down syndrome have a variety of neurological, biochemical, physiological, and psychophysiological problems that may stress the caregiving system and result in homeostatic failure. For example, their slower maturation of reflexes and of organ systems impairs the development of reliable sleep-wake patterns (Cicchetti and Beeghly, in press). Moreover, the confluence of neuromuscular hypotonia, poor eye contact, dampened affect intensity, higher arousal thresholds, "noise" in the emotion signaling system, and absence of crescendoing during face-to-face interaction provides significant stressors on the caregiver-infant communicative system (Berger, in press; Cicchetti and Sroufe, 1978; Emde, Katz, and Thorpe, 1978). Despite the difficulties that occur in the early months, most caregivers of infants with Down syndrome are able to accommodate to their infants' behavioral and physiological anomalies and to develop a mutually adaptive signaling system over the course of the first year of life (Sorce and Emde, 1982).

Vietze and others (1980) have conducted the only prospective investigation of parent-child interaction prior to the diagnosis of failure-to-thrive. Using a transactional perspective, they collected and evaluated data related to the infant's early environment. Although no significant differences were found on numerous dimensions between mothers whose infants were later diagnosed as having failure-to-thrive and those in the comparison group, certain features of dyadic behavior observed during the neonatal period discriminated infants who subsequently developed failure-to-thrive from physically healthy children who were also from high-risk environments. Mothers in the growth failure group spent significantly less time visually attending to their infants than did the other mothers. Also, although infant initiation or termination of dyadic interaction was not differentiated by diagnostic category, the analysis of maternal contribution to the interchange did show significant differences.

Mothers of male infants with subsequently diagnosed failure-to-thrive were more likely to drop out of simultaneous interaction. Moreover, mothers of males with growth failure were less likely than comparison mothers to maintain a behavior when the infant was not responding. This association of specific social interactional patterns with the subsequent development of failure-to-thrive is unique in the literature and has clear implications for the development of homeostasis and adaptive arousal modulation. Decreased visual attention, in concert with the lack of investment implicit in maternal inability to sustain contact, could potentially contribute to initial growth failure and to disorders of homeostasis. Homeostatic difficulties including excessive irritability, passivity, muted signaling of need states, or inability to be readily calmed or soothed have all been associated with failure-to-thrive.

In an important study of the impact of depression, Cohn and Tronick (1983) investigated the face-to-face interaction of normal mothers with their three-month-old infants. In one of the experimental conditions, mothers were requested to simulate depressive affect during interaction with the baby. During periods of simulated depression, infants evidenced wariness, protest, and gaze aversion. Cohn and Tronick (1983) concluded that even simulated depression could result in negative infant affectivity, subsequently impairing the infants' capacity to engage in effective self-regulation. These findings revealed that the flexibility in rhythms evidenced during sequences of normal interaction were significantly impaired during phases of simulated depression. In addition, Field (1984a) compared dyadic interactions between a sample of mothers suffering from postpartum depression and a sample of normal mothers simulating depression. A difference in coping strategy emerged, with infants in the postpartum group evidencing resigned, passive, and mimicking behavior, while infants in the simulated depression group were active in their protests (Field, 1984a). Data from the Rochester Longitudinal Study (Sameroff, Seifer, and Zax, 1982) demonstrated that offspring of depressed parents have lower Apgar scores, poorer tonus, and greater difficulty with self-quieting than infants with nonaffectively ill parents. In sum, studies indicate that differences in homeostatic regulation can emerge very early in the lives of infants exposed to a depressed parent. Although this does not suggest that infant depression results directly from parental depression, the impact of depressive symptomatology on the acquisition of developmental competencies is clear.

Management of Tension (Cognitively Produced Arousal) and the Differentiation of Affect (Four to Six Months). With the emergence of the social smile, a qualitatively new phase of development and behavioral organization emerges (Emde, Gaensbauer, and Harmon, 1976). Mastery of homeostatic regulation and the development of reliable patterns of signaling result in an increased capacity to attend to the environment. As a result, the infant begins to engage with the animate and inanimate world in a more organized manner (Sroufe and Waters, 1976). Behaviors that were previously endogenously stimulated and primarily reflexive become replaced by contingent response styles. This state is characterized by increased intensity and differentiation in the expression of affect (Sroufe, 1979b). The infant's ability to elicit maternal responsivity and maternal sensitivity to infant cues are critical for successful negotiation of this issue.

Once again, the biological system difficulties that exist in infants with Down syndrome present special challenges for the caregiver. Infants with Down syndrome are slower to develop laughter to a variety of stimuli presented by their mothers (Cicchetti and Sroufe, 1976), and these infants cannot process the incongruity of these stimuli with sufficient speed to generate the tension (that is, cognitively produced arousal— Sroufe and Waters, 1976) required for laughter. Likewise, Cicchetti and Sroufe demonstrated similar delays in the emergence of full-blown fear expressions. Importantly, the lags in the emergence of extreme forms of positive and negative affect cannot be accounted for simply on the basis of cognitive factors. Infants with Down syndrome laugh and cry far less often than mental-age matched normal babies, underscoring the role of biological, cognitive, and affective systems in the unfolding of a differentiated emotional system (Cicchetti and Sroufe, 1978). As noted above, the caregivers become increasingly able to negotiate patterns of communication that facilitate the successful resolution of this task (Sorce and Emde, 1982).

At three months infants who later exhibit failure-to-thrive are irritable and difficult to calm. Consequently, much of the dyads' time will be devoted to attempts to restore harmony, as opposed to exploration and shared enjoyment. Concurrently, nutritional status, which is often compromised in failure-to-thrive children, also may affect social responsiveness and hence influence the quality of parent-child interaction (Pollitt and Thomson, 1977).

The central role of affect in depressive disorders suggests that the differentiation of affect in infancy could be a task subject to disruption in children with a depressed parent. Although very little empirical information exists about this important issue, data from the Rochester Longitudinal Study found that four-month-old offspring of depressed parents were less responsive to others and that their mothers were less spontaneous, less happy, less vocal, and less proximal to their infants (Sameroff, Seifer, and Zax, 1982).

Development of a Secure Attachment (Six to Twelve Months). The development of a secure attachment relationship with the primary caregiver is a stage-salient issue that has generated considerable research (Ainsworth and Wittig, 1969; Bowlby, 1969). It is marked by increased attention and attunement to interpersonal interactions (Stern, 1985). Although the capacity for attachment originates in earlier stages, overt manifestations of this issue reach ascendancy in the latter half of the first year of life (Sroufe, 1979a). Dyadic interactions, marked by relatedness and synchrony, resiliency to stress, and appropriate affective interchange, are associated with successful adaptation during this stage (Sroufe, 1979b). In the absence of regular contingent responsivity, neither infant nor caregiver develops feelings of efficacy, and the development of a secure attachment relationship may be impeded (Ainsworth, Blehar, Waters, and Wall, 1978).

Despite their constitutional anomalies, the attachment system of infants with Down syndrome is organized in a manner similar to that of cognitively matched nonhandicapped youngsters. The majority of these children form secure attachment relationships with their caregivers (Thompson, Cicchetti, Lamb, and Malkin, 1985). In addition, the interrelation among the attachment, fear and wariness, exploratory, and affiliative behavioral systems is strikingly similar for children with Down syndrome and their cognitively matched counterparts (Cicchetti and Serafica, 1981).

Employing a laboratory paradigm with only one mother-child separation but otherwise quite similar to Ainsworth, Blehar, Waters, and Wall's (1978) "strange situation," Gordon and Jameson (1979) found that significantly more failure-to-thrive infants were insecurely attached to their mothers than a control group of children who had been hospitalized due to accidents they had incurred. Fifty percent of the failure-to-thrive infants were classified as insecurely attached as compared with 15 percent of the controls.

In a more elaborate analysis of these same data, Gordon (1979) found three variables to be particularly associated with insecure attachment status: mother's depression, infant temperament, and low socioeconomic status (SES). One subgroup of failure-to-thrive infants was of particular interest. Five of these babies were rated as low on the persistence dimension of temperament and had depressed mothers and came from the lowest SES backgrounds. All five of these infants formed an insecure attachment relationship. These results concur with those of a study by Drotar, Malone, and Nowak (1985), in which nearly half of a sample of twelve-month-old failure-to-thrive infants who had been hospitalized and then received psychosocial intervention were found to be insecurely attached.

In keeping with a transactional model, one must consider additional factors other than parent-child interaction that may contribute to secure versus insecure attachment. For example, preliminary analyses of factors that differentiate secure versus insecure attachments (Drotar, 1985) indicated that infants with insecure attachments had more chronic failure-to-thrive than the infants who were securely attached. Insecure attachment also was associated with a greater number of family stresses at intake. The mechanisms by which these factors affect the quality of attachment in failure-to-thrive children are not yet clearly understood.

A study by Ramey and others (1975) suggests that one major interactional deficit in failure-to-thrive may involve response-contingent stimulation from mother to child. Results of their study of nine infants ranging in age from 6.0 to 16.5 months suggest that both quality of nutrition and opportunity to receive increased response-contingent stimulation in a social context contribute significantly to the remediation of developmental retardation commonly associated with failure-to-thrive.

Although these findings do not establish lack of contingent responsiveness as a cause of failure-to-thrive, the implications for intervention are significant. Poor response-contingent stimulation is so commonly associated with failure-to-thrive that determination of cause versus effect often seems an exercise in futility. On the other hand, improving response-contingent stimulation may serve to prevent the development of progressive cycles of disengagement previously described.

Insecure attachments are frequently associated with less stable caregiving environments (Gaensbauer, 1982). In view of the cyclicity of depressive illness, it is reasonable to expect attachment patterns to be adversely affected in offspring of depressed parents. Data documenting a greater likelihood of insecure attachments in children of depressed mothers is beginning to accumulate. For example, in an important study, Radke-Yarrow, Cummings, and Kuczynski, and Chapman (1985) found that insecure attachments were infrequent in children of normal parents or in children of parents experiencing a minor depression. However, offspring of depressed mothers did evidence disturbances in attachment, which were primarily insecure avoidant or insecure avoidant/ambivalent. In addition, children of bipolar (manic-depressive) mothers evidenced the highest percentage (79 percent) of insecure attachments.

The vast majority of maltreated infants form insecure attachment relationships with their primary caregiver, with estimates of insecurity ranging from 70 percent to 100 percent across studies (Crittenden and Ainsworth, in press). Over time, there is a striking tendency for these attachments to become anxious avoidant (Type A—see Ainsworth, Blehar, Waters, and Wall, 1978) in quality (Schneider-Rosen, Braunwald, Carlson, and Cicchetti, 1985).

Development of an Autonomous Self (Eighteen to Twenty-Four Months). The toddler's emerging acquisition of a sense of self, which encompasses both affective and cognitive dimensions, is a significant developmental task (Lewis and Brooks-Gunn, 1979; Stern, 1985). The evolution of this ability enables the toddler to understand environmental occurrences more fully. Moreover, a well-differentiated sense of self provides the toddler greater comprehension of personal functioning as a separate and independent entity. Empathic acts also begin to emerge at this time, again a manifestation of the realization that the self can have an impact on others (Zahn-Waxler and Radke-Yarrow, 1982). Caretaker sensitivity and ability to tolerate the toddler's strivings for autonomy, as well as the capacity to set age-appropriate limits, are integral to the successful resolution of this issue.

Toddlers with Down syndrome evidence visual self-recognition in the mirror-and-rouge paradigm (Lewis and Brooks-Gunn, 1979) when they reach a mental age of approximately two years. Moreover, upon viewing their rouge-altered noses in the mirror, the toddlers with Down syndrome show the concomitant positive affective changes observed in cognitively equivalent nonhandicapped infants (Mans, Cicchetti, and Sroufe, 1978). The positive affect accompanying their visual self-recognition suggests that these children feel good about themselves.

Data from the collaborative National Institute of Mental Health (NIMH)/Colorado studies coalesce to provide information on the regulation of emotion in young offspring of depressed parents (Gaensbauer, Harmon, Cytryn, and McKnew, 1984; Zahn-Waxler, Cummings, McKnew, and Radke-Yarrow, 1984). Overall, children having a parent (mother or father) with a bipolar disorder evidenced socioemotional difficulties and were less competent in interpersonal relationships than were the control group children. The range of difficulties and their impact on adaptation were interpreted as reflecting poor modulation of affect (Zahn-Waxler, Cummings, McKnew, and Radke-Yarrow, 1984). Similar difficulties in the regulation of affect were found in toddlers of mothers with major depressive disorders (Radke-Yarrow, Cummings, Kuczynski, and Chapman, 1985). Heightened emotionality in the toddlers of depressed parents was assessed as being disruptive to social interactions.

The affective responses of maltreated children to their rouge-altered mirror images are strikingly different from those of a matched sample of nonmaltreated toddlers. Specifically, in contrast with most children from the middle-and lower-social classes (as well as children with Down syndrome) who manifest positive affective responses to their altered images, nearly 80 percent of maltreated youngsters show neutral or negative affect (Schneider-Rosen and Cicchetti, 1984). These results suggest that maltreated toddlers either attempt to mask their feelings or experience themselves in primarily negative ways.

Egeland and Sroufe (1981) assessed a toddler's emerging autonomy, independent exploration of the environment, and ability to cope with frustration at twenty-four months and found that physically abused maltreated children were more angry, frustrated with mother, noncompliant, and less enthusiastic than controls. Furthermore, the physically abused maltreated toddlers exhibited a higher frequency of aggressive, frustrated, and noncompliant behaviors and a lower frequency of positive affect than the neglected maltreated children they studied.

Symbolic Representation and Further Self-Other Differentiation (Twenty-Four to Thirty Months). Between twenty-four and thirty months, toddlers develop the ability to construct even more differentiated mental representations of animate and inanimate objects (Greenspan and Porges, 1984). Investigations in the areas of play, language, and cognition have burgeoned (Bretherton, 1984; Rubin, Fein, and Vandenberg, 1983). Additionally, the use of language and play to represent early conceptions of self and other is an age-appropriate manifestation of children's growing awareness of self and other.

Beeghly and Cicchetti (1987) found that although emerging at a delayed pace, the symbolic play of children with Down syndrome progresses through the same developmental sequences of decentration, decontextualization, and integration in object and social play that characterize the play development of normal children (Bretherton, 1984). Moreover, close correspondences were found between affective and cognitive dimensions of symbolic play (see also Motti, Cicchetti, and Sroufe, 1983). Affective motivational play style (persistence, enthusiasm, positive affect) significantly correlated with level of cognitive development, symbolic play maturity, and social play. These results attest to the coherence of development in children with Down syndrome.

Finally, children with Down syndrome show increasingly differentiated concepts of self and other in play. During play, their self-related language (for example, talking about their ongoing activities and internal states, using personal pronouns, and so on) was related to advances in both symbolic and cognitive development. In addition, parallel advances were found in their ability to use language as a communicative social tool (Beeghly and Cicchetti, 1987).

There is very little substantive research on the development of language and symbolic representation in failure-to-thrive children. Studies by Drotar (1985) are the only investigations to look specifically at symbolic play and language development in failure-to-thrive children. Although language and symbolic play scores in the Drotar (1985) sample were normal at both twelve and eighteen months, Drotar did identify numerous predictors and correlates of both symbolic play and language development in failure-to-thrive children (for example, higher income predicted play; maternal to child vocalizations predicted language).

We believe that the deficits manifested by the failure-to-thrive children may be more emotional or psychological rather than cognitive or intellectual. In other words, although failure-to-thrive children may indeed have normal language ability, the more important question may be whether they choose to utilize their linguistic skills. The research conducted to date has made it difficult to make this differentiation.

Dyadic discourse has emerged as a forum for exploring the self-conceptions of offspring of depressed parents. It is possible to assess parental impact on the development of the self by examining natural discourse and resultant child self-references and behavior. Radke-Yarrow, Belmont, Nottelmann, and Bottomly (in press) selected affectively disordered mothers (thirteen unipolar, four bipolar) and control group mothers (no psychiatric disorder) in order to explore mother-child discourse. Although this study revealed that depressed mothers were similar to nondepressed mothers in the quantity and content of attributions, depressed mothers conveyed significantly more negatively toned affect in their attributions. This occurred most often with respect to negative attributions about child emotions. In addition, depressed mother-child dyads evidenced higher correspondence of affective tone of attributions and of self-reference than did control dyads. These results are interpreted as suggesting that the children had heightened vulnerability to maternal attributions (Radke-Yarrow, Belmont, Nottelmann, and Bottomly, in press). The potential for increases in negative self-attributions for these children and the impact of these increases on the development of a depressive disorder are important issues for further study.

Investigations of the self-system in maltreated children were conducted by researchers interested in internal state language. Maltreated toddlers use proportionately fewer internal state words and attribute internal states to fewer social agents than a matched group of nonmaltreated children (Cicchetti and Beeghly, 1987). That is, maltreated youngsters talk less about their emotions and describe the emotional states of their parents and other adults less frequently than do matched groups of nonmaltreated toddlers. Moreover, the maltreated children's internal state utterances were more context-bound, focusing on the here and now and not on absent persons or objects. These findings enable us to identify areas of incompetence requiring intervention.

Implications for Intervention

In recent decades, utilization of early intervention to prevent the emergence of future psychopathology in at-risk populations is becoming a priority. A transactional model suggests a "Process-Person-Context" mode of intervention (Bronfenbrenner and Crouter, 1983). Attention should be directed toward the context in which a child is developing; the constitutional, biological, and psychological characteristics of the child and his or her caregiver(s); and the transactional processes through which development is occurring (see also Cowan, Chapter One).

As previously noted, the conditions we have chosen for illustrative purposes in this chapter can be conceptualized along such a continuum of reproductive and caretaking casualty (Sameroff and Chandler, 1975), with Down syndrome, failure-to-thrive, offspring of depressed parents, and child maltreatment progressively increasing in the relative importance of caretaker characteristics and decreasing in their respective weighting of reproductive casualty. Although articulation of the interrelationships among the parent-child-environment levels of the system is inherent in the transactional model, it is clear that the contribution of these various components and the manner in which they contribute to the ontogenetic process varies across conditions. Therefore, even if one component of the parent-child-environment system is chosen for an initial intervention, we should expect consideration of transactions among all levels of the system to be necessary.

Furthermore, while we are not suggesting that etiology necessarily governs intervention, it is the case that etiological considerations become increasingly important when planning preventive interventions (Cowan, Chapter One). Since our suggestions focus on infancy and toddlerhood (birth to three years) we are concerned primarily with prevention and early intervention. It is therefore necessary to remember that interventions also must reflect developmental changes and that techniques need to vary in accordance with developmental level (see Nannis, Chapter Two). In addition, since development is an integrated process, intervention must be broad-based in focus, and we believe that intervention should contain components that tap each developmental domain.

In this chapter, we presented illustrations of how the negotiation of stage-salient issues can be adversely affected in a variety of conditions of early childhood. Unfortunately, the vast majority of the research conducted to date has been cross-sectional in nature, thereby precluding us from asserting that the early dysfunctions will necessarily result in subsequent task failure. Even if longitudinal methodologically sound data were available, developmental discontinuities are possible. However, because early structural deviations are incorporated into the overall developmental process, early failures increase the probability of subsequent failure in task resolution. Moreover, because these tasks are not only stage-salient but also continue in different form across the life span, early maladaptation with respect to a given issue may result in lifelong difficulties with its resolution. For example, because attachment is a lifelong issue, negative internal working models in this area could lead to continual or repeated difficulties with relationship formation and intimacy. This underscores the importance of early identification of problems and early intervention.

In accordance with the transactional model, we will stress the importance of attending to the interactions between diagnosis and stage-salient issues. For example, interventions suggested for a child with a maltreating parent and for a child with a depressed parent must reflect diagnosis of the parents even though both children may experience similar stage-specific maladaptations. We cannot yet provide clear guidelines for how practitioners should intervene in order to achieve the identified goals. However, we believe that the ideas we have presented will promote the application of theory-driven interventions.

Interventions for Different Conditions

Children with Down syndrome load heavily on reproductive casualty. During the early months, numerous problems exist in their self-regulatory and in their communicative signaling systems. Concomitant with these child-systemic difficulties, parents of infants with Down syndrome have been reported to experience a grieving process in the initial months following the birth of an infant with Down syndrome (Emde and Brown, 1978). A model of intervention designed to address all of these areas is indicated.

In many ways, parents of infants with Down syndrome are very receptive to intervention and in fact experience fewer psychological difficulties associated with their role as parents than do parents of failure-to-thrive, offspring of depressed parents, or maltreated infants. Therefore, interventions that focus on facilitating understanding of and responsivity to their infants' cues may be successful. An educational approach designed to provide information about the developmental difficulties experienced by infants with Down syndrome, in conjunction with dyadic modeling around these issues, may prove to be productive. For example, using videotapes to help parents identify muted infant signaling systems and to respond contingently can be helpful. Parent groups that provide support for parents during the stressful months following the birth of an infant with Down syndrome also have been suggested (Spiker, in press) and may facilitate parental ability to accommodate to the developmental issues related to parenting an infant with Down syndrome and to deal with their own grief.

Due to the significance of reproductive casualty in children with Down syndrome, consideration of medical issues when working with these parents also is important. For example, apprising parents about the medical complications that often accompany Down syndrome is an issue that needs to be handled sensitively. Although an informational component is needed, it is important that parents not be inundated with negative information during an already stressful period.

Interestingly, despite the early deficits of infants with Down syndrome, parents are able to accommodate to these infant liabilities in growth-producing ways. Of the four conditions of infancy and toddlerhood chosen for review, it is only infants with Down syndrome who exhibit primarily secure attachment relationships with parental figures.

Failure-to-thrive infants evidence attachment disturbances that may be related to a lack of response-contingent stimulation and to earlier failures to attain mutually satisfactory regulation of the infant-caregiver relationship. Multiple hospitalizations and the resulting inconsistency in the caretaking environment also may exacerbate difficulties in the establishment of a secure attachment relationship. It is apparent that the infant requires ongoing intervention in order to ensure physically appropriate development.

Efforts to improve dyadic interaction through modeling also are indicated. Parents require help in learning to recognize weak or confusing signals and in learning to enjoy and to experience positive feelings about infants who are frequently irritable, apathetic, and passive. Therapeutic intervention with the caregiver may be necessary, because parents of failure-to-thrive children may be experiencing a psychiatric condition that affects their caretaking capacities. Affective disorders and character disorders may affect the emotional availability of the caregiver and the nature of the caregiver's interactions with the infant. Likewise, because failure-to-thrive children experience poor-quality caretaking, it is important to provide them with a visiting nurse, homemaker, or case manager. These individuals can help ensure that the family adequately utilizes resources that are available to them and can help educate the family in areas such as child development, child care, and taking care of a home. Moreover, these individuals often serve to provide some relief to an overtaxed, stressed mother, thus enabling her to be more emotionally available to her child.

An intervention strategy for offspring of depressed parents rests on altering environmental and caretaking characteristics. Parent psychotherapy and/or medication may be needed. However, the rate of development during infancy and its place as a vulnerable period of development suggest the need for providing alternate caregivers during parental depressive episodes (for example, day care, support of relatives). It should not be assumed that the nondepressed spouse can serve this function; he or she may be overwhelmed and unable to maintain adequate distance from the impact of the affective disturbance. Because there is much tension between couples with a depressed spouse, the other spouse may be less than desirably cooperative in treatment.

As with offspring of depressed parents, the insecure attachment relationships exhibited by maltreated children suggest the need for a comprehensive intervention strategy if future maladaption is to be prevented. Due to the heterogeneity of factors associated with maltreatment, including diverse etiology, intergenerational transmission, and developmental sequelae, treatment of maltreated children must be broad enough to address all components of the maltreating system. The role of the parent and his or her ability to alter dysfunctional patterns of interaction must be assessed accurately. An armamentarium of services, including psychotherapy, parent skill building, and support groups is indicated (Cicchetti and Toth, 1987). The impact of significant environmental stressors also needs to be addressed through the provision of increased social supports and home-based management programs (Olds and Henderson, in press). In cases where parents present as especially recalcitrant, temporary or permanent out-of-home placement may be the only mechanism likely to prevent the continuance of developmental dysfunction in the maltreated child.

The data concerning maltreated toddlers reveal very early deficits in the development of autonomy and self-regulation. These self-system difficulties portend poorly for future adaptation. Bemporad, Smith, Hanson, and Cicchetti (1982) documented a high incidence of early maltreatment in children later diagnosed with borderline syndromes, a disorder viewed by many to be a problem in the development of the self-system. Moreover, the concurrent relationship between childhood maltreatment and depression, another disorder that is affected by and affects self-esteem, was described by Kazdin, Moser, Colbus, and Bell (1985). Accordingly, it is imperative that work with parents, homemakers, and day-care teachers focus on fostering the development of a positive sense of self in the maltreated child. If intervention occurs during these early phases, severe future dysfunction may be prevented. A transactional model of intervention again must consider parental responsibility and amenability to change. Environmental supports designed to decrease parental stress and provide more positive caretaking supplements are likely to be needed.

The data on offspring of depressed parents and maltreated toddlers can be used to suggest stage-salient intervention strategies. An increase in correspondence between the affective tone of attributions made by toddlers and by depressed parents is an important finding, in which the links are potentially modifiable. Broadening the toddlers' experience base so that the depressed parent is not the primary channel of attribution communications is one possibility. Additionally, sensitizing the depressed parent to the nature of his or her own self-statements and to the impact of these references on the developing child may prove to be a significant area for change. Because cognitive behavior therapy with adults has been demonstrated to alter self-statements made by depressives (Beck, 1979), utilization of a similar approach with the parent-child dyad in order to modify parental statements is a potentially rich arena for intervention.

The tendency for maltreated toddlers to use fewer internal state words may stem from parental disapproval of the expression of affect or of a certain class of affects. These children may become overcontrolled in efforts to meet parental demands. Because a maltreating parent may have difficulty tolerating affective displays, alternate caregivers again may be necessary. However, the fact that the overcontrolled stance of maltreated children is likely to serve as an adaptive coping strategy for the maltreated child must not be disregarded (Schneider-Rosen, Braunwald, Carlson, and Cicchetti, 1985). For example, if a child is taught to verbalize anger, the parent must be able to deal with increased expression adaptively rather than punitively. Altering the toddlers' mode of interacting without assuring the environment's ability to tolerate this change would be a disservice. Therefore, intensive work with the parent must precede a more child-focused intervention. In lieu of this, the use of alternative caregivers or permanent foster placement may need to be considered.

Conclusion

It is clear that dysfunctions in the negotiation of stage-salient issues can emerge during the early years of life and that these difficulties may affect future adaptation. Based on current research, a transactional model of intervention designed to prevent the emergence of future psychopathology was proposed. Illustrative conditions of infancy and toddlerhood and related stage-salient deficits were used to suggest possible developmentally timed and focused strategies of intervention. In many ways, our ability to apply these principles to the development of theoretically sound interventions is in a very early stage. We believe that the approach presented here will generate future exploration and much needed research into developmentally specific methods of intervention.

References

Aber, J. L., and Cicchetti, D. "Socioemotional Development in Maltreated Children: An Empirical and Theoretical Analysis." In H. Fitzgerald, B. Lester, and M. Yogman (eds.), *Theory and Research in Behavioral Pediatrics.* Vol. 2. New York: Plenum Press, 1984.

Ainsworth, M., Blehar, M., Waters, E., and Wall, S. *Patterns of Attachment.* Hillsdale, N.J.: Erlbaum, 1978.

Ainsworth, M., and Wittig, B. A. "Attachment and Exploratory Behavior of One Year Olds in a Strange Situation." In B. M. Foss (ed.), *Determinants of Infant Behavior.* Vol. 4. New York: Wiley, 1969.

American Psychiatric Association Committee on Nomenclature. *Diagnostic and Statistical Manual of Mental Disorders.* Vol. 3. (rev. ed.) Washington, D.C.: American Psychiatric Association, 1987.

Beardslee, W. R., Bemporad, J., Keller, M. D., and Klerman, G. L. "Children of Parents with Major Affective Disorder: A Review." *American Journal of Psychiatry,* 1983, *140,* 825–832.

Beck, A. *Cognitive Therapy and the Emotional Disorders.* New York: Times Mirror, 1979.

Beeghly, M., and Cicchetti, D. "An Organizational Approach to Symbolic Development in Children with Down Syndrome." In D. Cicchetti and M. Beeghly (eds.), *Symbolic Development in Atypical Children.* New Directions for Child Development, no. 36. San Francisco: Jossey-Bass, 1987.

Bemporad, J., and Schwab, M. E. "The DSM-III and Clinical Child Psychiatry."

In T. Millon and G. L. Klerman (eds.), *Contemporary Directions in Psychopathology: Toward the DSM-IV.* New York: Guilford Press, 1986.

Bemporad, J., Smith, H., Hanson, C., and Cicchetti, D. "Borderline Syndromes in Childhood: Criteria for Diagnosis." *American Journal of Psychiatry,* 1982, *139,* 596-602.

Berger, J. "Interactions Between Parents and Their Infants with Down Syndrome." In D. Cicchetti and M. Beeghly (eds.), *Down Syndrome: The Developmental Perspective.* New York: Cambridge University Press, in press.

Bowlby, J. *Attachment and Loss.* Vol. 1: *Attachment.* New York: Basic Books, 1969.

Bretherton, I. (ed.). *Symbolic Play.* Orlando, Fla.: Academic Press, 1984.

Bronfenbrenner, U., and Crouter, A. C. "The Evolution of Environmental Models and Developmental Research." In P. Mussen (ed.), *Handbook of Child Psychology.* New York: Wiley, 1983.

Cicchetti, D. "The Emergence of Developmental Psychopathology." *Child Development,* 1984, *55,* 1-7.

Cicchetti, D. "An Historical Perspective on the Discipline of Developmental Psychopathology." In J. Rolf, A. Masten, D. Cicchetti, K. Neuchterlein, and S. Weintraub (eds.), *Risk and Protective Factors in the Development of Psychopathology.* New York: Cambridge University Press, in press.

Cicchetti, D., and Aber, J. L. "Early Precursors of Later Depression: An Organizational Perspective." In L. Lipsitt and C. Rovee-Collier (eds.), *Advances in Infancy.* Vol. 4. Norwood, N.J.: Ablex Press, 1986.

Cicchetti, D., and Beeghly, M. "Symbolic Development in Maltreated Youngsters: An Organizational Perspective." In D. Cicchetti and M. Beeghly (eds.), *Symbolic Development in Atypical Children.* New Directions for Child Development, no. 36. San Francisco: Jossey-Bass, 1987.

Cicchetti, D., and Beeghly, M. (eds.). *Down Syndrome: The Developmental Perspective.* New York: Cambridge University Press, in press.

Cicchetti, D., and Hesse, P. "Affect and Intellect: Piaget's Contributions to the Study of Infant Emotional Development." In R. Plutchik and H. Kellerman (eds.), *Emotion: Theory, Research and Experience.* Vol. 2. New York: Academic Press, 1983.

Cicchetti, D., and Olsen, K. "The Developmental Psychopathology of Child Maltreatment." In M. Lewis and S. Miller (eds.), *Handbook of Developmental Psychopathology.* New York: Plenum Press, in press.

Cicchetti, D., and Pogge-Hesse, P. "The Relation Between Emotion and Cognition in Infant Development: Past, Present, and Future Perspectives." In M. Lamb and L. Sherrod (eds.), *Infant Social Cognition.* Hillsdale, N.J.: Erlbaum, 1981.

Cicchetti, D., and Pogge-Hesse, P. "Possible Contributions of the Study of Organically Retarded Persons to Developmental Theory." In E. Zigler and D. Bella (eds.), *Mental Retardation: The Developmental-Difference Controversy.* Hillsdale, N.J.: Erlbaum, 1982.

Cicchetti, D., and Schneider-Rosen, K. "An Organizational Approach to Childhood Depression." In M. Rutter, C. Izard, and P. Read (eds.), *Depression in Young People: Clinical and Developmental Perspectives.* New York: Guilford Press, 1986.

Cicchetti, D., and Serafica, F. "The Interplay Among Behavioral Systems: Illustrations from the Study of Attachment, Affiliation, and Manners in Young Down Syndrome Children." *Developmental Psychology,* 1981, *17,* 36-49.

Cicchetti, D., and Sroufe, L. A. "The Relationship Between Affective and Cognitive Development in Down Syndrome Infants." *Child Development,* 1976, *47,* 920-929.

Cicchetti, D., and Sroufe, L. A. "An Organizational View of Affect: Illustration from the Study of Down's Syndrome Infants." In M. Lewis and L. Rosenblum (eds.), *The Development of Affect*. New York: Plenum Press, 1978.

Cicchetti, D., and Toth, S. "The Application of a Transactional Risk Model to Intervention with Multi-Risk Maltreating Families." *Zero to Three*, 1987, *7*, 1-8.

Cicchetti, D., and White, J. "Emotion and Developmental Psychopathology." In N. Stein and T. Trabasso (eds.), *Emotion-Cognition Interactions in Development*. Hillsdale, N.J.: Erlbaum, in press.

Cohn, J. F., and Tronick, E. L. "Three-Month-Old Infants' Reactions to Simulated Maternal Depression." *Child Development*, 1983, *54*, 185-193.

Cowan, P. A. "The Relationship Between Emotional and Cognitive Development." In D. Cicchetti and P. Hesse (eds.), *Emotional Development*. New Directions for Child Development, no. 16. San Francisco: Jossey-Bass, 1982.

Crittenden, P., and Ainsworth, M. "Attachment and Child Abuse." In D. Cicchetti and V. Carlson (eds.), *Child Maltreatment: Research and Theory on the Consequences of Child Abuse and Neglect*. New York: Cambridge University Press, in press.

Drotar, D. "Failure to Thrive and Preventive Mental Health: Knowledge Gaps and Research Needs." In D. Drotar (ed.), *New Directions in Failure to Thrive: Implications for Research and Practice*. New York: Plenum Press, 1985.

Drotar, D. "Failure to Thrive." In D. K. Routh (ed.), *Handbook of Pediatric Psychology*. New York: Guilford Press, in press.

Drotar, D., Malone, C. A., and Nowak, M. "Early Outcome in Failure to Thrive: Correlates of Security of Attachment." Presentation to Society for Research in Child Development, Toronto, Canada, Apr. 1985.

Egeland, B., and Sroufe, L. A. "Developmental Sequelae of Maltreatment in Infancy." In R. Rizley and D. Cicchetti (eds.), *Developmental Perspectives on Child Maltreatment*. New Directions for Child Development, no. 11. San Francisco: Jossey-Bass, 1981.

Emde, R. N., and Brown, C. "Adaptation to the Birth of Down Syndrome Infants." *Journal of American Academy for Child Psychiatry*, 1978, *17*, 299-323.

Emde, R. N., Gaensbauer, T., and Harmon, R. *Emotional Expression in Infancy: A Biobehavioral Study*. New York: International Universities Press, 1976.

Emde, R. N., Katz, E. L., and Thorpe, J. K. "Emotional Expression in Infancy: Early Deviations in Down Syndrome." In M. Lewis and L. A. Rosenblum (eds.), *The Development of Affect*. London: Plenum Press, 1978.

Engel, G. "The Need for a New Medical Model: A Challenge for Biomedicine." *Science*, 1977, *196*, 129-135.

Erikson, E. *Childhood and Society*. New York: Norton, 1950.

Field, T. M. "Early Interactions Between Infants and Their Postpartum Depressed Mothers." *Infant Behavior and Development*, 1984a, *7*, 517-522.

Field, T. M. "Follow-Up Developmental Status of Infants Hospitalized for Non-Organic Failure to Thrive." *Journal of Pediatric Psychology*, 1984b, *9*, 241-256.

Freud, A. *Normality and Pathology in Childhood*. New York: International Universities Press, 1965.

Gaensbauer, T. J. "Regulation of Emotional Expression in Infants from Two Contrasting Caretaker Environments." *Journal of the American Academy of Child Psychiatry*, 1982, *21*, 163-171.

Gaensbauer, T. J., Harmon, R. J., Cytryn, L., and McKnew, D. "Social and Affective Development in Infants with a Manic-Depressive Parent." *American Journal of Psychiatry*, 1984, *141*, 223-229.

Glasser, M., and Lieberman, A. F. "Failure to Thrive: An Interactional Perspective." In L. Zegans, L. Temoshok, and C. Van Dyke (eds.), *Emotions in Health and Illness*. Orlando, Fla.: Grune & Stratton, 1984.

Gordon, A. H. "Patterns and Determinants of Attachment in Infants with the Non-Organic Failure to Thrive Syndrome." Unpublished doctoral dissertation, Harvard Graduate School of Education, 1979.

Gordon, A. H., and Jameson, J. C. "Infant-Mother Attachment in Parents with Non-Organic Failure to Thrive Syndrome." *Journal of the American Academy of Child Psychiatry*, 1979, *18*, 96-99.

Gottesman, I., and Shields, J. *Schizophrenia and Genetics: A Twin Study Vantage Point*. San Diego, Calif.: Academic Press, 1972.

Greenspan, S. I. *Psychopathology and Adaptation in Infancy and Early Childhood*. New York: International Universities Press, 1981.

Greenspan, S. I., and Porges, S. W. "Psychopathology in Infancy and Early Childhood: Clinical Perspectives on the Organization of Sensory and Affective-Thematic Experience." *Child Development*, 1984, *55*, 49-70.

Hesse, P., and Cicchetti, D. "Perspectives on an Integrated Theory of Emotional Development." In D. Cicchetti and P. Hesse (eds.), *Emotional Development*. New Directions for Child Development, no. 16. San Francisco, Jossey-Bass, 1982.

Izard, C. *Human Emotions*. New York: Plenum Press, 1977.

Kaplan, B. "Meditations on Genesis." *Human Development*, 1967, *10*, 65-87.

Kazdin, A. E., Moser, J., Colbus, D., and Bell, R. "Depressive Symptoms Among Physically Abused and Psychiatrically Disturbed Children." *Journal of Abnormal Psychology*, 1985, *94*, 298-307.

Lewis, M., and Brooks-Gunn, J. *Social Cognition and the Acquisition of Self*. New York: Plenum Press, 1979.

Lewis, M., Feiring, C., McGuffog, C., and Jaskir, J. "Predicting Psychopathology in Six-Year Olds from Early Social Relations." *Child Development*, 1984, *55*, 123-136.

Lieberman, A. F., and Birch, M. "The Etiology of Failure to Thrive: An Interactional Developmental Approach." In D. Drotar (ed.), *New Directions in Failure to Thrive: Implications for Research and Practice*. New York: Plenum Press, 1985.

Main, M., Kaplan, N., and Cassidy, J. C. "Security in Infancy, Childhood and Adulthood: A Move to the Level of Representation." In I. Bretherton and E. Waters (eds.), *Growing Points of Attachment Theory and Research*. Monographs of the Society for Research in Child Development, no. 209. Chicago: University of Chicago Press, 1985.

Mans, L., Cicchetti, D., and Sroufe, L. A. "Mirror Reactions of Down's Syndrome Infants and Toddlers: Cognitive Underpinnings of Self-Recognition." *Child Development*, 1978, *49*, 1247-1250.

Motti, F., Cicchetti, D., and Sroufe, L. A. "From Infant Affect Expression to Symbolic Play: The Coherence of Development in Down Syndrome Children." *Child Development*, 1983, *54*, 1168-1175.

Olds, D. L., and Henderson, C. "The Prevention of Maltreatment." In D. Cicchetti and V. Carlson (eds.), *Child Maltreatment: Research and Theory on the Consequences of Child Abuse and Neglect*. New York: Cambridge University Press, in press.

Piaget, J. *Intelligence and Affectivity: Their Relationship During Child Development*. Palo Alto, Calif.: Annual Reviews, 1981.

Pollitt, E., and Thomson, C. "Protein Caloric Malnutrition and Behavior: A View from Psychology." In R. F. Wurtman and J. J. Wurtman (eds.), *Nutrition and Brain*. New York: Raven Press, 1977.

Radke-Yarrow, M., Belmont, B., Nottlemann, E., and Bottomly, L. "Young Children's Self-Conceptions: Origins in the Natural Discourse of Depressed and Normal Mothers and Their Children." In D. Cicchetti and M. Beeghly (eds.), *The Self in Transition.* Chicago: University of Chicago Press, in press.

Radke-Yarrow, M., Cummings, E. M., Kuczynski, L., and Chapman, M. "Patterns of Attachment in Two- and Three-Year-Olds in Normal Families and Families with Parental Depression." *Child Development,* 1985, *56,* 884–893.

Ramey, C. T., Starr, R. H., Pallas, J., Whitten, C. F., and Reed, V. "Nutrition, Response Contingent Stimulation and the Maternal Deprivation Syndrome: Results of an Early Intervention Program." *Merrill Palmer Quarterly,* 1975, *21,* 45–55.

Rubin, K., Fein, G., and Vandenberg, B. "Play." In P. Mussen (ed.), *Handbook of Child Psychology.* Vol. 4: *Socialization.* New York: Wiley, 1983.

Rutter, M., and Garmezy, N. "Developmental Psychopathology." In P. Mussen (ed.), *Handbook of Child Psychology.* New York: Wiley, 1983.

Sameroff, A. "Developmental Systems: Contexts and Evolution." In P. Mussen (ed.), *Handbook of Child Psychology.* Vol. 1: *Infancy.* New York: Wiley, 1983.

Sameroff, A. J., and Chandler, M. J. "Reproductive Risk and the Continuum of Caretaking Casualty." In F. D. Horowitz (ed.), *Review of Child Development Research.* Vol. 4. Chicago, Ill.: University of Chicago Press, 1975.

Sameroff, A. J., Seifer, R., and Zax, M. *Early Development of Children at Risk for Emotional Disorder.* Vol. 47.Monographs of the Society for Research in Child Development, no. 199. University of Chicago Press, 1982.

Sander, L. "Issues in Early Mother-Child Interaction." *Journal of the American Academy of Child Psychiatry,* 1962, *1,* 141–166.

Schneider-Rosen, K., Braunwald, K., Carlson, V., and Cicchetti, D. "Current Perspectives in Attachment Theory: Illustration from the Study of Maltreated Infants." In I. Bretherton and E. Waters (eds.), *Growing Points in Attachment Theory and Research.* Monographs of the Society for Research in Child Development, no. 209. Chicago: University of Chicago Press, 1985.

Schneider-Rosen, K., and Cicchetti, D. "The Relationship Between Affect and Cognition in Maltreated Infants: Quality of Attachment and the Development of Visual Self-Recognition." *Child Development,* 1984, *55,* 648–658.

Sorce, J. F., and Emde, R. N. "The Meaning of the Infant Emotional Expressions: Regularities in Caregiving Responses in Normal and Down Syndrome Infants." *Journal of Child Psychology and Psychiatry,* 1982, *22,* 145–158.

Spiker, D. "Early Intervention from a Developmental Perspective." In D. Cicchetti and M. Beeghly (eds.), *Down Syndrome: The Developmental Perspective.* New York: Cambridge University Press, in press.

Sroufe, L. A. "The Coherence of Individual Development." *American Psychologist,* 1979a, *34,* 834–841.

Sroufe, L. A. "Socioemotional Development." In J. Osofsky (ed.), *Handbook of Infant Development.* New York: Wiley, 1979b.

Sroufe, L. A. "Infant-Caregiver Attachment and Patterns of Adaptation in Preschool: The Roots of Maladaptation and Competence." In M. Perlmutter (ed.), *Minnesota Symposium in Child Psychology.* Hillsdale, N.J.: Erlbaum, 1983.

Sroufe, L. A., and Rutter, M. "The Domain of Developmental Psychopathology." *Child Development,* 1984, *55,* 17–29.

Sroufe, L. A., and Waters, E. "The Ontogenesis of Smiling and Laughter: A Perspective on the Organization of Development in Infancy." *Psychological Review,* 1976, *83* (3), 173–189.

Stern, D. N. *The Interpersonal World of the Infant.* New York: Basic Books, 1985.

Thompson, R., Cicchetti, D., Lamb, M., and Malkin, C. "The Emotional Responses of Down Syndrome and Normal Infants in the Strange Situation: The Organization of Affective Behavior in Infants." *Developmental Psychology,* 1985, *21,* 828–841.

Trad, P. V. *Infant Depression: Paradigms and Paradoxes.* New York: Springer-Verlag, 1986.

Vietze, P., Falsey, M., O'Connor, S., Sandler, H., Sherrod, K., and Altemeier, W. A. "Newborn Behavioral and Interactional Characteristics of Non-Organic Failure to Thrive Infants." In T. M. Field, S. Goldberg, D. Stern, and A. M. Sostek (eds.), *High Risk Infants and Children.* New York: Academic Press, 1980.

Zahn-Waxler, C., Cummings, E. M., McKnew, D. H., and Radke-Yarrow, M. "Altruism, Aggression and Social Interaction in Young Children with a Manic-Depressive Parent." *Child Development,* 1984, *55,* 112–122.

Zahn-Waxler, C., McKnew, D. H., Cummings, E. M. Davenport, Y. B., and Radke-Yarrow, M. "Problem Behaviors and Peer Interactions of Young Children with a Manic-Depressive Parent." *American Journal of Psychiatry,* 1984, *141,* 236–240.

Zahn-Waxler, C., and Radke-Yarrow, M. "The Development of Altruism: Alternative Research Strategies." In N. Eisenberg (ed.), *Development of Prosocial Behavior.* San Diego, Calif.: Academic Press, 1982.

Dante Cicchetti is associate professor of psychology and psychiatry at the University of Rochester, where he is director of the Mt. Hope Family Center. Mt. Hope specializes in the research, education, treatment, and prevention of child, adult, and family developmental psychopathology.

Sheree L. Toth is research associate and assistant professor of psychology at Mt. Hope Family Center of the University of Rochester. Her research interests are focused in the area of affective disorders in children and adolescents.

Marcy A. Bush is research associate and assistant professor of psychology at Mt. Hope Family Center of the University of Rochester. Her research interests are in the areas of infancy and in early precursors of maladaptive coping and pathology.

Janet F. Gillespie is research associate and assistant professor at the Mt. Hope Family Center in the Department of Psychology, University of Rochester. Her research interests are in the areas of children's social-cognitive skills, social competence, and the development of preventive interventions for high-risk groups.

Two main approaches to applying Piaget's theory of cognitive development to the study of child psychopathology are represented in this chapter. In one approach, the authors hypothesize relations between cognitive development and socioemotional development. In the other, the authors use the cognitive theory as a source of material, drawing selectively from it in order to construct a model of socioemotional development.

Possibilities and Pitfalls in Clinical Applications of Cognitive-Developmental Theory

Leonard Breslow

While the chapters in this sourcebook offer diverse approaches to the application of cognitive-developmental theory to clinical psychology, they share some assumptions in common. Within Cowan's typology of nine ways to explain normal and abnormal development, outlined in Chapter One, the present approaches may all be classified under the same heading. All adopt a primarily psychological, rather than biological or social interactional, perspective. All agree on the centrality of child-environment interaction in the determination of development. Not surprisingly, then, all of the contributors draw primarily on the interactionist theory of cognitive development proposed by Jean Piaget in attempting to relate cognitive development to developmental clinical phenomena.

At the same time, the approaches to applying Piagetian theory to clinical issues and concerns differ in fundamental respects. In all cases, social-emotional development is implicated in this application. In some cases (Nannis, Slotnick, Gordon), this application may be conceived on the metaphor of bridge building. That is, one tower, representing cogni-

E. D. Nannis, P. A. Cowan (eds.). *Developmental Psychopathology and Its Treatment.*
New Directions for Child Development, no. 39. San Francisco: Jossey-Bass, Spring 1988.

tive development, is linked by a bridge to another tower, representing social-emotional development. One might expand the metaphor to specify a series of bridges linking developmental levels of one tower to specific levels of the other (Nannis). Direction of traffic on the bridge may be thought to represent direction of influence. Nannis and Gordon discuss traffic or influence proceeding primarily from the cognitive domain to the social-emotional domain, while Slotnick posits two-way traffic or reciprocal influences of the two domains. In any of these cases, this approach is ambitious as well as hazardous, since the success of the resultant construction depends upon the strength of both towers or developmental domains and upon the strength of the bridges by which they are related.

In contrast to this approach, efforts by Noam and by Cicchetti, Toth, Bush, and Gillespie to apply cognitive-developmental theory to socioemotional-clinical issues may be conceived more in terms of the construction of a single tower than of a bridge between towers. The single tower represents social, emotional, or personality development. However, sections of this tower are copied more or less exactly from the cognitive-developmental tower. That is, elements or concepts from cognitive-developmental theory are selectively incorporated into the developmental framework the authors have constructed. Often they are modified in the process. In this approach, cognitive-developmental theory only serves as an analogy, model, or inspiration for concepts in the socioemotional theory or perspective. Not surprisingly, these authors place relatively greater emphasis on differences as well as similarities between cognitive and socioemotional development than the bridge builders. In general, this approach would appear to be the safer one, at least so far as the relating of cognitive and socioemotional development is concerned, since it is architecturally simpler. But it may be quite ambitious in other respects as we will see.

Evaluation of Piaget's Theory

For either approach, but especially for bridge building, a crucial step must be to evaluate the adequacy of the cognitive-developmental theory being employed—in the present chapters, the theory of Piaget. The major problem confronting anyone attempting to use Piaget's theory as a support to the understanding of socioemotional development and clinical phenomena is that the theory has been fundamentally challenged by many workers during the past decade or so (Brainerd, 1978). As Noam has suggested, researchers and clinicians working toward a clinical-developmental framework find themselves in the paradoxical situation of bringing to bear a theory already in question in the very field, developmental psychology, they most heavily draw from. While it is beyond the scope of this chapter to provide a detailed summary and evaluation of the criticisms of Piaget's theory, their fundamental importance to the consideration of the chapters in this sourcebook warrants at least a summary discussion.

One common criticism presupposes that Piaget's stage concept requires that cognitive attainments of the same stage develop in synchrony. Such synchrony is often not found (Gelman and Baillargeon, 1983). In my own view, Piaget explicitly eschews the notion of synchrony of attainment (Piaget, 1977). Instead, the stage construct is supported by Piaget in terms of the centrality of logicomathematical thought to other domains of thought (for example, physical, social and figurative, including memory, imagery, perception, and language). The influence of logicomathematical thinking on other domains does not imply synchrony because influence can occur even though there is a temporal delay between cause and effect. A second criticism of the theory concerns whether or not there is structural change in children's concepts. It often appears possible to find evidence for any concept among the youngest children that can be tested (Gelman and Baillargeon, 1983).

In general, with regard to these criticisms and others, it appears to me that Piaget is at his best where his ideas are expressed the most formally and also that his later ideas are typically superior to his earlier ones. Both detractors and supporters of the theory often do the theory a disservice by focusing on the more discursively or informally defined and less up-to-date features of the theory.

With regard to distinction between formally versus discursively, informally defined concepts, claims that the thinking of the preoperational child is egocentric and bound to perceptual appearances (two informal concepts) are soundly contradicted by the evidence (Shantz, 1983). In contrast, claims concerning more formalized concepts, such as claims that the preoperational child is unable to perform transitive inferences, understand class inclusion, or conserve number have, in my view, held up under massive scrutiny (Breslow, 1981; Halford, 1982). With regard to the transition to formal operations, the more formally defined attainments, such as proportionality and combinatorial reasoning, are typically not found prior to adolescence, while more discursively defined abilities, such as the consideration of possibilities, formation of hypotheses, and separation of variables, often are found prior to adolescence. For instance, while Inhelder and Piaget (1958) originally claimed that the ability of the preadolescent to generate possibilities was severely limited, if not nonexistent, Piaget (1987) in a posthumous work provided evidence for definite abilities to generate possibilities among preadolescents, albeit abilities more limited than those of adolescents. This revision concerning the discursive construct of possibilities in no way forces a revision of the formal specification of the stage structures.

In addition to considerations of the empirical evidence, there are theoretical reasons to consider the more formalized aspects of the theory to be the most central. The formalized structures are more precisely defined and are depicted more clearly as undergoing qualitative changes, crucial to the structuralist position, than are the more discursively, informally defined concepts. The latter are often employed in a more quantitative manner (for example, more or less egocentric or perceptually bound), inconsistent with the theory's premise of qualitative structural change. Further, the most central cognitive domain in the theory, the logicomathematical domain, is the one that is most formalized (Piaget, 1972). Also, filiations between concepts are more clearly elaborated for formalized concepts than for discursive ones (Piaget, 1942). In contrast, the more informally characterized concepts (for example, egocentrism) are typically dependent upon or even epiphenomena of the formally characterized concepts. For example, the ability to conceive of indefinite numbers of possibilities in adolescence is dependent upon the combinatorial formal operational structure. It is likely for these reasons that Piaget developed in his career from the use of more discursively characterized concepts (Piaget, 1929) to the reliance on ones that are formally defined (Piaget, 1972).

I have elaborated on this point because many of those who attempt to utilize Piaget's theory in the clinical domain or other applied domains frequently draw more heavily from the more discursive aspects of the theory than from the more formalized components.

With regard to the functional side of Piaget's theory, there is less question of utilizing formalized concepts since Piaget's functional concepts are less formalized than the structural ones. However, as with the structural side of the theory, there remains a tendency to draw from the less developed, up-to-date aspects of the theory when applying it to other domains. Concepts relating to the equilibration model of stage transition, in particular assimilation and accommodation, certainly have been invoked more than other functional Piagetian concepts by those positing relations and parallels between domains. Examples are to be found in Block (1982) as well as most of the contributors to the present volume. According to most of these authors, structural change proceeds directly from the interchange between the child's cognitive structures and the environment. A balance between active assimilatory and passive accommodatory modes of interchange are responsible for the equilibration productive of structural change. Circumstances or individual differences resulting in a predominance of one or the other of these modes—that is, for overassimilation and overaccommodation—are thought to impede developmental progress.

However, this account of equilibration does not reflect Piaget's latest and most elaborated accounts. Only in his early account of sensorimotor development did Piaget characterize equilibration in terms of phases of overassimilation, overaccommodation, and assimilation-accommodation balance (Piaget, 1952). In later work, Piaget (1970) described equilibration in terms of perturbations and compensations. Within a stage, the child both assimilates and accommodates to the world by means of his or her current cognitive structures. However, eventually the child finds some phenomena produce perturbations in the form of contradictions. Through a probabilistic process the child then accommodates to the world by constructing a new structure that resolves or compensates for the contradication or perturbation. This reliance on accommodation has been criticized for implying an empiricist learning model, inconsistent with Piaget's interactionism (Fodor, 1980). Piaget's latest account of equilibration, elaborated in the last decade of his life (Piaget, 1985), appears to meet this objection. Within a stage, direct interaction (roughly, assimilation and accommodation) with the environment produces schemes (empirical abstractions and generalizations) that will eventually be transformed into the next stage structure. The transformation process, however, is characterized by Piaget as an internal process of integration among schemes, rather than an assimilative-accommodation interaction with the environment (Piaget, 1985).

In sum, imbalances and balances between assimilation and accommodation do not play the central role in Piaget's later accounts of structural change that they played in the earliest account. What is more, even if balances between assimilation and accommodation were responsible for cognitive development, it is not clear how imbalances could be involved in the production of individual differences, such as personality differences and psychopathology. Such imbalances could only produce developmental delay. But individual differences and psychopathology are not generally reducible to developmental retardation (Cowan in Chapter One, Slotnick in Chapter Four).

The above considerations notwithstanding, aspects of Piaget's theory of cognitive development that are not well supported or not current can certainly play a legitimate role in theories of personality, socioemotional development, and psychopathology if those aspects are used as a basis for rough analogies rather than as a literal component in the latter theories. That is, as long as one is not positing actual similarities between cognition and other domains, one may still borrow and adapt aspects of cognitive-developmental theory for use in those domains. Assimilation and accommodation, for example, are certainly interesting concepts that have inspired creative conceptualizations outside the cognitive domain. In the personality domain, for example, overassimilation in the form of imperviousness to feedback from the social environment or overaccommodation in the form of overconformity and overresponsiveness to the environment are clearly maladaptive modes of functioning.

Further, individuals may have pervasive assimilative or accommodative styles of functioning. Such adaptations of concepts from Piaget's theory may prove to be productive even if the concepts are no longer relevant to their original domain of application.

Bridge Builders

Let us now consider the different contributions in this volume in turn, beginning with those that posit an actual relation or bridge between cognitive development and other psychological domains. After considering questions such as those discussed above relating to the adequacy of the cognitive-developmental theory or concepts being employed, the bridge builder must ensure the adequacy of the social, emotional, or clinical concepts to be incorporated in his or her construction as well as the adequacy of the link or bridge relating the two domains.

Gordon in Chapter Three posits relations between the structure of adolescents' reasoning and their social judgments and behavior—for instance, those related to pregnancy and classroom behavior. Specifically, she evaluates a number of adolescent psychosocial problems in terms of prerequisite cognitive abilities, such as the ability to envision alternatives or possibilities, to evaluate alternatives, to take another person's perspective, and to reason about chance. This approach offers the advantage of attempting to specify the logical structures presumably underlying social-emotional behavior. However, we will need to begin specifying these underlying structures in formal rather than discursive terms in order to produce a clear and testable model. That is, on the basis of the clinically based hypothesis that certain cognitive abilities that improve during the concrete-to-formal operations stage transition are involved in sexual or classroom decision making, it is premature to conclude that limitations in the adolescents' social decision making stem from a structural deficit in these cognitive abilities. Piaget normally does not posit that the child develops from no understanding at all of various concepts in the stage of concrete operations to fully adult knowledge in formal operations. Rather, the child's understanding undergoes incremental qualitative changes from one stage to the next. Thus, in order to demonstrate the dependence of a specific social ability on a formal operational understanding of a given concept, we will have to do more than determine that some understanding of the concept is involved in the social ability. Rather, it will be necessary to demonstrate that the specifically formal operational form of the concept is required for adaptive functioning and that the concrete operational form of the concept is not adequate for adaptive social functioning. For example, while some ability to generate possibilities is necessary for sexual or classroom decision making, it is not clear that a specifically formal operational level of that ability is necessary for adaptive behavior in these areas. Piaget (1987) provided much evidence that concrete operational children can generate many possibilities on a variety of tasks. What they cannot do is recognize that indefinitely many alternatives are possible in indeterminate situations or generate all possible alternatives on multidimensional problems where such generation requires combinatorial reasoning. It seems to me unlikely that the generation of alternatives to sexual intercourse (methods of birth control, refusing intercourse, and so on) or to putting on makeup in the classroom requires a formal operational level concept of possibility. On the other hand, the hypothesis that a formal operational understanding of chance may be necessary for an adequate understanding of the probability of becoming pregnant as a result of intercourse appears more promising. But in either case, a structural analysis of the adolescents' actual reasoning on these social problems, together with a consideration of the precise structure of cognitive concepts at different stages, is needed in order to assess the dependency of adaptive social functioning on a particular stage-level form of a given cognitive concept.

The question naturally now arises of how a child who possesses the necessary level of cognitive competence for adaptive functioning in a given social area can nonetheless reason poorly in that area and behave in a maladaptive manner as a partial consequence of that reasoning. The answer to this question must be that there are more determinants of cognitive performance than the child's structural level of competence. Various functional factors of a social nature (such as peer pressure), or of an emotional nature (such as motivation), or of a cognitive nature (such as attention and memory) can produce cognitive performance below the level of the child's structural competence. Cognitive biases must also be included under the category of functional factors. For instance, there is an extensive literature that most adults have difficulty reasoning probabilistically in concrete situations, tending to construe probabilistic phenomena as deterministic in nature (Kahneman, Slovic, and Tversky, 1982). Presumably, a substantial proportion of these adult subjects are formal operational in competence and can demonstrate probabilistic reasoning under certain circumstances. Clearly, their problem is not one of structural delay.

In addition to functional factors, deficiencies in reasoning may result from deficiencies in the content of thought, such as a paucity of relevant knowledge, or from incorrect information, rather than from the structural immaturity of thought. The structural logical apparatus may be intact, but the apparatus may have limited or faulty information to use as premises. Certain adolescents may be unable to conceive of certain possibilities, not because they lack combinatorial reasoning but because they lack relevant knowledge upon which the combinatorial can be applied. Lack of knowledge may be due to lack of experience—for instance, as a result of social isolation or a homogeneous social sphere. Alternatively, knowledge may remain inaccessible to reasoning for emotional reasons, as the Freudian conception of unconsciousness implies. Gordon describes ways in which functional deficits and limitations in experience may produce structural delay or asynchrony. I am suggesting that we also consider the possibility that social-behavioral problems may result from functional deficiencies or knowledge limitations in the absence of structural deficits.

The issue of whether fallacious reasoning is due to deficiencies in structure or in content has clear clinical implications. If the reasoning difficulties are due to limitations in content, then the therapist needs to act either as an educator or as a facilitator of the uncovering of unconscious ideas, depending on the source of the limitation. For instance, if the adolescent is simply ignorant of the probability of becoming pregnant due to intercourse, then she must be provided with the relevant facts. However, if the problem is produced by structural deficiencies, the therapist must act to promote structural change by stimulating the equilibration process responsible for such change. In the present example, the therapist would attempt to help the adolescent develop a general formal operational understanding of the nature of probabilistic phenomena. The attempt to induce structural change is probably considerably more difficult than the provision of information or ideas that are assimilable within existing structures and is thus best reserved for problems where the contribution of structural cognitive immaturity has been clearly established.

The second bridge builder, Nannis, in Chapter Two provides the most thorough analysis of a social cognitive domain based on her own and others' research on the development of children's concepts of emotions. Nannis suggests that an understanding of children's concepts of emotions has important implications for the therapeutic process. Insofar as therapy produces changes in social and emotional functioning through the patient's acquisition of insight into his or her emotions, we have at least an indirect link between concepts of emotions and emotions themselves. Certainly the ability to reflect on one's own emotions and on those of other people is likely to be highly adaptive for socioemotional functioning. As Nannis points out, insight-oriented therapy must take into account developmental limitations in the child's ability to conceive of emotions.

However, Nannis does well to mention that one cannot assume that the development of children's concepts of emotion resembles the development of their emotions themselves. Indeed, there is some reason to believe they do not. While the ability to conceive of emotional ambivalence, for instance, does not develop before approximately eleven years, the experience of conflicting emotions is likely present in infancy. Research on attachment in infancy (Ainsworth, Blehar, Waters, and Wall,

1978) has distinguished a pattern of attachment, called resistant attachment, characterized by the infant's emotional ambivalence toward its mother. Similarly, with regard to the time course of emotions, Harris and Olthof (1982) provide evidence for major differences between the development of emotional concepts and the emotions themselves. It is not clear whether emotional development proceeds through structurally similar stages to emotional conception, only much more rapidly, or whether emotional development is structurally quite different from emotional conceptual development, perhaps not manifesting structural transformation at all.

In either case, the lack of structural correspondence between these two domains points to a certain conception of unconsciousness similar to that proposed by Piaget (1976) in his book *The Grasp of Consciousness*. Piaget argued that children's motor activity often develops in advance of their ability to conceive of that activity. As a result, children will often be unable to reflect on their own actions and to that extent will remain unconscious of their actions. Similarly, if young children can experience emotional ambivalence but not conceive of it, they can be said to be unconscious of their ambivalent emotions. This cognitive unconscious is quite distinct from the Freudian conception of unconsciousness. In the Freudian conception, the repression of feelings in unconsciousness is motivated and emotionally determined. A censoring agency is motivated to keep certain emotions out of conscious reflection. Unconsciousness is further maintained by the expression of the forbidden emotions in a form, determined by primary process thinking, that is too primitive for the rationally guided conscious mind to understand. In the cognitive conception of unconsciousness, in contrast, unconsciousness is neither motivated nor emotionally determined. In addition, the unconscious emotions do not escape conscious scrutiny because they are too primitive, as in the Freudian conception but, on the contrary, because these emotions are too complex for the conscious conceptual system to comprehend.

There are clearly some clinical dilemmas that derive from this view of unconsciousness. Even though a four-year-old cannot conceive of ambivalence, his or her emotional problems may nonetheless stem from ambivalent feelings. Therapy cannot be directed toward allowing the child to gain insight into the ambivalence, because the child's conceptual level will not permit such insight. But the therapist must nonetheless find some other way to deal with the child's ambivalent feelings.

In addition to positing relations between emotional conceptions and emotional-social functioning, Nannis posits dependencies of the development of emotional concepts on the development of Piagetian logico-mathematical-physical concepts. Questions confronting these hypothesized dependencies are similar to those confronting dependencies proposed by Gordon. That is, the concepts are sometimes discursive and relatively quantitative ones from Piaget's theory (for example, perceptual-boundedness, systematicity of thought) or sometimes formally defined concepts from the theory used in a discursive or quantitative manner (for example, conservation of weight). In any case, Nannis's ideas concerning the development of reasoning about emotions and its relevance to clinical issues does not depend crucially on the existence of relations between emotional reasoning and Piagetian structural cognition.

Of the bridge builders, Slotnick in Chapter Four is the one most centrally concerned with Piagetian cognition, specifically in the logico-mathematical domain of classification. While many researchers have found various functional (Breslow and Cowan, 1984) and structural (Schmid-Kitsikis, 1976) cognitive deficits in autistic children, Slotnick attempts to study the relation between these two areas of deficit. At the same time, she examines the role of social problems as a possible factor contributing to the cognitive deficits. Her basic approach is to match autistic and normal children on the structural level of their classification ability as assessed by unstructured sorting tasks and then to compare the groups on other areas of their functioning on both the unstructured and structured tasks. The assessments have the advantage of being nonverbal in nature, obviating the impediments to assessment created by the language deficiencies of autistic children. Both functional strengths and weaknesses of autistic children, as well as possible contributions of social impairments to their cognitive deficits, were determined on the basis of the assessments.

A major challenge confronting this approach is the problem of distinguishing between structural competence and functional abilities. Given that competence can only be assessed through performance and that the performance of autistic children is likely influenced by one or more of the functional deficits they are known to have (in perception, memory, and so on), it is difficult to assess accurately their structural competence. In Slotnick's study, autistic and normal children were said to be matched for structural level on the basis of their performance on the unstructured classification task. But it was also partly on the basis of this task that evidence for functional deficits was obtained. Could not the functional deficits have influenced the assessment of structural level? Indeed, the autistic children performed at a higher level on the nonsocial structured task than on the unstructured task used as a basis for assessment of structural level, suggesting that the former task may provide a more accurate assessment of the children's competence than the latter task. However, the improvement obtained in the structured task appears to have been a within-level improvement in the quantity of sorting activity. A more serious problem is posed by the fact that perceptual boundedness was one functional deficit the autistic children were found to have relative to the matched normals. But perceptual boundedness is one characterization of the structural level of the two groups. Specifically, their structural level is operationalized, following Sugarman (1982), in terms of the inability to sort objects into two class groups in mixed sequence. As Slotnick notes, this behavior can be characterized as a type of perceptual boundedness. Could not the autistic children possess a higher level of structural competence than they are credited with possessing, the limitations in their cognitive performance arising principally from the functional deficit of perceptual boundedness?

It should be emphasized, however, that many of the problems faced by the clinical psychologist in assessing the structural level of atypical children are similar to those confronting the developmental psychologist attempting to assess the competence of normal children. In the latter case as well, controversy arises concerning whether developmental changes in cognitive performance should be attributed to changes in functional capacities such as short-term memory or to changes in competence (Breslow, 1981; Trabasso, 1977). With regard to the present topic, it might be argued that the apparent structural cognitive trends reported by Sugarman (1982) for normal children really reflect changes in perception and attention that reduce the children's perceptual boundedness. Although I think there is some reason to reject this interpretation (Sugarman, forthcoming), the point I am making is that the clinical psychologist is here faced with many of the same problems as the developmental psychologist. The optimistic side of this situation is that each of them may learn from the other. The pessimistic side is that the clinical psychologist is faced with the double problem of distinguishing structure from function, in the determination of both the normative structural sequence and the position a particular atypical child occupies within that sequence. Central to the resolution of both of these problems will be the development of a unified structural-functional theory that can predict performance. We are far from having such a theory at present.

Tower Builders

The tower builders, drawing selectively from Piaget's theory and adapting it as they deem necessary, have a less difficult task than the bridge builders, at least with regard to relating cognitive-developmental theory to the social, emotional, or personality domains. However, in other respects their work is equally as ambitious as that of the bridge builders. In fact, the tower builders come closest to providing original theories of socioemotional development and psychopathology.

Noam in Chapter Five offers an outline for a theory of psychopathology focusing on the development of the self. Acknowledging Piagetian and social cognitive theorists' contributions to theories of the self, Noam goes beyond a structural description of stages of the self. He examines structural development, which he terms self-complexity, and structural integration, which he terms self-strength.

Pathology is conceived as a resistance of integration into a higher-order system of experiences. In particular, specific biographical or life experiences, called encapsulations, are construed in terms of the structure that prevailed at the time of the original experience and are not revised even as the individual progresses to more advanced stages. Although the encapsulated experience resists being assimilated to the more advanced structure of the self-system, it interacts with and influences the self-system, producing different effects at each stage in the latter's development. In vertical encapsulation, the encapsulated experiences simply remain fixated at an earlier stage. In horizontal encapsulation, these experiences change with development but they change in some aberrant fashion. While the nature of horizontal encapsulation is not entirely clear to me, it appears to represent a departure from the Freudian conception of fixation in which certain early experiences are simply frozen in a past stage as in a vertical encapsulation. In either case, therapy is directed toward enabling the self-system to assimilate the encapsulated content into its mature structure. Finally, perpendicular to the stage dimension is the dimension of core themes, which provides further elaboration of individual differences. An individual has a number of particular themes, different from those of others, that persist throughout the person's lifetime.

Differences between Noam's theory and Piaget's theory are apparent. Noam acknowledges that Piaget admits the existence of asynchronies between domains and coexistence of multiple stage levels within a domain. However, he capitalizes on this internal inconsistency to a greater extent than Piaget in attempting to explain personality differences. The divergence from Piagetian theory is even sharper with regard to the relation between structure and content. Whereas for Piaget experiences retained in memory are revised in terms of newly acquired stage structures (Piaget and Inhelder, 1973), Noam argues that experiences interpreted according to an early structure of the self-system may persist unrevised, encapsulated, despite the emergence of new structures. In this regard, his perspective is close to Freud's notion of fixation, with the qualifications indicated in the preceding paragraph.

Noam also argues that stage transition in the personality domain need not be associated with progress as it usually is thought to be in the cognitive domain. Stage transition produces greater complexity of the self but also presents opportunities for reduced integration of the self if certain contents resist assimilation to the new structure. Although it is not clear, Noam may be espousing another view of development close to Freud's and contrasting with Piaget's. The idea is that one must complete each stage in a satisfactory fashion in order to progress to the next stage without bearing carry-overs from the earlier stage that will impair one's functioning in the new stage. In any case, the idea that higher stages can bring new problems as well as progress represents an important divergence from the usual view of cognitive development. This idea was mentioned also by Nannis and is represented in recent work on depression (Garber, 1984) showing that many symptoms of depression (guilt, feelings of worthlessness and helplessness, suicidal ideas) become more prominent at higher developmental levels.

The theoretical sources of the ideas of Cicchetti, Toth, Bush, and Gillespie in Chapter Six are less explicitly stated but may be easily inferred. Their model, like that of Noam, has both similarities and differences from Piaget's theory and does not explicitly specify relations between cognitive and social-emotional development. One Piagetian aspect of their model is the characterization of social-emotional development in terms of a series of stages, each marked by an organizational unity. These stages characterize not only normal development but also changes in the symptoms of various atypical populations. Stage-appropriate interventions also are indicated.

The model in Chapter Six is also neo-Piagetian in that it is interactionist, or in their terminology transactional. Four childhood problems are discussed, ranging from predominantly constitutional etiology (Down syndrome) to predominantly environmental etiology (maltreatment). In all four cases, however, the authors argue that child, parent, and environment are all involved at least to some extent in the maintenance, if not the origination, of the problem. Intervention must, likewise, be directed to changing child, parent, and environment. Even where the problem is primarily organic in origin, as in Down syndrome, intervention with the parent can be beneficial to the child's development. The authors thus apparently support Cowan's position that the etiology of a problem does not necessarily dictate the appropriate course of treatment.

In some respects, however, Cicchetti and his colleagues draw more from psychoanalytic theory and ego psychology than from Piagetian theory, often in ways similar to Noam. The authors characterize each stage in terms of specific stage-appropriate tasks, such as homeostatic regulation, management of tension, attachment, development of an autonomous self, and so on. The child goes on to the next stage no matter how well or poorly he or she has mastered the tasks of the previous stage. But poor mastery in one stage will adversely influence the child's ability to master the tasks of subsequent stages. However, the authors depart from psychoanalytic theory in claiming that a task remains a viable concern in the child's life beyond the stage in which it first arises. Presumably the authors would consider the nature of the task to change with development. This leaves open the possibility that a task that was poorly mastered in the stage it first appeared may be mastered later without the reliving and reworking of experiences from the distant past.

Conclusion

I have discussed the present papers in terms of two main methods by which Piagetian cognitive-developmental theory may be applied to clinical issues either directly or via socioemotional domains. The first is by positing actual relations or bridges between the cognitive-developmental domain and the target domain. The second is by utilizing Piaget's theory as a source of ideas that may be adopted or adapted as appropriate in the target domain.

With regard to the first approach, a number of recommendations follow from the preceding discussion. First, one must utilize Piaget's theory accurately and utilize it as its best. Where predictions of the theory are not in conformity with available evidence, the theory must be revised. There can be no question at this stage of the field of cognitive development of simply adopting Piaget's theory as is. Second, one needs a good understanding, based on both empirical evidence and structural analysis, of the target phenomenon, be it social, emotional, clinical, or some combination of these. Third, one must analyze the target phenomenon in terms of well-established constructs from the cognitive-developmental domain in a manner that is true to the nature of those constructs. For example, to demonstrate that a cognitive concept of a given stage is required for a given social task, it is necessary to analyze successful task performance structurally to show that it involves the concept and that the concept's predecessor in the preceding stage is not adequate for performance.

Those adopting the second approach, the tower builders, are not positing any relation between domains, be it structural or causal. Their responsibility in drawing on theory from the cognitive-developmental domain is only the scholarly responsibility to characterize the theory accurately. Of course, their job is as challenging as that of anyone else attempting to construct a theory of social, emotional, or personality development or of developmental psychopathology without the inspiration of cognitive-developmental theory. It is beyond the scope of the present chapter to offer guidelines for adequate theory building in these domains.

Whether one is building bridges or towers, differences between cognitive development and social-emotional development will necessarily limit the relevance of Piaget's theory to the latter. A number of such differences have been noted in the preceding discussion and by some of the volume contributors. I have indicated a difference between the Piagetian and psychoanalytic concepts of the unconscious as well as between the development of concepts of emotion and of emotions themselves. Noam and Nannis have argued that in the area of personality-social development, higher stages are not necessarily better stages characterized by more adaptive functioning, in contrast to the typically assumed case in cognitive development. Noam and Cicchetti and his colleagues both posit the existence in children of carry-overs of content or functioning from earlier stages even after they have progressed to more advanced stages, a notion more similar to psychoanalytic than to Piagetian theory. In addition to these differences and although not suggested by the present authors, a possibility should be raised that certain areas of emotional, social, or personality development may not be best characterized in terms of structural change at all.

Various clinical applications of structural-developmental theory have been proposed in the volume papers. Structural change is a normative dimension that interacts with such individual differences as psychopathology in a number of ways. Symptoms of a given problem predictably change with developmental level. A full understanding of an individual patient therefore requires the assessment of his or her level of development. Similarly, intervention strategies must be determined in part in terms of developmental level. One example of this discussed earlier relates to the importance of understanding the child's level of conception of emotions in therapies that depend upon the child's attaining insight into his or her emotions.

But there appear to be limitations in the ability of structural-developmental theory to account for individual differences, be they personality differences or forms of psychopathology. Since the theory is largely concerned with normative development common to most children, individual differences are primarily conceived in terms of developmental delay or advance. At best, one can point to developmental delays in certain domains but not in others. But, as Cowan notes, psychopathology is not reducible to developmental delay.

Other aspects of cognition may be more useful in the explanation of individual differences. These may be classed into the categories of functional aspects and content of cognition. Functional aspects include the various information-processing faculties (such as memory, attention, perception, and so on) biases, strategies, algorithms, regulatory processes, and emotional factors (such as motivation). Content includes learning, specific nonstructural knowledge, and skills. Possible roles for both of these nonstructural aspects of cognition in the production of behavioral and emotional problems in children and adolescents have been discussed. What is lacking is a unified theory of cognitive development that integrally incorporates structure, function, and content. Such a theory would provide a firmer basis for a cognitive theory of individual differences and psychopathology.

It must be emphasized that the absence of a unified theory of this sort is not simply a gap in cognitive-developmental theory preventing it from explaining phenomena that it might be hoped to explain (for example, individual differences). Rather, I believe that the absence of an integrated whole weakens the strength of the part. Structure is a hidden construct accessible only through performance. Without a theory specifying the relationship between performance factors (such as functions and content) and structure, the assessment of cognitive structure will retain some degree of speculativeness. One consequence of this deficiency in cognitive-developmental theory in my view is that we cannot at present meaningfully raise the question of whether certain individuals suffering from psychopathology develop through stages that are structurally different from those of normals. Generally, these individuals suffer from various functional deficits as well as structural retardation. Since we currently know so little about structure and function and especially about their relationship in normals, we are much less likely to be able to distinguish accurately between structural and functional divergence from normality in pathological cases.

Most of this volume has been devoted to the consideration of possible contributions of cognitive-developmental theory to the understanding of social-emotional development. But what the foregoing discussion indicates is that cognitive-developmental theory can in turn benefit from the effort to apply it to other domains. Such efforts, as we have seen, can magnify certain of the current limitations in the theory, such as its inability to distinguish and relate structure and function, and thus point to potential growing points for the theory. Further, while differences that have been proposed in the volume between socioemotional development and cognitive development as depicted in Piaget's theory may often reflect differences inherent in the respective domains, they may also sometimes point to inadequacies in Piaget's theory. That is, it may be that cognitive development bears a greater similarity to social-emotional development in certain respects than the theory allows.

References

Ainsworth, M.D.S., Blehar, M. C., Waters, E., and Wall, S. *Patterns of Attachment.* Hillsdale, N.J.: Erlbaum, 1978.

Block, J. "Assimilation, Accommodation, and the Dynamics of Personality Development." *Child Development*, 1982, *53* (2), 281–295.

Brainerd, C. J. *Piaget's Theory of Intelligence.* Englewood Cliffs, N.J.: Prentice-Hall, 1978.

Breslow, L. "Reevaluation of the Literature on the Development of Transitive Inferences." *Psychological Bulletin*, 1981, *89* (2), 325–351.

Breslow, L., and Cowan, P. A. "Structural and Functional Perspectives on Classification and Seriation in Psychotic and Normal Children." *Child Development*, 1984, *55*, 226–235.

Fodor, J. "Fixation of Belief and Concept Acquisition." In M. Piattelli-Palmarini (ed.), *Language and Learning: The Debate Between Jean Piaget and Noam Chomsky.* Cambridge, Mass.: Harvard University Press, 1980.

Garber, J. "The Developmental Progression of Depression in Female Children." In D. Cicchetti and K. Schneider-Rosen (eds.), *Childhood Depression.* New Directions for Child Development, no. 26. San Francisco: Jossey-Bass, 1984.

Gelman, R., and Baillargeon, R. "A Review of Some Piagetian Concepts." In P. H. Mussen (ed.), *Handbook of Child Psychology*. Vol. 3: J. H. Flavell and E. M. Markman (eds.), *Cognitive Development*. New York: Wiley, 1983.

Halford, G. S. *The Development of Thought*. Hillsdale, N.J.: Erlbaum, 1982.

Harris, P. L., and Olthof, T. "The Child's Conception of Emotion." In G. Butterworth and P. Light (eds.), *Social Cognition*. Chicago: University of Chicago Press, 1982.

Inhelder, B., and Piaget, J. (A. Parsons and S. Milgram, trans.) *The Growth of Logical Thinking from Childhood to Adolescence*. New York: Basic Books, 1958. (Originally published 1955.)

Kahneman, D., Slovic, P., and Tversky, A. *Judgment Under Uncertainty: Heuristics and Biases*. Cambridge, Mass.: Cambridge University Press, 1982.

Piaget, J. (J. Tomlinson and A. Tomlinson, trans.) *The Child's Conception of the World*. London: Kegan Paul, Trench, Trubner, 1929. (Originally published 1926.)

Piaget, J. *Classes, relations et nombres: Essai sur les "groupements" de la logistique et la reversibilite de la pensee* [Classes, relations, and numbers: Essay on the logical groupings and the reversibility of thought]. Paris: Vrin, 1942.

Piaget, J. (M. Cook, trans.) *The Origins of Intelligence in the Child*. New York: International Universities Press, 1952. (Originally published, 1936.)

Piaget, J. "Piaget's Theory." In P. Mussen (ed.), *Carmichael's Manual of Child Psychology*. New York: Wiley, 1970.

Piaget, J. *Essai de logique operatoire* [Essay on logical operations]. Paris: Presses Universitaires de France, 1972.

Piaget, J. (S. Wedgwood, trans.) *The Grasp of Consciousness*. Cambridge, Mass.: Harvard University Press, 1976. (Originally published 1974.)

Piaget, J. "The Stages of Intellectual Development in Childhood and Adolescence." In H. E. Gruber and J. J. Voneche (eds.), *The Essential Piaget*. New York: Basic Books, 1977. (Originally published 1956.)

Piaget, J. (T. Brown and K. J. Thampy, trans.) *The Equilibration of Cognitive Structures: The Central Problem of Intellectual Development*. Chicago: University of Chicago Press, 1985. (Originally published 1975.)

Piaget, J. *Possibility and Necessity*. Vol. 1: *The Role of Possibility in Cognitive Development*. Minneapolis: University of Minnesota Press, 1987. (Originally published 1981.)

Piaget, J., and Inhelder, B. (A. J. Pomerans, trans.) *Memory and Intelligence*. New York: Basic Books, 1973. (Originally published 1968.)

Schmid-Kitsikis, E. "The Cognitive Mechanisms Underlying Problem-Solving in Psychotic and Mentally Retarded Children." In B. Inhelder and H. Chapman (eds.), *Piaget and His School: A Reader in Developmental Psychology*. New York: Springer Verlag, 1976.

Shantz, C. U. "Social Cognition." In J. H. Flavell and E. M. Markman (eds.), *Handbook of Child Psychology: Cognitive Development*. Vol. 3. New York: Wiley, 1983.

Sugarman, S. "Developmental Change in Early Representational Intelligence: Evidence from Spatial Classification Strategies and Related Verbal Expressions." *Cognitive Psychology*, 1982, *14*, 410–449.

Sugarman, S. "Young Children's Spontaneous Inspection of Negative Instances in a Search Task." *Cognitive Psychology*, forthcoming.

Trabasso, T. "The Role of Memory as a System in Making Transitive Inferences." In R. V. Kail and J. W. Hagen (eds.), *Perspectives on the Development of Memory and Cognition*. Hillsdale, N.J.: Erlbaum, 1977.

Leonard Breslow is assistant professor of child psychology at the University of Minnesota. He was a National Science Foundation Postdoctoral Fellow at the University of Geneva, Switzerland, in the academic year 1982–83.

Index

A

Aber, J. L., 125, 127, 140, 141
Accommodation. *See* Assimilation and accommodation
Achenbach, T. M., 6, 25, 92, 119
Ackerman, N. W., 20, 25
Adaptation: and formal operations, 52; research linking cognitive deficits to, 53–54
Adelson, E., 19, 27
Adolescents: and cognitive-developmental theory, 152–154; emotional understanding of, 32–33, 34, 41–43; and formal operations, 51–73
Affect, as stage-salient issue, 129–130
Aggression, in attachment theory, 19
Ainsworth, M.D.S., 130, 131, 132, 140, 142, 154, 162
Altemeier, W. A., 145
Alternatives: envisioning, 56–57; evaluating, 57–58
American Psychiatric Association, 7, 25, 76, 78, 87, 126, 140
Anderson, B., 91n
Andrea, 56–57, 58, 60
Anthony, E. J., 93, 119
Arend, R., 19, 25
Asberg, M., 11, 25
Assimilation and accommodation: by autistic children, 83, 84–85, 86; in cognitive-developmental theory, 150–152; and emotional understanding, 37; in formal operations, 52, 53, 54, 63–67, 68, 69–70; imbalance in, 64–65; and interactions, 16–18; intercoordination of, 65–67; lack of opportunity for, 63–64; and social development of self, 107–110, 111, 115
Attachment: relationship view of, 18–19; as stage-salient issue, 130–132
Atwood, G. E., 93, 119
Autistic children: analysis of cognitive development of, 75–90; assimilation and accommodation by, 83, 84–85, 86; background on, 75–76; cognitive deficits in, 80–83; cognitive-developmental study of, 78–80, 156–157; described, 76, 78–79; and developmental patterns, 8; flexible regulation for, 82–83; implications of findings on, 84–87; interventions for, 86–87; perseveration in, 81–82, 85–86; research review on, 76–78; similarities of, to younger children, 80–81; social disturbances in, 83–84; structural and functional differences of, 79, 81–83
Autonomous self, as stage-salient issue, 132–134

B

Baillargeon, R., 149, 163
Baldwin, A. L., 13, 25
Baldwin, C. P., 13, 25
Baldwin, J. M., 96, 104, 119
Bandura, A., 14, 26
Baron-Cohen, S., 77, 87
Barry, W. A., 18, 28
Bates, J. E., 19, 26
Bateson, G., 20, 26
Beardslee, W. R., 126, 140
Beattie, O. V., 114, 119
Beck, A. T., 67, 73, 93, 119, 139, 140
Beedy, J., 106, 121
Beeghly, M., 126, 128, 134, 135, 140, 141
Belief systems, and self, 109
Bell, R., 139, 143
Belmont, B., 135, 144
Bemis, K., 69, 72
Bemporad, J., 126, 139, 140–141
Bennett, E. M., 28
Berger, J., 128, 141
Bernstein, A. C., 15, 26
Bertilsson, L., 25
Beth, 45–46
Bettelheim, B., 13, 26
Biography, and self, 94–95, 104, 108, 111, 118